Consciousness Beyond Consumerism

Consciousness Beyond Consumerism

A Psychological Path to Sustainability

Terence Sexton

Published in 2021 by
Aqumens Publishing
Ashford, Kent, UK

Disclaimer

The contents of Consciousness Beyond Consumerism: A Psychological Path to Sustainability (the Book), such as text, graphics, images and other material contained within or accessed through the Book (the Content), are for informational and educational purposes only. The Content is not intended to be a substitute for professional medical advice, diagnosis or treatment. Always seek the advice of your physician or qualified healthcare provider regarding any medical condition that could be affected by engaging with the activities contained in the Book. You assume all responsibility and risk for your use of and reliance upon any Content contained within or accessed through the Book.

Design & Formatting: Artbully Ltd
Editor: Camille Bramall

Print Edition: ISBN 978-1-9168938-0-1
E-book Edition: ISBN 978-1-9168938-1-8

www.consciousnessbeyondconsumerism.org

For my wife, Kate, and
my daughters, Jessica and Amy.

CONTENTS

LIST OF FIGURES

LIST OF TABLES

ACKNOWLEDGEMENTS

I offer my thanks to all those who have helped me on my journey to writing this book. They include my university tutors, the psychotherapists I worked with as I explored different therapies and the people I met at Schumacher College, both faculty and fellow students, who inspired me so greatly. They also include the authors of numerous books, which have deepened my knowledge, understanding and insight in a wide range of areas, including psychology, ecology, economics, philosophy, religion, spirituality, business and management. In particular, I would like to thank my colleagues, Jill Chapman and Gary King, who helped me improve techniques to develop leaders' consciousness. Without all of these people, this book would not have been possible.

I am also very grateful to my friends and family who have beta read this book and helped with many edits. These include Graham Read, Kate Sexton, Amy Sexton, Ellen Wilson, Rob Porter, Mike Green and Julie Brooks. I thank them for their feedback, guidance, support and encouragement.

INTRODUCTION

The poem 'Hieroglyphic Stairway', by Drew Dellinger, had a significant impact on me when I read it a few years ago.[1] It is about a man who lies awake at 3.23 am because his great-great-grandchildren ask him questions in his dreams, such as: 'what did you do when the earth was unraveling? [...] what did you do once you knew?'

What if one day my grandchildren ask me 'What did you do when you knew?' Would my answer be, 'I did nothing'?

I am not an economist, politician, ecologist or environmentalist. I am a psychologist. I cannot save the planet. So, I carried on with business as usual. But the poem would not leave me. The line 'what did you do once you knew?' became an earworm until, one day, logic hit:

> Our society is unsustainable.
> Who creates our society? *Our leaders.*
> Therefore, our leadership is unsustainable.
> What is my work? *I develop leaders.*
> *I must be part of the problem.*
> *If I am part of the problem, I can also be part of the solution.*

With this logic in mind, I set about developing and delivering programmes to enable people to demonstrate more sustainable leadership. Leadership to regenerate rather than plunder the planet, which creates communities and fosters good mental health. Through this work, I realised our consciousness has been industrialised to the extent that we have been conditioned to be consumers. The more we consume, the more we serve industry.

How we perceive, understand and relate to our world is seen only through the lens of our consciousness. We are 'subject' to it. It is nearly impossible to 'objectively' recognise that our minds have been conditioned to serve industry. This book endeavours to make 'object' what, for most people, has always been 'subject'. It aims to free our minds from our industrialised bias and open a window into an alternative way of seeing, thinking and being; a way that enables us to create a more sustainable future.

Even though our Earth has been suffering for decades, our consciousness has not allowed us to see it. If we are to create a more sustainable society, we must now develop our consciousness beyond consumerism. In this book, I aim to give you the background as to how and why our consciousness has been industrialised; explanations as to the damage this is causing; and ways to develop your consciousness beyond consumerism. If we are to survive as a species, our consciousness now needs to develop faster than the problems it creates.

We are at the tipping point of destroying what makes our planet habitable for humans and many other life forms. Only with objective awareness will we have the choice to take a different path. If we develop our consciousness, we can choose a different future. If we do not, no matter how many sustainability initiatives we employ, or how many ideas for a new economy are developed, there will be little genuine change. We will likely just 'industrialise' and overconsume the solutions we put in place, leading to unintended consequences we are yet to foresee. We will continue down the same destructive path, perhaps at a slower rate, but it will ultimately lead to the same ruin.

In Chapter 1, I explore the pain of the environmental crisis, inequality and mental illness caused by the industrialisation of our consciousness. Many psychologists believe pain is the universe letting us know that the way we live is out of balance and we need to change. We tend to resist change until the pain is too great, hoping it will go away. Society has reached a point where the pain may force a change.

In Chapter 2, you will be able to assess the extent to which your consciousness has been industrialised in terms of your separation from nature, other people and yourself. For these self-assessments, I will ask some difficult questions. Difficult because, as mentioned before, we are 'subject' to the industrialisation of our consciousness. By considering these questions, I hope you will be able to view the industrialisation process objectively and, therefore, be able to decide to de-industrialise your mind or continue with business as usual. It is your choice. But without objective awareness of the process, you have no choice.

In Chapter 3, I will take you through the processes by which our consciousness has been industrialised. We will explore the influences of religion, philosophy, science, economics, psychology and management. Knowing where we went wrong can inform the decisions we make in the future. As we progress through history, I will build a picture of our industrialised consciousness based on the Triangle Model below (see Figure 0.1). I was inspired to create this diagram after watching a lecture by the American ecopsychologist Andy Fisher. He used the same foundation for his model to describe different types of psychology. I have taken his foundation and developed it in another direction.

Figure 0.1 The Triangle Model – Base

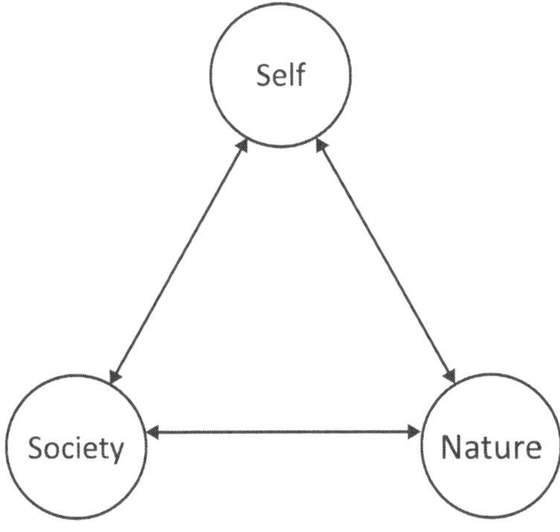

Chapter 4 introduces the fourth and final aspect of the industrialisation of our consciousness, our conditioning to be consumers. I will outline the devastating impact our increasing separation from nature, each other and ourselves has had on our psychology. As a result, we are left vulnerable to business techniques used to condition us into becoming prolific consumers of products and services. The chapter outlines the techniques used and demonstrates how they work on our psychology.

Industrialising our consciousness was necessary to drive a consumer-led economy, providing people with jobs, incomes and pensions. We know this type of economy is unsustainable and cannot continue much longer. Our economic system's durability is addressed in Chapter 5, as it explores the relationship between the economy, society and consciousness. We have many ideas for a more sustainable economy but are unable to make any significant change. It is our collective consciousness that is holding us back. Establishing a new economic system requires us to evolve a new collective consciousness across our society.

Chapter 5 completes Part 1, which focuses on exploring how our consciousness has been industrialised and its impact on our environment, society and mental health. Part 2 addresses how we can develop consciousness beyond consumerism.

Chapter 6 explores the nature of consciousness to lay the foundation for the development of consciousness beyond consumerism. In doing so, I seek to answer the questions what, why and how. What is consciousness, why do we have it and how is it produced? These are hard questions to answer and have kept philosophers and scientists busy for centuries. Nevertheless, we need to understand what we are working with.

In Chapter 7, I demonstrate that changes in our consciousness are natural and that they happen throughout our lives. The changes are part of growing and maturing psychologically. Yet, most people's psychological growth extends only as far as what is deemed normal in our society. Normal is what supports our industrialised, consumer-led economy and damages the environment. If we are to change the economy and change our path, we need people who can develop and grow their consciousness beyond normal. We need to develop a critical mass of people with a new type of consciousness. Does that include you?

If you want to develop beyond what society currently sees as the norm, to help the environment, our communities and ourselves, then carry on reading. Chapter 8 outlines some of the methods that research has shown to be effective in developing people's consciousness. Coincidently, they include reconnecting with nature, each other and ourselves. They also include developing how we think, feel and behave in preparation for taking on developmental challenges.

If we are to create a new, more sustainable economy, waiting for enough people to develop and grow their consciousness in isolation will take too long. Therefore, in Chapter 9, I address what can be done in society to accelerate the process. I advocate changing the focus of education, encouraging businesses to develop people psychologically alongside giving them knowledge and skills, and encouraging political leaders to lead by example. If we are to create a new sustainable society, we need to do this together.

Although I am critical of our current economic system, this is not a pessimistic book. It is a book of hope. I do not suggest that the industrialisation of our consciousness has been a planned and intentional process. Instead, it has emerged and progressed over centuries as a natural evolution of our society. It has delivered many benefits, but it has been overdone and is now threatening our future. It is time to create a more sustainable society. It is time to develop our consciousness and change paths.

In many ways, this is a technical book exploring the work of philosophers, scientists, psychologists, economists and management theorists. There are many details that will help you to understand how our consciousness became industrialised and the process of de-industrialisation. However, the technical details will not speak to your heart or connect with your unconscious. For this reason, I have written a short mythical story to accompany the technical detail called 'Sophia and the Three-Headed Dragon'. The mythical story will help you understand the technical book, and the technical book will help you find a deeper meaning within the mythical story. The two go hand-in-hand.

Throughout history, and across cultures, many mythical stories appeared when people needed to make sense of changes happening around them. They have been used to guide people through change or transition from one world to the next. As we are struggling to make sense of what is happening around us, and if we are to survive, our society needs to make a transition. We are in great need of new mythical stories that will speak to our emotions. When learning is attached to an emotion it enhances our ability to remember. As powerful tools for learning, mythical stories are handed down through the generations. However, myths are more powerful than stories because they go deeper into our psyche. They connect with elements in our unconscious that Carl Jung (1875–1961) called 'archetypes'.[2] Jung described these as the universal, archaic symbols and images that derive from the collective unconscious. Myths contain archetypal figures like the great mother, father, child, devil, God, wise old man, wise old woman, trickster, warrior or hero, and events such as the apocalypse, flood and the creation, etc. Archetypes are inborn tendencies that shape our behaviour and, because they come from our collective unconscious, they unite us.

'Sophia and the Three-Headed Dragon' will start in this Introduction and unfold at each chapter's beginning. It is written in italics to differentiate it from the rest of the book. If you like mythical stories, you may wish to read all of these sections before turning to the book's technical aspects. Alternatively, you may wish to read each chapter of the mythical story before each chapter of the technical book. Reading the mythical story in this way will give you a more in-depth introduction to each chapter. Equally, if you do not like mythical stories, you may prefer not to read the story at all. The choice is yours.

The subtitle of the book is *A Psychological Path to Sustainability*. I thought long and hard about using the term 'sustainability'. In doing so,

I am not advocating ways in which we can sustain our current lifestyles. On the contrary, we need to change. We need to find new ways of living that are able to sustain our natural environment, our communities and our psychological well-being. This requires change. In fact, before we can become sustainable in these ways, we will first need to regenerate our environment, communities and psychological well-being. Rather than creating a 'consumptive' society, we need to create a 'generous' society – one that gives back to the resources that sustain us.

Post the global Covid-19 pandemic, we have the opportunity to build back better. Yet if we do not develop our collective consciousness, we will continue to behave in the same way we have done since the Industrial Revolution. Although our intention may be to create a sustainable future, we will end up doing the same things while expecting different results. Our collective madness will continue to destroy the environment upon which our lives depend.

SOPHIA AND THE THREE-HEADED DRAGON

Wiping blood from her finger, Sophia pondered how she had ended up an apprentice in her parents' tailor's shop. She was continually pricking or cutting herself and the reality of her future life was becoming painfully obvious.

Sophia lived in Halkeld, a small town somewhere north of nowhere. On a clear day, if you climbed the encircling walls and squinted westward, you could just make out the watchtowers of the nearest settlement, Onwick, through a distant haze. Halkeld was one of the oldest towns in the country. There had been a settlement here for over 800 years due to the clear spring water that bubbled up through the bedrock. The town was enclosed behind high stone walls, which everyone lived within for fear of being called an outsider. According to Sophia, the main problem with Halkeld was that nothing ever happened. It simply ticked along monotonously, day in day out, through seasons and years. Routine was its lifeblood. As a town, it was virtually self-sufficient. Surrounding fields provided enough food for everyone, nearby forests provided fuel, and within the walls were every trade and profession anyone who didn't think too creatively would ever need. There was no need for trade with neighbouring towns, so there was minimal contact with the outside world. Visitors were few and far between. One summer's day, that all changed.

PART 1

THE INDUSTRIALISATION OF OUR CONSCIOUSNESS

CHAPTER 1

THREE CRISES OF OUR SOCIETY

'Don't get blood on that collar!' shouted her father.

Suddenly Sophia heard a commotion. Dropping her work and running outside, she found a group of five or six outsiders being harangued by locals. They were in a terrible state, as if they had travelled for days without food or shelter, and their clothes hung from their malnourished bodies.

'It was the dragon,' said one of the strangers, 'A three-headed dragon. The town's gone, all gone, we can't go back. We lost everything.'

With that, Sophia's mother grabbed her arm and bustled her back into the shop.

A few days later, another 10 outsiders arrived, more bedraggled, also from Onwick, Halkeld's nearest neighbour. In the following week, 30 strangers arrived from other places but with the same story. A three-headed dragon had attacked their towns. What started as a trickle of outsiders became a torrent. They fled to Halkeld because it had a defensive wall. Initially, the townsfolk made room in their houses for the newcomers. Now, though, just a few weeks later, things were different. Tents were erected in parks to accommodate the influx of people. An emergency meeting was convened to discuss the crisis.

'We can't keep taking these people in. We haven't got the space!' bellowed a man from the back of the room.

A small woman at the front stood up and said, 'Yes, and what about the food? At this rate, we won't have enough to see us through winter.'

The hall erupted in roars of agreement.

'Order! Order! We must have order!' the Mayor shouted as he banged his gavel on the table.

Sophia raised her hand to speak, but her father pulled it down sharply.

'I want to say something.'

'We'll talk when we get home,' her father replied.

With that, the Mayor declared, 'I've made my decision. We must close the gates. We can't take any more outsiders. Meeting closed.'

'We can't leave people outside the gate without food or shelter!' Sophia shouted at her father.

'The Mayor has made his decision and that's final,' he replied.

But for Sophia, that was not an acceptable solution. 'Then someone needs to do something about the dragon,' she implored.

Her father looked at her sympathetically and said, 'Look Sophia, it's not our problem; there's no dragon here.' With that, he stood up and walked out of the hall.

The injustice of the situation troubled Sophia deeply and an overwhelming desire to do something welled up inside her, preventing any thought of sleep that night. Had anyone tried to talk to the dragon, she wondered. It might be a challenge, but it seemed a logical solution. In any case, she should go and assess the problem. The next morning, very early, she packed a rucksack with a tent, warm jumper and a torch. What else did she need? She might have to fight it if she couldn't reason with it. If it were like Medusa, she would need a mirror. She wrapped one in a sock and stuffed it in a pocket. In the kitchen, she found her mother making sandwiches.

'Off to fight dragons, are you?' Sophia chose not to answer. 'You'll need this then,' her mother said, handing over a pile of food she'd prepared. 'Best you take these as well,' she said, passing Sophia a small throwing axe and coil of rope. 'Good luck little one,' said her mother as Sophia silently closed the street door.

She managed to get through the gates, as the guards had orders only to stop people entering, and set off towards the town on the horizon, Onwick. This is where the dragon had first appeared and, hopefully, where she would find it.

It was two days' walk away and, being mid-summer, they were hot and long. The heat didn't bother Sophia, she was used to it, but the flies got on her nerves. On the second day, as she neared the town, things started to change. There were no more insects, and it became eerily quiet without any birdsong. As she crossed fields near the town, she saw that the fruit and vegetables had all flowered and died. As she walked, the temperature rose. The earth became scorched and barren; there couldn't have been any rain here for weeks. At the edge of town, two elderly people staggered towards her.

'Give us some food; we are starving,' the man said. Sophia opened her rucksack, broke off some bread and gave it to the couple.

'Thank you and God bless,' said the old woman, tucking it into the folds of her dress. Then they scuttled away as if frightened they would be robbed.

In Onwick, Sophia found that people had built high fences around their properties. Curiosity getting the better of her, she peered through a hole. Behind the fence, she could see piles of food. She went to another; it was exactly the same. As she stared, someone nearby shouted, 'Get back; you won't get a warning next time.'

Sophia jumped back and looked up to see a man standing above the fence, waving a broom.

'I won't tell you again, now scram!' he shouted.

She ran, past other houses, and saw the same everywhere. People on top of their fences defending piles of food. Scuffles were breaking out where the hungry had managed to scale a fence. Abruptly, the fighting ceased as a man, dripping in gold and silver, came striding down the road. People stood and smiled at him in recognition and admiration. Then, when he had gone, the fighting resumed.

'That's how you get stuff in this place,' Sophia heard a voice behind her.

It was a boy, about 15 years old and slightly taller than her. He wore a few gold and silver adornments, but not as many as the man who had walked by.

'It's no good fighting for food, you've got to trade, and for that, you've got to look the part. You've got to look like you've got stuff; otherwise, no one will want to know,' he told her. 'If you're good at trading you can get more stuff, then you look better and can trade some more. That's how you work your way up.' Sophia looked confused, so he went on. 'That man you saw, he worked his way to the top. He's got stuff and he's got respect. No one's going to touch him. Now look at you, you've got nothing on show; no one's going to trade with you. You're just going to get done over.'

Sophia turned and ran away as fast as she could, until she collapsed, completely out of breath, in a narrow alley between two boarded-up houses. There she sat, for what seemed like hours, watching people without them noticing her. It appeared that most of the town's inhabitants lived alone. They spent their time pushing people away, defending their stuff. And it wasn't just food they were defending; it was all sorts of things. She guessed it was anything they thought they could trade. Occasionally, a person would walk down the street, head held high, strutting. These 'peacocks' adorned themselves with anything that would signify status. Gold and silver were best, but if you didn't have these, then anything shiny or sparkly was a useful substitute. A person's lack of gold and silver could also be offset by their confidence. The more they strutted, the more they were admired. And the boy was right; these people could trade. They bargained for food and baubles with ease.

While the people of Onwick appeared to be solitary, one thing united them: they all looked miserable. Underneath their anger or confidence, she sensed a deep sadness. People walked around like empty shells. Did the dragon do this to people? Unnerved by what she saw in their empty eyes and not seeing any sign of the dragon, Sophia started home to Halkeld. What sort of dragon could wreak so much damage? she mused. Perhaps her father was right. Maybe there was nothing to be done.

INTRODUCTION

Human beings are members of a whole,
In creation of one essence and soul.
If one member is afflicted with pain,
Her members uneasy will remain.
If you have no sympathy for human pain,
The name of human you cannot retain!

A poem written by the 13th-century Persian poet Sa'adi (rhyming translation by M. Aryanpoor). This poem is at the entrance of the United Nations in Manhattan.

When most people hear about creating a more sustainable society, they tend to think of environmental sustainability. Of course, this is a major concern, but it is not the complete picture. We also have to consider psychological sustainability and the sustainability of our communities. It is no coincidence that we are simultaneously experiencing an environmental crisis, a crisis of community and a psychological crisis. They are interrelated. Sustainability is fundamentally a matter of relationships: our relationships with nature, each other and ourselves.

As our consciousness increasingly became industrialised, we became more and more separated from nature, each other and ourselves. These separations have provided opportunities for industry to continually grow businesses and the economy to provide products, services and financial security for us all. While we have enjoyed these benefits for decades, we have not noticed the flip side. The industrialisation of our consciousness has blinded us to increases in environmental degradation, inequality and mental illness. This chapter demonstrates how industry exploits our separation from nature, each other and ourselves for profit and economic growth, and highlights the benefits this gives us. It then explores the flip side of these benefits in terms of the environmental, community and psychological crises.

ENVIRONMENTAL CRISIS

For centuries, world economies have been based on the seizure and processing of natural resources, often called 'capturing the commons'. These are resources shared by all members of society, including natural elements such as air, water, land, etc. There was a time when no one owned the planet's natural resources. Everyone, humans and non-human, shared them. We co-existed together, foraging for only what we needed. Gradually, natural resources fell into private ownership. First, through staking claims to land for farming; next through sharing the spoils of war following a conquest; and then through industrial acquisition. Today, virtually all of planet Earth's natural resources are privately owned. Natural resource-based economies rely on industry taking what we once collectively owned, adding value through some sort of processing and selling them back to us in the form of products. For instance, water companies charge for, and profit from, the water they have stored, cleaned and distributed. Countries vie for ownership of the seabed to drill for oil. Companies gain the rights to destroy mountains in the search for valuable metals, rocks and fuels. For economies to grow, industry must continually capture more 'commons' and convert them into more products for us to buy.

This capturing of the commons extends beyond the boundaries of our planet. The 1967 Outer Space Treaty declared outer space to be a common good for mankind.[1] However, this is now largely ignored. Amongst other exploitations of space, we rush to put tens of thousands of satellites into a low Earth orbit; thereby risking light pollution, significantly increased greenhouse emissions and further pollution of our atmosphere, all for the promise of improved internet access or faster communications.

We enjoy the benefits of the products and the financial security gained from a growing economy. We do not want to know about the flip side of these benefits. To fully enjoy the economic benefits, our consciousness needs to blind us to the pain we are causing nature. As a society, for decades, we have found it acceptable to let companies carry out deforestation, destroy the seabed, overfish seas, extract minerals, turn oil into plastic, spray pesticides, create mountains of rubbish, use non-sustainable intensive farming, etc. It is vital that, as a consumer society, we do not feel nature's pain and react en masse to prevent its exploitation and destruction. Maintaining our consumerist lifestyle requires us to separate from nature. Some people believe we have gone too far in the destruction of the Earth and reached the tipping point.

Probably the most famous research into environmental unsustainability is the planetary boundaries research carried out by the Stockholm Resilience Centre at Stockholm University, in collaboration with the Australian National University and the University of Copenhagen.[2] This research presents a set of nine boundaries within which humanity can continue to develop and thrive for generations to come. First introduced in 2009, it has since been updated and was published in the journal *Science* on 16 January 2015. These boundaries are the processes and systems that regulate the stability and resilience of the Earth system. The interactions of land, ocean, atmosphere and life provide conditions upon which our society depends. Scientists found that four of the nine planetary boundaries have now been crossed due to human activity. These four are climate change, loss of biosphere integrity, land system change and altered biogeochemical cycles (phosphorus and nitrogen). Lead author of the report, Professor Will Steffen, stated that transgressing a planetary boundary increases the risk that human activities could inadvertently drive the Earth system into a much less hospitable state, damaging efforts to reduce poverty and leading to a deterioration of human well-being in many parts of the world, including wealthy countries. For a more detailed explanation of planetary boundaries, please see Appendix 1.

None of this is new. We have known about the looming environmental crisis for decades. In 1992 the United Nations Framework

Convention on Climate Change (UNFCCC) was signed at the Rio Earth Summit. Since then, the Conference of the Parties (COP) has taken place every year, with negotiators trying to put in place a plan of action to address climate change. Yet year on year, carbon levels in the atmosphere continue to rise, and climate change marches on unabated. In 2018 the UN Intergovernmental Panel on Climate Change (IPCC) warned we only have 12 years to take the action necessary to keep global warming to a maximum of 1.5°C, beyond which even a small increase will significantly worsen the risks of drought, floods, extreme heat and poverty for hundreds of millions of people.[3] We know this, but do we change our ways? No. Not collectively and not to the extent needed to make a difference.

Individually many of us are trying to change our ways. We recycle, switch to a renewable energy supplier or buy an electric car. Yet, despite all these individual efforts, the global environmental crisis continues at pace. We are simply tinkering around the edges of the problem, not tackling its root cause. It is a problem of consciousness. With our industrialised minds, we simply cannot stop consuming the Earth. At the current level of consumption, we need 1.7 Earths to sustain us (Global Footprint Network, 2017).[4] By 2050, we will need 3 Earths to meet our consumption levels (United Nations, 2018).[5] Of course, some people argue that resources will not run out any time soon. Instead, they believe technology will advance to find new ways to capture and exploit Earth's ever-dwindling resources. Fracking is an example. While they may be right, we also have to consider the cost. Do we really want to destroy the entire natural world so that we can continue to consume at ever-increasing rates? What about the side effects of exhausting the Earth's resources, all the pollution caused and rubbish accumulated? The Earth can no longer process what we have produced already. We cannot continue to consume at the current rate.

Continual consumption means increasingly encroaching on wildlife habitats, land degradation, wildlife exploitation, resource extraction and climate change. The encroachment on wildlife habitats has led to a rise in zoonotic diseases such as Ebola, Middle East Respiratory Syndrome (MERS), severe acute respiratory syndrome (SARS) and coronaviruses. Epidemiologists have been warning for decades of the presence of an extensive reservoir of SARS-CoV-like viruses in wildlife populations. The United Nations Environment Programme (UNEP) says that some two million people, mostly in low- and middle-income countries, die from neglected zoonotic diseases every year.[6] The recent Covid-19 pandemic has clearly demonstrated that all countries are exposed to zoonotic diseases. If we continue exploiting wildlife and destroying ecosystems to capture and use natural resources, these figures will likely increase in the future. The next pandemic may be even more deadly.

If Earth is to remain hospitable to humans, both in terms of living within the planetary boundaries and preventing future pandemics, there needs to be greater protection, and reverence, for wildlife, their habitats and the natural environment. Industries cannot continually capture common natural resources and convert them into products. Economist Kenneth Boulding (1910–1993) once said, 'Anyone who believes exponential growth can go on forever in a finite world is either a madman or an economist.' For continual, sustainable economic growth, industries need to find, capture, process and sell us commons that are not limited and environmentally precious, natural resources.

CRISIS OF COMMUNITY

We are seeing a transition to the capture and exploitation of non-finite resources. Capturing the 'commons' of our social relationships for economic growth is already happening. For example, the care of children and the elderly used to be performed by the family, the local community or the government. It is now increasingly carried out by commercial businesses. Equally, healthcare and education were once provided within the local community or by the state. In many countries today, they are wholly, or partially, in the hands of commercial businesses. Social media is another example of industry capturing, processing or selling our social relationships for economic growth, i.e. Facebook and dating apps.

We allow our relationships to be captured by businesses because we enjoy the benefits sold back to us. We can choose to be home carers or pursue other careers and outsource some of the caring roles. Through an explosion of social media, we can share our thoughts, ideas and creations with other people without leaving our sofa. We can meet people online more easily than in our neighbourhood. What we do not experience is the flip side of these benefits. We are losing our communities. Our consciousness is becoming more and more industrialised; we do not see the impact the increasing loss of community has on our psychology.

An increasing loss of community means we increasingly become separated from each other. Consequently, we become progressively more individualistic and competitive, creating an ever-widening gap between winners and losers in our societies. In 2015, income inequality in OECD countries (35 countries in the Organisation for Economic Co-operation and Development) was at its highest for 50 years.[7] The average income of the wealthiest 10% of the population was around nine times that of the poorest 10% across the OECD, up from seven times 25 years ago. In January 2020, Oxfam published a report stating that the world's 2,153 billionaires have more combined wealth than 4.6 billion people who make up 60% of the planet's population.[8] Why does this matter?

Even though globalisation has reduced inequality between nations, it appears to have increased inequality within nations, leading to higher rates of health and social problems. In their book *The Spirit Level*, Richard Wilkinson and Kate Pickett present findings from research into economic inequality and its impact on society.[9] They found that countries with the highest levels of inequality also suffered from high levels of health and social problems. In more equal societies, people are more likely to trust each other, be more engaged in their community and form higher levels of social cohesion.

Health and social problems affect us all. In the face of difficulties, the most affluent can use their wealth to separate themselves from the rest of society. In doing so, they imprison themselves behind high gates and walls. They suffer from the fear of crime caused by inequality. No matter how wealthy we are, we cannot build sustainable happiness upon the suffering of others.

PSYCHOLOGICAL CRISIS

Alongside capturing the commons of our natural resources and relationships, industry is also capturing the commons of our psychology for economic gain. This is being done by medicalising normal and everyday psychological conditions.

The *Diagnostic and Statistical Manual of Mental Disorders* (DSM) defines and classifies mental disorders in order to improve diagnoses, treatment and research.[10] The forerunner of the DSM was created in 1917 and contained just 22 diagnosable psychological conditions. Over the years, the number of diagnosable psychological conditions has grown to 265 in DSM-5, the latest edition. Although our understanding of psychological disorders has increased over the years, this substantial increase has been attributed to the pharmaceutical industry's influence. Psychiatrists are increasingly concerned that diagnostic thresholds are being lowered and too many new conditions are being introduced. Consequently, there is a fear that once relatively normal and common psychological conditions, such as shyness, are now being medicalised. Once a condition is included in the DSM, the pharmaceutical industry can sell us medication for its treatment.

The pharmaceutical industry is not the only industry looking to capture the commons of our psychology. Self-help is an industry that has grown significantly over the past few decades, selling books, seminars, apps and coaching, etc. In 2000, the self-help industry was estimated to be worth $2.48 billion per year in the US.[11] By 2016, this had increased to $9.90 billion, and it is expected to grow to $13 billion by 2022. These statistics are likely to be replicated in other westernised countries. In 2015 the Global Wellness Institute estimated the industry to be worth $3.72 trillion and identified that the market was growing at 5–6% per year.[12] Meditation is particularly popular and, according to Marketdata Enterprises Inc., is estimated to be growing by around 11.4% per year and set to be worth $2.08 billion by 2022.[13]

By capturing the commons of our psychology, the pharmaceutical and self-help industries can create and grow their markets. It is in their interest to create psychological crises. They must simply convince the 'worried well' they are experiencing a psychological problem that can be remedied by their products and services. For this to happen, we need to become separated from ourselves.

The pharmaceutical and self-help industries may be responding to what some people argue is an epidemic of mental illness, especially in westernised societies. Alternatively, as other people argue, the reported increases may be statistical anomalies and the prevalence of mental health conditions may not have changed for decades. Nevertheless, most people agree that a considerable number of people suffer from mental illness worldwide. Regardless of the pharmaceutical and self-help industries' marketing efforts, it appears our way of living in westernised societies is leading to a psychological crisis.

According to the World Health Organization (WHO), mental health conditions are increasing worldwide.[14] Between 11 and 18% of people in 2015 are estimated to have experienced a mental or substance abuse disorder, a rise of 13% in 10 years. Of these one billion people, anxiety disorder was the most prevalent, estimated to affect around 4% of the population. Even taking population increases into account, the numbers are huge and mental illness is a significant issue in our societies.

These statistics are replicated in the UK. According to the Mental Health Foundation, 70 million workdays are lost due to mental illness, including anxiety, depression and stress-related conditions.[15] Mental illness is the leading cause of sickness and absence from work. An independent review carried out by Lord Dennis Stevenson and Paul Farmer in 2017 found that around 15% of people at work in the UK are struggling with their mental health.[16]

Of most significant concern is the decreasing mental health of children. The WHO has estimated that between 10 and 20% of the world's children and adolescents have a mental health condition.[17] A UK survey by NHS Digital into the mental health of children and young people in 2020 found that one in six (16.0%) children aged 5–16 years were identified as having a probable mental disorder, increasing from one in nine (10.8%) in 2017.[18] The increase was evident in both boys and girls.

SUMMARY AND CONCLUSION

Nations are heavily reliant on capturing and exploiting natural resources to expand their economies. To allow this to happen, we needed to become separated from nature. If we are to survive as a species, economic growth through the overexploitation of the natural world must end. Countries and business leaders recognise this need and are turning their attention to capturing and exploiting other 'commons'. Social relationships are being captured, processed and sold back to us. For this to happen, we must become separated from each other. Our own psychology is also being captured, processed and sold back to us. To allow this to happen, we have had to become separated from ourselves. This increasing separation from nature, each other and ourselves enables economies to continue to grow, providing the jobs, pensions, products and services we desire.

While we have enjoyed the fruits of continued economic growth for decades, if not centuries, we are starting to experience the flip side. With increasingly frequent heatwaves, wildfires, floods and violent storms, we see our weather's volatility due to climate change. Viral pandemics are causing huge levels of death and suffering. As people find they cannot survive in inhospitable climates, migration will continue to place an additional burden on governments struggling to maintain their inhabitants' well-being. Increased conflicts within and between nations will be inevitable. High levels of inequality are ripping societies apart, causing a wide range of social problems. All of this, and much more, is feeding into the decline of our psychological well-being.

Governments are fully aware of the environmental, community and psychological crises facing us today. Strategies are being formulated, initiatives implemented and money invested in tackling each one. However, what is missing is a recognition of their interconnectivity. Even though we are aware of how the environmental crisis and inequality impact our psychological well-being, there is no talk of how inequality and mental illness fuel the environmental crisis. There is no recognition that all of these crises are being driven by something much deeper, our industrialised consciousness. As Albert Einstein (1879–1955) is purported to have said, 'No problem can be solved from the same level of consciousness that created it.' We need a new level of consciousness, and we need it now.

CHAPTER 2

THREE PSYCHOLOGICAL SEPARATIONS

As Sophia began her trek home, she saw an old man approaching on her right. She quickened her pace and tried to avoid him; she'd had enough of people for one day. But no matter how fast she walked, it was obvious that they would cross paths at the same time.

'Where are you headed?' enquired the old man.

'Home!' Sophia replied.

The man stroked his grey beard and replied, 'That surprises me, a young woman like you with a task still to do.'

Sophia tried to sidestep the old man, but somehow she couldn't get around him.

'Let me introduce myself,' he said, 'I'm Mimir. I come from your true north.'

What a strange way of talking, she thought. 'I'm Sophia,' she replied.

'Glad to meet you, Sophia.'

A silence ensued, which lasted so long it became too much for Sophia to bear. She asked the old man, 'Have you seen the damage in the town?'

'I have; I hear it was a three-headed dragon.'

'Something needs to be done.'

'I agree, so what do you intend to do?'

'Me? Why me?'

'As you said, something needs to be done, and I'm too old, so that leaves you.'

Mimir sat and beckoned Sophia to sit, and he continued, 'Listen to me carefully. The dragon resides in a land to the east, on the other side of the great river. Once across the river, you will find three paths. The Way of Nature, the Way of People and the Way of Self. Each one of these paths will take you to the three-headed dragon. You must decide which path you take.'

Sophia listened intently and asked, 'But which path is best?'

'To know that you must first look inside.' Then he stood up, turned around and walked back the way he had come.

He's an unusual man, she thought, but somehow, she trusted him. Surprisingly, she felt happy to return to the task. By now, it was getting late; she would start for the river in the morning. Sophia pitched her small tent and climbed in. She ate some food and stowed the rest. Then, with the axe beside her, she settled down to sleep, exhausted by the day's events. As she drifted into slumber, she thought about Mimir's words. To choose her way, she must first look inside. What did he mean by that? On the verge of sleep, her mind began contemplating her relationship with nature, with other people and herself.

INTRODUCTION

> A human being is a part of the whole, called by us 'Universe', a part limited in time and space. He experiences himself, his thoughts and feelings as something separate from the rest – a kind of optical delusion of his consciousness. This delusion is a kind of prison for us, restricting us to our personal desires and to affection for a few persons nearest to us. Our task must be to free ourselves from this prison by widening our circle of compassion to embrace all living creatures and the whole of Nature in its beauty. Nobody is able to achieve this completely, but the striving for such achievement is in itself a part of the liberation and a foundation for inner security
>
> Albert Einstein (1879–1955), translation by *The New York Times* (29 March 1972)

So, what has Einstein's view of the human experience got to do with the industrialisation of our consciousness? He has described precisely the task we face if we are to avoid destroying our future and that of generations to come. We must free ourselves from the delusion that we are separate from the rest of the universe if we are to live sustainably. This delusion comes from the industrialisation of our minds. A more sustainable society needs a new type of consciousness, one that reconnects us to the universe.

This chapter will enable you to explore the nature of your separation from the rest of the universe. In doing so, you will be asked to consider your psychological relationship with nature, other people and yourself. Considering these relationships will help you to determine the extent to which your consciousness has been industrialised. As we are all 'subject' to our consciousness, this will be a difficult process. You will be trying to bring 'objective awareness' to something you experience subjectively. Without awareness, you will have no option other than to continue to live with your industrialised consciousness. Awareness brings choice. You could go on to develop your consciousness and overcome the optical delusion that you are separate from the 'whole', the universe.

SEPARATION FROM NATURE

Have you ever gone into your garden, local park, woods, fields or mountains and just sat, doing nothing? I suggest you try it. Just be present and open all your senses to nature without trying to understand or label it. Bring the attention of all your senses to the aspects of nature that come into your awareness field. These may be the breeze, clouds, grass, plants, trees, stone, rocks, hills, mountains, insects, birds or mammals. Whenever I do this, I am filled with awe and wonder at the beauty of our natural environment. This feeling can grow and become all-consuming. Becoming overwhelmed by nature, I lose the sense of my own self-importance. I am not becoming insignificant – I am of equal significance to everything around me. I become fully integrated and feel connected with nature.

You may think this behaviour unusual; that this type of connection to nature is not normal in western society. Was a deep connection with nature ever normal? Other cultures live, or have lived, much closer to nature, for example, indigenous or First Nation communities. They are part of nature and live more sustainably within it. As a child, I spent many hours in woodland, so simply sitting in nature feels normal for me. Many children grow up without spending much time in nature, yet studies show spending time in green environments has a hugely beneficial impact on our mental health.

But what is nature? In the broadest sense, it is everything natural in the universe, from the smallest bacteria to the greatest solar system in a far-off galaxy and everything in between. When picturing nature, we tend to see flowers, trees, birds, wild animals, rivers, hills, mountains, etc. Everything untouched by human design. We would tend not to include a field containing genetically modified crops or a building made from limestone as being natural and part of nature. We see nature as pre-agricultural and pre-industrialisation. But it includes the natural resources that feed industry and create the products we use. Coal and oil are natural products, along with rain before it is processed and distributed to our homes.

If nature is everything natural in the universe, we must be nature. So how can we have been separated from it? When I talk about our separation, I am describing how we have been psychologically separated from nature.

Your Point on the Path of Separation from Nature

Is nature psychologically alive?

Before you try to answer this difficult question, we should explore the meaning of 'psychologically alive'. Psychology is the study of the mind and how it influences behaviour. So, I am essentially asking, does nature have a mind? At this stage, it is best not to confuse the mind with the brain. I am not asking if nature has a brain; I am asking if nature has a mind. The mind is our 'experience' of thinking and feeling; it is where we find consciousness. Scientists and philosophers call consciousness the 'hard problem' and do not agree on its make-up and origin. Nevertheless, they would agree it includes self-awareness (our thoughts and emotions) and awareness of our environment (our perception). So, is nature conscious? Does it have self-awareness, and is it aware of its surroundings?

Here I should also introduce soul and spirit. These are often interchanged. In some traditions, they are viewed as one, whereas they are seen as tangibly different in others. Consequently, definitions of soul and spirit are wide-ranging. Here I define the soul as the immaterial part of a being, a distinct entity, separate from the body. Thus, many religions consider the soul immortal and present in another plane of existence after death. Spirit, on the other hand, I define as 'life force' or the spark of life, present in every living thing and, therefore, connecting us. Chinese philosophy and religions would call this Chi. Our soul connects us to our spirit, which in turn connects us to everything else. So, if you think nature has consciousness, soul or a spirit, then, to you, nature is psychologically alive.

You might argue humans have consciousness, a soul and spirit, but a lump of granite does not. Humans are psychologically alive, but rocks are not. If so, where would you draw the line? Are animals psychologically alive?

These are tough questions. In November 2017, the UK Parliament grappled with the same problems as part of the EU Withdrawal Bill. The focus of the debate was animal sentience. Do animals feel pain and emotion? In conclusion, they voted to reject the inclusion of animal sentience into the Bill. In doing so, the UK Parliament aligned themselves with the 17th-century philosopher René Descartes, who is alleged to have asserted animals are without feelings, physical or emotional. Yet, most pet owners would claim their animals are sentient, having experienced their personalities, emotions and desires. Despite the UK Parliament's decision, most scientists agree animal sentience is proven, pointing to over 2,500 research studies on the subject.

So, what about trees and plants? Are they psychologically alive? In his book, *The Hidden Life of Trees*, Peter Wohlleben argues that we need to recognise trees are 'wonderful beings' with innate adaptability, intelligence, and the capacity to communicate with and heal other trees.[1] This suggests trees are psychologically alive. Wohlleben cites research that found mother trees suckle their young. Trees are connected by tiny roots, which grow assisted by a network of mycelium. The root tips have highly sensitive brain-like structures that can distinguish whether another root it encounters is from its own tree, from another species or from its own species. Upon encountering its own kind, sugar molecules flow between them, sharing food and energy.

So, are rocks psychologically alive? It might be helpful to consider the psychological aliveness of a rock as different from a human. I doubt anyone would argue that rocks have the same complex psychological attributes as humans. Yet many philosophers and scientists have argued that everything material, however small, has an element of consciousness. This is called 'panpsychism', which ascribes a primitive form of consciousness to entities at the fundamental level of particle physics. Panpsychism is one of the oldest philosophical theories, dating back to Thales and Plato, and has had a recent revival due to an increasing interest in consciousness. Panpsychism argues that consciousness permeates every aspect of reality rather than being a unique feature of the human experience. For panpsychists, consciousness is the foundation of the universe and is present in every quantum particle; therefore, all physical matter. This view does not mean a particle has the same level and type of consciousness as a human. On the contrary, the consciousness of a particle is believed to be incredibly simple. However, when particles combine in complex ways, entities develop more complex forms of consciousness, such as that found in humans. A rock does not demonstrate the consciousness of humans because it lacks the complex combinations of particles. Nonetheless, panpsychism holds that each particle in the rock is conscious, at an extremely simple level. Planet Earth is, therefore, a conscious entity along with everything on it.

If humans, animals, trees and rocks all have consciousness, do they have soul and spirit? From a panpsychism perspective, it could be argued that consciousness, being the foundation of the universe, is the life force, the spirit. Even so, most panpsychists are unlikely to argue this gives humans, animals, trees and rocks a soul. Attributing a soul to animals, plants, inanimate objects and natural phenomena is known as animism. For many indigenous peoples, animism is a key part of their belief systems. As with panpsychism, animism does not merely focus on isolated and independent entities, it deems that everything in the universe has a soul. In many philosophies and religions, especially eastern, there is an intrinsic connection between all things on the planet. The world is a single living entity, containing all other living entities, all related and interconnected. The Earth's soul, anima mundi, is the living aspect of its material existence.

There is a theory that challenges the psychological aliveness of everything, even humans. It is called eliminism, also known as eliminative materialism. This theory purports that our understanding of the mind is false, and the mental states we believe we experience do not exist. The logic behind eliminism is based on whether different mental states can be traced back to neural activity. The theory asserts that what we believe to be consciousness is simply down to chemistry and physics in our brains. Eliminists argue that consciousness, soul and spirit do not exist anywhere.

So, is nature psychologically alive? You may believe humans and animals are psychologically alive, but plants and rocks are not. You may think nature is conscious but does not have a soul or spirit. Your answer may be a combination of these.

Whatever your answer, you should be able to position your belief along a continuum from eliminism at one end to panpsychism/animism at the other (see Figure 2.1).

Figure 2.1 *Eliminism–Panpsychism/Animism Continuum*

Eliminism	Panpsychism / Animism
No material basis for psychological aliveness in nature	Nature has consciousness, soul and spirit

My next question is:

Are humans an equal part of, or separate and superior to, nature?

Perhaps, this is a more straightforward question, though maybe one you have not been asked before. Your answer will probably be a result of unconscious bias, i.e. beyond your objective perception. We all see the world subjectively rather than objectively.

You might believe humans are superior and separate from nature, an anthropocentric view. This view holds that human beings are the most important species and separate from the rest of nature. Therefore, we can, and have the right to, control nature through technological and economic advances. You may believe that nature is cruel and indifferent and, therefore, we humans need to be separated and protected from it. Anthropocentrism assumes all phenomena should only be interpreted through human values and experiences. Critics of anthropocentrism, such as the psychologist James Hillman, philosopher Lynn White and ecologist Arne Naess (1912–2009), argue that our propensity to see nature purely from the human perspective is the root cause of our current environmental crisis. Proponents of anthropocentrism counter this argument with the view that the environmental crisis is due to society not being anthropocentric enough. Deeper anthropocentrism, they contend, will make the world more suitable for humans. So, while anthropocentrism is being blamed for the environmental crisis, a lot of environmental activism and actions are taken from an anthropocentric perspective. If you believe humans are separate from nature, then you are far from alone. Anthropocentrism is considered to be profoundly embedded in most modern human cultures.

However, if you think humans are an equal and integral part of nature, you have an ecocentric viewpoint. Ecocentrism is nature-centred, as opposed to human-centred, in its values system and, therefore, sees no tangible division between human and non-human entities.

Ecocentrism is ecosphere (biosphere) egalitarianism; all life is equal and has the same value. The concept of ecocentrism was conceived by the environmentalist Aldo Leopold (1887–1948) and developed in the deep ecology movement founded by Arne Naess.

Your answer may lie between anthropocentrism and ecocentrism. For example, you may believe humans are an integral part of nature, but we are superior to other entities due to our higher levels of consciousness and intelligence.

You should be able to plot your answer along a continuum from anthropocentrism at one end and ecocentrism at the other (see Figure 2.2).

Figure 2.2 Anthropocentrism–Ecocentrism Continuum

Anthropocentrism
Humans are separate to, and above, nature
Ecocentrism
Humans are a part of, and equal to, nature

By combining these two continuums, a two-by-two matrix is formed (see Figure 2.3). By plotting where your beliefs lie on each, you can determine which of the four quadrants best suits your relationship with nature. For example, the plots below describe a spiritual ecologist.

To label each quadrant, I have used the theories that best fit the characteristics.

> **Spiritual ecologist:** Spiritual ecologists recognise the unity and interrelationship of all creation. Early proponents include Rudolf Steiner (1861–1925) and Pierre Teilhard de Chardin (1881–1955). Steiner created a philosophy and movement called anthroposophy that seeks to guide the spiritual development in humans with spiritual development in the universe. Teilhard de Chardin, a French Jesuit and palaeontologist, spoke of a

transition towards a consciousness of the divinity within every particle of life, even dense minerals. More recent proponents include David Suzuki, an ecologist and environmentalist, who stated the way we see the world shapes the way we treat it.[2] If we see resources rather than spiritual entities in nature, we are more likely to exploit rather than preserve them.

Gaia theorist: Gaia theorists assert that living organisms and their inorganic surroundings interact to form a complex system. Chemist James Lovelock formulated this theory in the late 1960s.[3] The theory argues that Earth's systems self-regulate global temperature, the salinity of seawater, atmospheric oxygen levels, the maintenance of a hydrosphere of liquid water and other environmental variables to ensure sufficient stability is maintained for life. Every entity on the Earth is interrelated. Yet, there is no indication each of the entities is psychologically alive. On the contrary, it merely recognises symbiotic relationships combine to create a living planet without suggesting the Earth is psychologically alive.

Earth steward: Earth stewards see entities in nature as psychologically alive but humans as superior. For instance, a shepherd provides stewardship over a sheepdog, another psychologically alive entity, or foresters have stewardship over trees. Earth stewardship is associated with ecologist Terry Chapin and focuses on shaping the future relationship between people and nature to the benefit of both. The Earth steward's goal is not to protect nature from people but to protect nature for human welfare, an anthropocentric view.

Utilitarianist: Utilitarians believe the most ethical choice is the one that will produce the greatest good for the greatest number of people. Philosopher Jeremy Bentham (1748–1832) described utility as 'that property in any object, whereby it tends to produce benefit, advantage, pleasure, good, or happiness (all this in the present case comes to the same thing) or (what comes again to the same thing) to prevent the happening of mischief, pain, evil, or unhappiness to the party whose interest is considered'.[4] It is a viewpoint often used in business because it accounts for costs and benefits. However, the costs and benefits are always taken from the human perspective, seeing nature simply as a resource to be utilised for human well-being and happiness.

Figure 2.3 Relationship with Nature Matrix

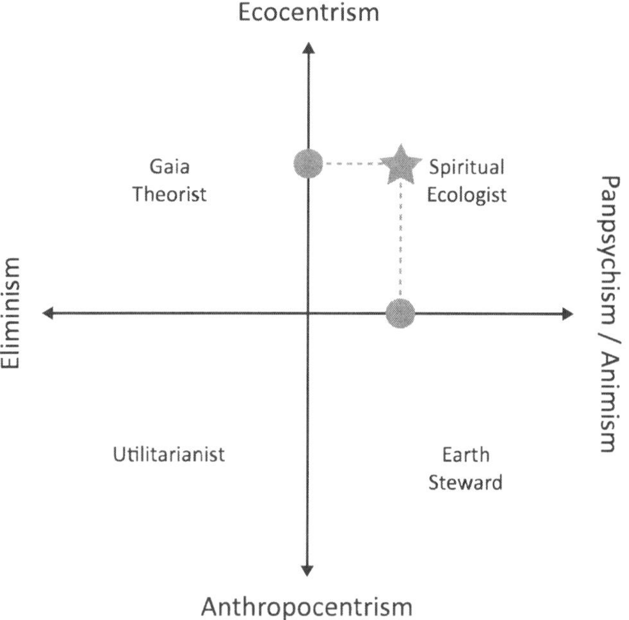

Our Separation from Nature – The Rise of Utilitarianism

Most westernised societies have been on a path from spiritual ecology towards utilitarianism. Centuries ago, we collectively experienced nature as a living and spiritual presence. Today nature is in danger of becoming merely a utilitarian means to an end.

Our increasing separation from nature allows industry to freely consume and destroy it. We no longer feel its pain. Ecologist Stephan Harding says, for the western mind, the Earth, including its non-human inhabitants, has become no more than a dead machine to be exploited for our own benefit.[5] There has been such a significant human impact on Earth's geology and ecosystems that our current geological era has been named the Anthropocene; the human-made.

SEPARATION FROM EACH OTHER

How often do your conversations become debates? Is there a winner and a loser? How many times have you changed your mind to align with the argument put forward by the other person? I suspect, like most people, it does not happen often. When we lose a debate, it is like losing a battle but not the war. Instead, we go away to rethink our argument and find more supportive evidence before re-engaging once again. Debates rarely lead to consensus, more in-depth understanding or creating something new. Instead, they drive us apart. Often, the more we debate, the more our views become entrenched and polarised. So why do we do it so frequently? To protect our self-esteem. When people disagree with us, we feel less valued. Therefore, we compete with each other to maintain our self-esteem. Debating is ingrained in western societies. It is encouraged in school, academia and business. We see it every day in politics and journalism. Of course, a debate of this nature is often necessary to scrutinise the decisions of leaders. But has it gone too far? Our need to compete, to maintain our self-esteem, is driving us apart.

In considering our increasing separation from each other, I am talking about a psychological separation. Our psychological relationships collectively form our society. They shape how we get along with each other and work together to create our society. Our views on economics and politics influence our psychological relationships. For most people, the link between our political opinions and our psychological relationships with other people may not be conscious. Our views are often the result of our cultural and social conditioning. However, in this section, I argue that our increasing psychological separation from each other is also the result of our consciousness's industrialisation.

Our separation from each other provides business opportunities. For industry to fully exploit the Earth's natural resources, we had to be separated from nature as we have seen. Equally, for economic activity to fully exploit our social relationships, we must be separated from each other. There is money to be made when society breaks down and loses its community. Our social interactions, or lack of them, form the foundations of new economic activity.

In this section, I ask you to consider how you relate to other people. My argument is that we have increasingly become psychologically separated from each other.

Your Point on the Path of Separation from Each Other

Do you consider yourself an individual or part of a collective?

Answering this question is like being asked in an interview: Do you work best on your own or in a team? In an interview, you may try to give the impression you work well in both situations. In reality, you will have a preference influenced by your psychology, political views, religion and culture. Before you answer the question, we should explore what is meant by 'individualism' and 'collectivism' and how their manifestation is changing worldwide.

Individualism emphasises the moral worth of individuals, independence, self-reliance and liberty. It rejects any external interference on an individual's choices by society, the State or any other group in its purest form. As a political ideology, individualism advocates that the interests of the individual take precedence over the State's interests. Instead, the State's role is to protect each individual's liberty, as long as the individual does not infringe on another's liberty. Individualism champions the right of a person to freedom and self-realisation, and is opposed to tradition, religion or any other form of external moral standard being used to limit an individual's choice and actions. It relies on, and emphasises, the individual's own conscience and reasoning for moral guidance and judgement. Although not inherently selfish, individualism argues that people are not duty-bound to adhere to a socially imposed standard of morality. Pure anarchism is an extreme example of individualism, which holds that the pursuit of self-interest should not be constrained by any collective body, including a democratic government.

Conversely, in collectivism, the individual is seen as being subordinate to a group, whether that be a State, nation, race, social class, family or team, etc. Collectivists value emotional dependency, group solidarity and compliance with the group decision. Social rules focus on selflessness and doing what is right for society. People who subscribe to collectivist perspectives tend to find common values and goals that unite them and demonstrate 'in-group' behaviour to prevent them from being excluded. At its purest, collectivism is based on replacing the identity of the individual with the group identity. The individual must submit to the authority of the collective group. Totalitarian government is an extreme example of collectivism, restricting individual opposition to the State and exercising an extremely high degree of control over public and private life.

It is often said that eastern countries, such as China, Japan, Indonesia, North Korea, South Korea, India, etc., have more collectivist cultures. In contrast, countries in the west, such as the USA, Canada, the UK, etc., are said to have more individualist cultures. In eastern cultures, the individual is generally not conceived to be a unique entity but is seen as a part of a wider society. In western cultures, people tend to consider themselves unique individuals with their own views, ideas and achievements. Across Europe, individualism and collectivism vary according to religion. Protestant countries tend to be more individualist, while Catholic countries tend to be collectivist. Educational systems, derived from the dominant philosophical and political beliefs, also have a significant influence.

Gerard Hendrik (Geert) Hofstede (1928–2020), a Dutch social psychologist, made comparisons across the continuum from individualism to collectivism.[6] Between 1967 and 1973, he surveyed national differences in values involving 117,000 IBM employees worldwide. Hofstede found that both wealth and climate are major predictors of whether a country will value individualism or collectivism. Wealthier nations tend to be more individualistic, and poorer countries more collectivistic. Colder climates tended to favour individualism, whereas warmer climates favoured collectivism.

So, now do you consider yourself an individual or part of a collective?

You may value your freedom, independence and self-reliance or solidarity, selflessness and mutual support. Your answer may be a combination of these.

Whatever your answer, you should be able to position your preference along a continuum from individualism at one end to collectivism at the other (see Figure 2.4).

Figure 2.4 Individualism–Collectivism Continuum

Individualism
Freedom of action for individuals over the group

Collectivism
Priority of the group over the individual

The next question I would like to ask is:

Are you inherently more competitive or co-operative?

I have included the word 'inherently' because the people around you will influence your behaviour. If they are co-operating, you may co-operate. If they are competing, you are likely to compete. According to Ernst Fehr, a Swiss behavioural economist, 70% of the population in western societies are naturally more co-operative than competitive.[7] His research showed that in games where all participants are co-operators, the group would look for win–win solutions where no one loses and all benefit equally. However, if a competitive person joins the game, bringing their 'I win/ you lose' approach, gradually, all the co-operators become competitive, and the result is to win or lose.

In western societies, the competitive 30% are more likely to rise to the top of an organisation or society and set the rules for everyone else. Their rules tend to benefit competitive people, giving them an advantage over the co-operative 70%. Western society has developed in line with the rules of the competitive 30% rather than the 70% who are collaborative.

Competition can be seen in young children in western societies, as they compete for attention or toys. Growing older, we are encouraged to compete for the best grades or in competitive sports. We compete on social media to have the most exciting profile. We compete at work for promotion or to avoid redundancy. Popular television programmes involve competition rather than people working together for the common good.

There is an often-quoted and misinterpreted phrase, 'survival of the fittest', attributed to Charles Darwin (1809–1882). From this, many believe it is natural for us to compete to improve our lives. Ironically, the phrase was coined by Herbert Spencer (1820–1903) in his book *Principles of Biology* published in 1864 and attributed to Darwin.[8] Russian anarchist Peter Kropotkin (1842–1921), in his book *Mutual*

Aid: A Factor of Evolution, stated that the concept of 'survival of the fittest' supports co-operation rather than competition.[9] He argued that the struggle is against natural conditions unfavourable to the species and not against each other. Therefore, the species that could draw upon mutual aid attained the greatest development. This mutual aid is seen in animals living in colonies, packs or groups, etc. In terms of human society, he theorised that mutual aid was one of the dominant factors in our evolution.

Competition can simply be a matter of greed. Some people compete to gain more than they need, even though this will deprive others. As Abraham Maslow (1908–1970) pointed out in his Hierarchy of Needs, once our basic survival needs are met for food and shelter, we may then compete for relationships, esteem and power.[10]

Co-operation, on the other hand, involves people working together for mutual benefit. This benefit can be in terms of meeting their economic, social or cultural needs and aspirations. We co-operate for reasons such as supporting our family, to receive immediate benefits or to build later reciprocity. In fact, since the earliest tribes, co-operation has been at the heart of our social groups and now our workplace. It is a way for societies to organise work and allocate tasks. In economics terms, this is division of labour. It allows a person to specialise in one area, knowing others can be called on for other types of work.

Much evidence shows a correlation between enjoyment, performance and competition. John Tauer at the University of St Thomas and Judith Harackiewicz at the University of Wisconsin-Madison observed hundreds of young children taking free throws at a basketball hoop.[11] There were three situations in the study:

1. The children played co-operatively with a partner, trying to achieve as many baskets as possible together.

2. They played alone against a partner, trying to score more baskets than him/her.

3. They played with a partner against another pair.

They found the children enjoyed situation three the most, i.e. mixing the co-operation and the competition, and they performed best in this context.

So, combining co-operation with competition is the key to triggering enjoyment and increasing performance. However, competition can increase our performance when we work alone. In 2003, Matthew Rhea and his colleagues at Arizona State University studied weightlifters.[12] They found the athletes bench-pressed more when competing against another person than when lifting by themselves. Businesses often prefer to recruit competitive people for this reason.

Coming back to the question, are you inherently more competitive or co-operative? Please consider aspects such as how much you enjoy competing in sport, striving to deliver the best performance at work or increasing your wealth. Alternatively, you may enjoy building things with others, helping people or sharing rewards. You may be in the middle. For instance, enjoy winning as part of a co-operative team.

You should be able to position your preference along a continuum from competitive at one end and co-operative at the other (see Figure 2.5).

Figure 2.5 *Competitive–Co-operative Continuum*

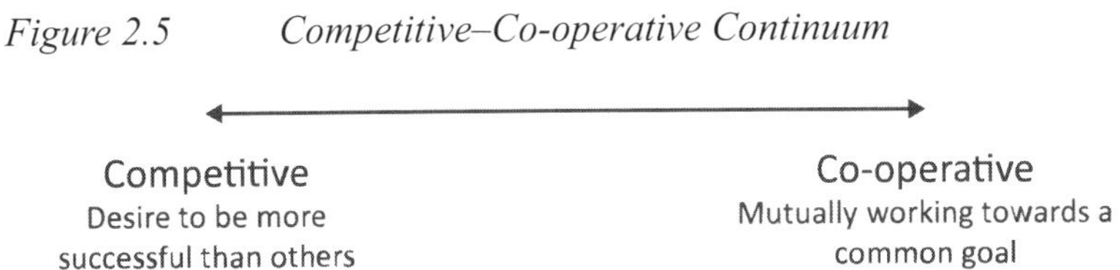

Combining these two continuums forms a two-by-two matrix (see Figure 2.6). By plotting where your preferences lie on each, you can determine which of the four quadrants best suits the nature of your relationship with other people.

Figure 2.6 Relationship with Each Other Matrix

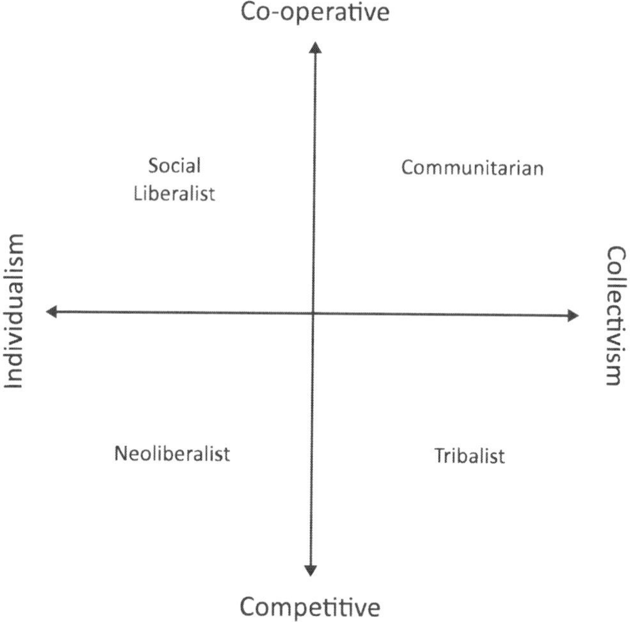

Communitarian: Communitarians emphasise the connection between the individual and the community. Their core belief is that a person's identity is a reflection of their relationships. Communitarianism stresses common interests, shared values and the well-being of all in the community. It opposes policies that give the individual precedence and benefits over and above everyone else.

Social liberalist: Social liberalism is a social and political philosophy and can be considered as an economic philosophy. It differs from classical liberalism because it favours collective rights such as social welfare and justice. Social liberalists emphasise the freedom of the individual and balance liberty with social equality.

Tribalist: Tribalists hold a collectivist and competitive worldview. At first glance, a competitive collectivist would appear to be an oxymoron. However, the tribe is defined by the level, from individual to the community, at which the competition occurs. Tribalism is where society divides into groups whose members are united by a shared belief and, as a result, form a collective. Competition then naturally arises between the groups over differences in beliefs or the psychology of in-group/out-group behaviour. As Henri Tajfel (1919–1982) and his colleagues found, when we are in a group, we quickly discriminate in favour of the people within our group and against those outside.[13] This gives us a sense of protection and belonging. If our group performs favourably against another, our self-esteem is enhanced. Identity politics is a form of tribalism in which people prioritise concerns on the grounds of race, religion, gender, class, culture, outlook or interests, etc. They then form alliances with others who share this identity rather than engaging in more broad-based party politics. Examples include Extinction Rebellion, the alt-right, Momentum, etc.

Neoliberalist: Neoliberalism, like social liberalism, is an economic, social and political philosophy. Neoliberalists emphasise the freedom of the individual but, additionally, free-market competition. Competition is seen as a natural aspect of human relations, and they seek to protect the natural freedom of individuals from the power of government. As such, they believe that allowing free-market competition is the most efficient way to allocate resources and this gives everyone what they deserve. Attempts to limit competition by the government are taken as an infringement on liberty. Inequality is seen as necessary, virtuous, and as a motivator for utility, efficiency and entrepreneurship.

Neoliberalists believe wealth trickles down, and everyone benefits eventually. Efforts to create a more equal society are seen as counterproductive and morally corrosive.

Our Separation from Each Other – The Rise of Neoliberalism

Most societies are moving towards neoliberalism. Centuries ago, we would have lived in tribal societies. As communication links improved, tribes began co-operating, and communities were established. With much-improved communication, people move away from friends, family and local communities. Consequently, societies are increasingly fragmented. This has facilitated a decline in co-operative collectivism and paved the way for more competitive individualism.

As societies have developed and changed over the past 100 years, there has been tension between the liberty of the individual and the common good. Various methods of managing this have been attempted around the world. More socialist methods gave priority to co-operation and collectivism, whereas libertarians gave priority to competition and the individual. There have also been a plethora of combinations of these two positions. Nevertheless, in the past decades, political parties from both the left and right have worked towards societies becoming more neoliberal in the western world.

In Europe and the USA, with collectivist forms of government such as fascism and communism having been defeated, there has been a rise of liberalism in both politics and economics. Early proponents of neoliberal policies were Margaret Thatcher in the UK and Ronald Reagan in the USA. Although more centrist liberals such as Bill Clinton, Tony Blair and Angela Merkel have pushed back against some aspects of neoliberalism, it has remained mostly intact. Due to globalisation and neoliberal policies at the International Monetary Fund (IMF), neoliberalism has spread across the globe.

Globalisation is the interaction and integration of people,

companies and governments, allowing increased trade and cultural exchange between nations. Combined with neoliberalism, globalisation has led to local and national economies being integrated into a global unregulated market economy. The IMF identifies four basic components of globalisation: trade and transactions, capital and investment movements, migration and movement of people, and the dissemination of knowledge. Created in 1945, the IMF comprises 189 countries and seeks to foster global monetary co-operation, secure financial stability, facilitate international trade, promote high employment, sustain economic growth and reduce poverty. Due to its practices of forcing debtor countries to open up their markets to free-market competition and adopt austerity measures, the IMF has been regarded as one of the key organisations driving the increase of neoliberalism around the world. Neoliberalist polices are generally supported because, globally, our cultures are becoming increasingly individualistic.

In 2017, Henri Santos, Michael Varnum and Igor Grossman published an article called 'Global increases in individualism'.[14] Examining 51 years of data on individualist practices and values across 78 countries, they found individualism appeared to have increased by 12% over the past several decades. Only four countries seemed to be headed away from individualism in their practices: Cameroon, Malawi, Malaysia and Mali; while only Armenia, China, Croatia, Ukraine and Uruguay headed away from individualism in their values. By far the most potent factor to influence individualism was socio-economic development. As education, income and the proportion of white-collar jobs increased, so did individualistic practices and values. Generally, countries not showing an increase in individualistic values rated lowest in socio-economic development. China was the only exception.

This research begs the question, does socio-economic development increase neoliberalism, or vice-versa? Whatever the answer, it suggests economic growth is associated with individualism and competitiveness. Our separation from each other may be growing the economy. As I outlined previously, with the increasing protections on natural resources restricting economic growth, the shortfall can be made up by selling services to replace our social interactions. Industry is now capturing, processing and selling us our community. In the process, we are increasingly separating from each other.

Our Separation from Each Other – The Possible Fall of Neoliberalism

The global financial crisis of 2007–2008 demonstrated the fragility of neoliberalist economies. With the supply of money drying up, governments turned to more 'collective' forms of economic policy to kickstart a recovery. Governments who had previously been embarking on privatisation programmes now found themselves essentially nationalising banks to prop up the financial system and save the economy. Many hoped this financial shock would herald a significant change in government policy, economics and society. Yet neoliberalism soon returned with business as usual, albeit with increased regulation in the financial sector.

This lack of change was one factor that inspired many protests, such as the anti-capitalist demonstrations at the Group of Eight (G8) and Group of Twenty (G20) summits and, most notably, the Occupy Movement. This was an international pressure group that sprang up in opposition to high social and economic inequality levels and a lack of real democracy. Its primary concern was how large corporations control the world and operate to benefit the wealthy minority. The first Occupy protest was in Zuccotti Park, near Wall Street, which began on 17 September 2011. By October, there were Occupy protests in 951 cities across 82 countries. Gradually these were broken up, and the financial sectors of major cities returned to normal. Did the Occupy Movement make a difference? The answer is debatable. Although large corporations have not radically changed their practices, and inequality remains high in neoliberalist countries, there is a trend towards more values-driven behaviour in business, especially in the financial sector. It could be argued that Occupy inspired Extinction Rebellion, which has become a global entity, challenging neoliberalist policies on climate change and sustainability.

As mentioned earlier, the IMF is regarded as one of the main drivers of neoliberalism. They give countries financial assistance and loans on the condition neoliberal reforms be implemented. However, in June 2016, the IMF's *Finance & Development* journal warned that neoliberalism is jeopardising the future of the world economy. In an article entitled 'Neoliberalism: Oversold?' its authors Jonathan D. Ostry, Prakash Loungani and Davide Furceri, from the IMF's Research Department, stated that 'instead of delivering growth, some neoliberal policies have increased inequality, in turn jeopardising durable expansion'.[15] They acknowledged that while the liberalisation of trade has helped lift many out of poverty, and some privatisations have raised efficiency, the costs of inequality have been prominent. Consequently, the benefits of increased growth have been difficult to establish when looking across a broad group of countries. The article highlights that inequality hurts the level and sustainability of growth, and neoliberalist policies increase economic volatility and crisis frequency. The authors conclude that the benefits of some important parts of the neoliberal agenda have been somewhat overplayed.

The Covid-19 pandemic demonstrated again the fragility of the neoliberalist system and its inability to cope with crises. Countries reliant on globalised supply chains found they could not procure the personal protective equipment (PPE) needed to fight the virus, treat the sick and care for the vulnerable. As it took hold, countries increasingly adopted protectionist measures to retain products within their borders. Many governments abandoned competition regulations to enable pharmaceutical companies to collaborate to search for a vaccination and develop treatments. Governments intervened in the economy to financially support individuals and businesses. In the short term, people became less individualistic and competitive, forming community groups to support the vulnerable and collectively demonstrating their gratitude and support for front-line workers.

Even though neoliberalism has repeatedly bounced back over the past 40 years, it does appear to be coming to the end of its useful life.

SEPARATION FROM OURSELVES

Have you ever witnessed yourself? Have you ever observed your thoughts, emotions and behaviour? Most of the time, we are our thoughts, emotions and behaviour, so much so that we become them. Witnessing yourself is like being on a balcony at a nightclub and looking down at yourself on the dance floor. Would you feel embarrassed? This embarrassment is probably why we do not generally witness ourselves, but it can be done. Why not give it a go now? Just follow these simple instructions:

- Become aware of your breathing. Just notice the physical sensations in your body as you breathe. Notice who is doing the noticing.

- Become aware of how you are feeling, right now. Notice where you are experiencing this emotion within your body. Notice who is doing the noticing.

- Become aware of your thoughts. Just notice them and let them on their way, like clouds crossing a clear blue sky. Notice who is doing the noticing.

In doing this simple exercise, you will have experienced that there is part of you that is having the experience, the body sensation, emotion or thought, and there is a part that is noticing that you are having the experience. From this exercise, you find there are at least two of you (selves) within your psychology. All of us have multiple selves.

Psychologists have mapped our psyche and created several different elements and selves. Consequently, when I talk about becoming separated from ourselves, I am talking about how the selves within our psyche have become separated. For simplicity, I am calling these separated selves our ego and our Self. Do not worry about the psychological terminology. I will define the terms as we begin to work with them. In this section, I argue that the increasing separation of our ego from our Self has resulted from the industrialisation of our consciousness.

First, I will ask how you generally relate to aspects of your psyche. I recognise this will be difficult and I am not expecting you to provide answers to my questions. It is an opportunity to reflect on your psychology. From this exploration, I will show that we are losing connection with our Self and becoming overly attached to, and critical of, our ego.

Your Point on the Path of Separation from Yourself

In plotting the path of separation from ourselves, it is useful to consider how you relate to different elements of your psyche. Ask yourself the following question:

Where is my centre of gravity? Is it closer to my ego or my Self?

This question is difficult to answer. First, because of the terminology. What are ego and Self? I will explore these definitions later in this section. Second, most people have not developed the self-awareness to enable them to identify where they gravitate to the most, Self or ego. For most people in the west, their centre of gravity will be closer to their ego than their Self, unless they have done a lot of spiritual or self-development work. The question simply aims to help you explore aspects of your psyche and start to understand how, over the centuries, we have moved from being close to our Self to being close to our ego.

Philosophers and psychologists have developed their own models of the psyche (the entirety of our psychological functioning). Unfortunately, the same terminology can mean different things in different models. For example, when the Greek philosophers were using the word 'soul', they often referred to our 'psyche'. In Sigmund Freud's (1856–1939) model, the ego equates primarily to our conscious processes, whereas in Carl Jung's (1875–1961) model, the persona is generally considered to be the ego and, like Freud's model, the ego is the seat of consciousness. The other complication is our common language. For example, when we talk about someone's ego, we often speak in derogative terms. We also use the word soul without definition or in a religious context. Some psychologists, such as Roberto Assagioli (1888–1974), prefer not to use the word 'soul' due to the religious connotations and instead, use the word 'Self' with a capital 'S' and then refer to the seat of consciousness as 'self' with a lower-case 's'. This whole area of models of the psyche can be hugely confusing.

Some of these problems were caused by translations. Many models were developed in different languages, and meanings changed in translation. Some models are very old, and our understanding of the psyche has changed over time. With all this confusion, it is important to keep in mind that none of the models is the truth. They are simply representations of something too complex and intangible. They are just different ways to help us try to understand the complexities of our minds.

To avoid confusion, I will use consistent terminology when discussing the models put forward by philosophers and psychologists. I may not be using the terms the originators would have used, but, for simplicity, here are the terms I will use and their definitions:

> **Psyche:** This represents the entirety of our psychological life. It is the totality of the human mind. Our psyche contains our ego, soul and witness consciousness as well as our thoughts, emotions and desires. It includes what is conscious and unconscious.

Ego: This is the constructed identity we like to present to the world. It is our self-image or mask. In everyday language, when we use the word 'me', we are often referring to our ego. It is our self-identity.

Self: This is the core of our being, not conditioned by everyday life experiences, and it does not need defending. It is often referred to as being the 'higher Self' or the 'soul'. It is also the gateway to 'non-dualism', where the distinction between subject and object disappears. Everything becomes connected as one unifying whole. Our Self can, therefore, connect us to our spirituality.

Witness consciousness: This is the awareness of both our external and internal worlds and is often called 'pure awareness' or 'conscious self'. When we use the word 'I' in everyday language, we are often referring to our witness consciousness. It is not to be confused with the contents of the consciousness, such as thoughts and emotions; instead, it is the part of our psyche that can witness these. You will use your witness consciousness to see if your centre of gravity is closer to your ego or Self.

Our ego is steadily constructed throughout our lives as we determine how our behaviour interacts with the world. Gradually, we adopt behaviours that work well for us. These behaviours become habitual and then form our personality, how other people see us. Genetics also plays a part, influencing the nature of the behaviours we try out in the world in the first place. We adapt our behaviour following on from our experience. Therefore, our ego is our adaptive behaviour. As these behaviours become habitual, they become who we are, our personality. When we identify with our personality, we become our ego. This identification gives us our self-respect and self-esteem. These are highly valuable to us and, consequently, need defending from perceived attacks and threats. We protect ourselves through various psychological techniques called ego defences, for example, denial or projection (seeing our own weaknesses in others). Just as we have habitual behaviours, we also have our favourite ego defences and these also become part of our personality. They are how we keep ourselves safe.

Although most people identify with their ego, some people are more able to identify with their Self. They achieve this through years of spiritual and psychological development or extraordinary events, such as a near-death experience. Nonetheless, we all experience our Self doing its work. The more we can move towards Self, the more we move away from being driven by our ego.

Witness consciousness is often strong in children. As much is new, children tend to experience things directly without judgement or preconceived ideas. Getting older, we see things as we expect them to be, take cognitive short-cuts and group things together in schemas (representations or models). We also tend to get caught up and identify with thoughts and emotions. We spend our time planning ahead, or worrying about the past, rather than living in the present. We believe our thoughts are true and make them our reality; for instance, I am good at this and bad at that. We identify with our emotions, such as I am worried or I am happy. We then become that emotion; for instance, I am a worrier, or I am a cheerful person. Gradually, our witness consciousness gets submerged beneath a sea of thoughts and emotions. When we develop our witness consciousness, we can surface and observe our ego and the workings of our Self. We can then determine where we spend most of our time, where our centre of gravity lies. Our 'witness consciousness' can move up and down a continuum between the ego and the Self, being aware of each. However, it is likely to feel more comfortable identifying more with one than the other.

Coming back to my question: where is your centre of gravity? Towards your ego or your Self? As I said, this is a difficult question to answer, but please indicate on this continuum where you think your centre of gravity is (see Figure 2.7).

Figure 2.7 *Centre of Gravity between Ego and Self*

Ego ⟷ Self

My next question is:

Are you more self-critical or self-compassionate?

You will be aware when you are being critical of other people or when you are demonstrating compassion. Nevertheless, you may not be aware of whether you are being self-critical or when you are practising self-compassion. For you, these may be simply part of the way you manage yourself and have become an unconscious habit. While you consider your answer, I am going to unpack these terms.

Both self-criticism and self-compassion are forms of self-evaluation, comparing yourself against standards of behaviour or the progress you would like to make towards achieving your goals. They can be done objectively. The difference is how you use the results of the evaluation.

Self-criticism tends to focus on one's flaws. This evaluation is also often in comparison with other people. It can be directed to various aspects of the self, such as behaviour, achievement, thoughts, emotions, appearance, intellect, etc. If we are being self-critical and believe we do not meet our own expectations, this can spur us on to try to do better. However, while it can be a motivator, the act of self-criticism can hurt. So, with self-criticism, the motivator is to avoid pain. We avoid the pain by continually trying to meet our own standards, achieve our own goals or just do better than other people. Consequently, self-criticism is strongly related to competition. We either compete with ourselves or against others. People who employ a lot of self-criticism are usually high achievers and use it as a pre-condition for self-improvement and growth. They set themselves high targets and work hard to achieve them.

Recognising the negative impacts of self-criticism, psychologist Kristen Neff has proposed self-compassion.[16] This is about turning inwards the compassion we usually extend outwards when we see other people suffering. Self-compassion is first about refraining from being harsh on ourselves and, instead, being gentle and warm. Second, rather than competing with others, it is about recognising that we are human and that part of the human condition is that we are not perfect and we make mistakes. Third, self-compassion is about holding our emotions in an open and balanced way, without bias or exaggeration.

So back to the question: do you tend to be more self-critical or more self-compassionate when evaluating yourself? Whatever your answer, you should be able to position your preference along a continuum from self-critical at one end and self-compassionate at the other (see Figure 2.8).

Figure 2.8 Self-compassionate–Self-critical Continuum

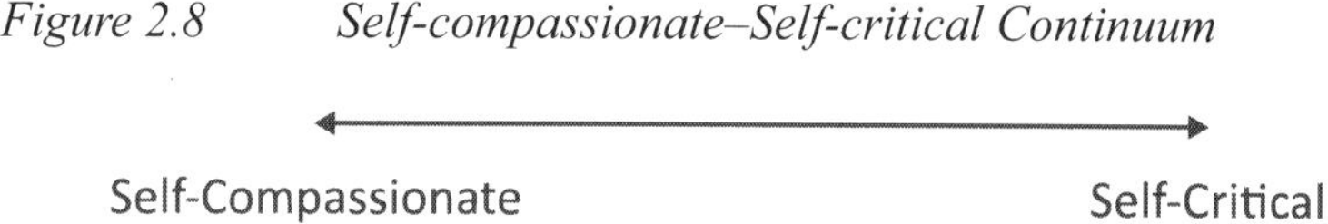

When we combine these two continuums, a two-by-two matrix is formed (see Figure 2.9). By plotting where your preferences lie on each continuum, you can determine the nature of your connection with your own psychology.

Transcender: Transcendence involves expanding your personal boundaries, connecting with something beyond your ego, considering yourself to be an integral part of a unifying whole and acting accordingly. It is about relating to, and connecting with, something greater than yourself, such as other humans, nature, the universe or a spiritual consciousness. Transcending your ego and identifying more with your Self is likely to have enabled you to find true meaning and purpose in your life. Transcendence is often associated with the highest and most inclusive levels of human consciousness. At its highest level, the Self connects with the spirit, the life force, and non-duality (the dissolution of subject–object and self–other) is realised.

Actualiser: Actualisation is the growth of your ego towards self-fulfilment through achieving its potential. It involves you accepting who you are rather than striving to become your ideal self. Therefore, you are likely to be more compassionate with yourself than critical. This self-acceptance will likely have afforded you a relatively high level of psychological robustness, allowing you to be motivated by personal growth rather than being focused on overcoming any deficiencies.

Denier: If you are a denier, it suggests you have connected more with your Self than your ego and you practise self-criticism more than self-compassion. You stand outside of yourself, look back in and take a critical perspective. As denial is the act of letting go of the ego and forgoing personal pleasures, you are likely to be critical of your own needs, desires and pleasure-seeking. In some religious traditions, self-denial is seen as a virtue and a path towards God. It is about recognising the God-given will and prioritising this over one's own will. This can be achieved through the renunciation of certain pleasures.

Esteemer: This suggests you tend to be self-critical as a way of ensuring you continually maintain and strengthen your own ego. Your self-esteem comes from competing against other people and yourself in terms of appearance, capability, achievements, etc., and generally coming out on top. However, you will tend to feel shame when your self-evaluation does not meet the validation criteria you have set compared to others or by your own standards. Since our ego does not like to feel shame, you may try to protect yourself by becoming defensive, promoting your own achievements or working harder.

Figure 2.9 *Relationship with Ourselves Matrix*

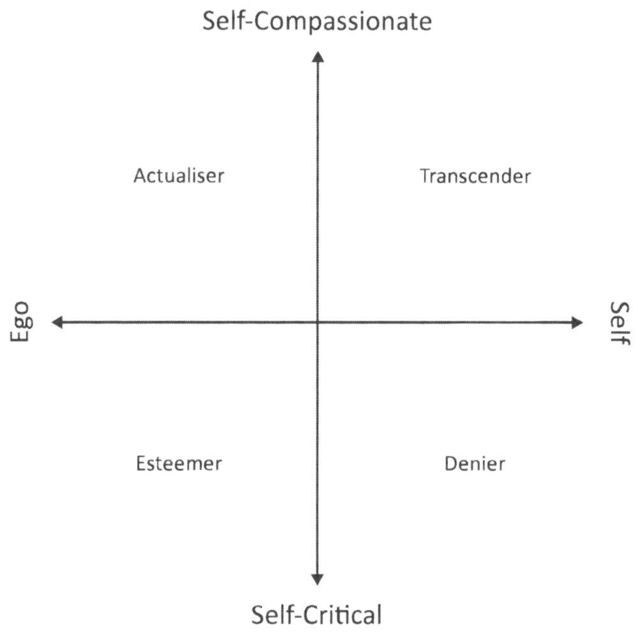

Our Separation from Ourselves – The Rise of Self-esteem

Most societies worldwide are gravitating towards people being driven by the need to continually maintain and increase their self-esteem (esteemers). In neoliberal western societies, as we grow and develop, our well-being often stems from having a strong sense of who we are. This equates to having a secure ego. When I speak about our separation from ourselves, I am talking about our ego being separated from our Self and then the ego being held up separately for criticism. Both of these are forms of separation in our psyche. Society's increasing emphasis on self-esteem is the result of us increasingly becoming separated from ourselves.

While the phrase 'self-esteem' was coined by the philosopher and psychologist William James (1842–1910) in 1890, it has been a popular concept for research and application since the 1960s and developed into a 'movement' in the 1980s. The movement advocates parents and teachers should point out a child's positive behaviours and tell them how special they are to increase their self-confidence and motivation to achieve their goals. It proposes that self-esteem is the key to success in life. This approach is often criticised because it does not necessarily reward hard work and achievement or encourage children to evaluate their own behaviour and performance against their standards and goals. When overused, a focus on increasing self-esteem can lead to perfectionism.

Perfectionism should not be confused with conscientiousness and diligence. People who are conscientious and diligent endeavour 'simply' to do a good job, while perfectionists endeavour to do a good job so they can feel good about themselves.

Numerous studies have found perfectionism is increasing in westernised societies. For example, a meta-analysis, carried out by Thomas Curran and Andrew Hill in 2019, of 164 research studies from 1989–2016 involving American, British and Canadian college students found an overall increase in perfectionism of 33%.[17] Socially oriented perfectionism showed the greatest increase reflecting the increasingly competitive nature of our society. It appears that increasing competition, especially in the form of social comparisons, makes people more self-critical. Other studies have found people with high levels of perfectionism tend to suffer from anxiety and depression.

SUMMARY AND CONCLUSION

This chapter explored how, in westernised societies, we have increasingly become separated from nature, each other and ourselves. Consequently, our relationship with nature is increasingly utilitarian, our relationship with each other is increasingly neoliberalist and our relationship with ourselves is increasingly focused on self-esteem. These three types of separation prime us to be conditioned into being consumers to support continuous economic growth.

By becoming separated from nature, each other and ourselves, we have allowed industry to capture our natural resources, community relationships and our psychology to fuel continuous economic growth. This growth has provided benefits such as employment, pensions and an ever-wider range of consumable goods. However, we are now suffering the consequences, including increasing degradation of the environment, huge social inequality and growing levels of mental illness.

CHAPTER 3

EVOLUTION OF SEPARATION

Sophia woke early, ate the remainder of her food and set off towards the great river. On reaching the bank, she found the river in flood.

'It's going to be a dangerous crossing,' said the old ferryman. 'It's the last one today, and I doubt I'll be crossing tomorrow neither. There's been rain in the mountains. It'll get worse before it's done with us, mark my words. So, if you cross, you won't be getting back for a while.' Sophia hesitated for a few minutes. 'Are you coming or not? I can't hang around.'

Sophia clambered aboard the small punt, and they set off into the torrent. The strong current dragged the small vessel downstream. The ferryman used all his wiry strength not to let the punt be upturned and washed away. Progress was slow and arduous. Sophia grabbed a bucket and started bailing when waves threatened to sink them. Finally, exhausted, they reached the far bank and safety. Sophia paid the ferryman then sat on the bank to get her breath back. It was just past midday, and the heat of the sun would soon dry her clothes.

As she rested, she saw the old man push off from the bank and begin his return across the fast-flowing water. There was no turning back for her. She must continue her journey and face the three-headed dragon.

Mimir was right; this was indeed a strange landscape. Leading away from the river were three diverging paths, just as he had described. The one on the left led into a dense forest from which she could just make out unfamiliar bird calls. The middle path was rocky and crowded. Large groups of travellers appeared to be helping each other over large, scattered boulders blocking the route. The path to the right appeared from its narrow width to be the least used. It wound steeply upwards and disappeared into the mist on the side of what must be an exceptionally large hill or even a mountain. She couldn't see much of this path, but it appeared deserted.

Mimir had advised her to look inside to find the correct path. So, after some time for contemplation, she decided to take the path to the left, the Way of Nature, through the forest.

'Who's that?' Sophia asked. Something had caught her attention. As she peered through the undergrowth, she could just make out a man sitting on the forest floor. His hair was thick with leaves, and his skin a blue-green colour that was hard to describe. 'What are you doing?'

'Nothing,' replied the man. 'I'm being.' Sophia waited for him to complete his sentence, but clearly, he had forgotten what he was going to say.

'Being what?'

'Just being.'

He's obviously not in a talking mood, thought Sophia, and she went on her way. Soon she heard male voices ahead on the path. There were three of them. As she drew close, she saw a father and his two sons. The young men were arguing.

'I'm telling you, God put nature on Earth to sustain us.'

'No, you've got it the wrong way round. God put us on Earth to look after nature.'

Sophia opened her mouth, ready to join the argument, but the father gave her a resigned look and shook his head. So, without a word, she went past them. The sons were so entrenched in their argument they didn't acknowledge her.

For an hour or so, Sophia walked through the forest without seeing anyone else. She was enjoying the experience of seeing and smelling the vast array of plants and trees in the forest. Birdsong and the sound of insects provided a welcome musical accompaniment to her journey. Then, around a bend in the path, she came upon a group of men. They were stripping leaves from trees, netting insects and digging for worms. Gathered items were being dissected and examined under microscopes set on a large table. Suddenly there was a roar of excitement.

'What is it?' enquired Sophia, approaching the table. One of the men scribbled a note on a piece of paper and passed it to a young boy who ran off down the path in the direction Sophia was headed. She followed as fast as she could, encumbered by her rucksack. The boy ran into a large clearing and handed the note to a man standing beside an enormous box-like machine.

'Finally! Over there, those ones!' he shouted, pointing to a group of tall oak-like trees.

Within seconds the trees were surrounded, and the forest filled with the sound of chopping and sawing. As Sophia watched, the felled trees were hauled away and fed into the giant machine. The process was repeated every ten minutes or so, with more notes arriving and different parts of the forest being fed into the mammoth engine. Sometimes they threw in rocks, sometimes plants and even animals. Sophia was both horrified and mesmerised. After what seemed like hours, she turned her gaze away, back to the path. Carefully she picked her way past the machine. Smoke billowed from its two chimneys and noxious waste spewed from its back. To Sophia's utter amazement, the most wonderful and desirable products were emerging from its gaping mouth. There were clothes, shoes, ornaments, cutlery and cooking utensils. Anything Sophia could possibly desire materialised from the depths of the machine. The items were loaded onto trucks, which lumbered away across the clearing and disappeared into the forest on the far side.

Sophia entered the forest once more. As she walked, she noticed the tree cover was becoming more and more sparse. The forest here let in streams of light. There was an eerie silence with no birdsong and few insects. After an hour, Sophia was walking across open grassland. This new landscape was dry and yellow; bare patches of earth became dust clouds which irritated her eyes when the wind blew. Peering through her fingers, she could see people running towards her carrying bags of money. They pushed past and sped on in the direction of the forest. With the sun beating down and with no shade to be had, Sophia stopped on the brow of a low hill to drink some of her water. The path went straight ahead into a vast desert and disappeared into the horizon. There was no sign of water anywhere. Turning round, she began to retrace her steps. She needed to fill her water bottle, and the river was the only source of water she had seen. The Way of Nature led only to desert. Surely no dragon could survive out there?

Fully refreshed at the river, Sophia decided she should attempt one of the other two paths. She chose the Way of People. After all, it was a popular path. Initially, she made good progress despite the boulders. There were always people nearby willing to help her navigate the huge rocks. However, as she progressed, she noticed that there were fewer groups of people around, and they were less helpful than those closer to the river. Ahead of her, she could see only individual travellers, no groups. It was harder to get over the boulders here, and there was no one to help her. A voice in the distance was shouting 'Ready, steady, go!' Getting closer, she could see a man directing races. As she went to walk by, the man stepped out and deliberately blocked her path.

'What do you think you're doing!' he boomed.

'Just walking the path,' replied Sophia, conscious that all eyes were now turned on her.

'We all want to do that, but you have to race, just like the rest of us,' said the man with such a menacing undertone that Sophia apprehensively

joined the queue for the start line.

'Ready, steady, go!' and they were off.

They only ran for about 100 metres. Even though she enjoyed running, Sophia didn't do too well due to the heavy rucksack on her back; she finished in the middle of the pack. Crossing the finish line, she was directed back to the starting line with everyone else. The only ones not to be sent back were those who finished the race in first, second or third place. Angry at not being able to continue on the path, Sophia used the bulk of her pack to push her way to the front of the waiting runners and looked around for a way to escape.

'What do you think you're doing!' the race director screamed, pointing his whistle at Sophia. 'You didn't come near to winning; get back to where you belong.'

Sophia kept shuffling backwards until he indicated she was in the correct place. Off they went again. This time Sophia finished far behind the main pack. For the next race, she had to start at the back. Runners here were angry and frustrated at their lack of progress. No matter how hard they tried, they could not progress through the throng. As soon as they finished one race, they had to start it again. There was much pushing and shoving as everyone tried to get an advantage. Sophia had one more race but made no progress. Exhausted and demoralised, she muttered to herself, 'I'm never going to get past these runners. I'll have to go back and try the third path. The Way of Self.'

This final path had a foreboding air. It climbed steeply and disappeared into thick cloud. How would she ever find her way? But it was the last path, so she had to try. There was no way of getting back across the river anytime soon. Setting off, to her surprise, felt good. Despite its steepness, Sophia climbed well, and the fresh air energised every step. This confidence remained as she entered into the mist. She could barely see ahead, but somehow, she knew the way. It was as though Mimir was whispering in her ear. She trusted herself and thought about the meaning and purpose of her journey. As the path got steeper and Mimir became quiet, Sophia gradually lost her confidence. To keep herself motivated, she set herself little tasks. Some she succeeded in and felt good. Growing in confidence, she set herself harder tasks, but her confidence ebbed, and her energy fell when she failed. To spur herself on and deeper into the cloud, she decided she should not go back to the easy tasks; instead, she must try to complete the harder tasks. Another voice replaced Mimir's in her ear. 'You're not good enough, Sophia. You should turn around and go back.' To drown out the voice, she whispered, 'I am the best mountain climber. I can follow this path.'

A woman appeared from the mist, descending the path. Sophia was startled for a second and, as they carefully manoeuvred around each other, she heard the woman muttering to herself, 'I can do this; I am the best person on this path.' As Sophia continued climbing, she continued with her mantra 'I am the best mountain climber. I can follow this path,' sometimes whispered, sometimes shouted depending on the terrain's difficulty. Occasionally she passed other people, but none looked at her. They were too absorbed in their own heads, their own worlds, trying to be the best climber on the mountain. Eventually, the climbing and battling with the voice in her head took its toll. Exhausted, she forced herself onwards and upwards; it was the only way.

INTRODUCTION

> You cannot control the world but you can control how you react to it.
>
> Maya Angelou

As I have reasoned, our increasing separation from nature, each other and ourselves has led us to have a utilitarian relationship with nature, a neoliberalist relationship with each other and a relationship with ourselves that focuses on increasing our self-esteem. These types of relationships have benefited industry and grown the economy. You may reasonably conclude businesses and governments have orchestrated these separations as part of a grand masterplan. Seeing the damage these separations continue to inflict on our environment, our communities and our psychological well-being, you may also be inclined to blame business or government. This chapter aims to demonstrate that these separations and the consequential industrialisation of our consciousness have not been planned. Instead, they result from the path society has trodden over the past 2,500 years, each step taken when someone came up with an insight or idea that solved a societal problem. Every step was built on its predecessor, allowing society to progress. Consequently, the gradual industrialisation of our consciousness is the result of evolution towards a supposed better society.

This chapter will identify some of the key people who have helped society move forward. These are religious leaders, philosophers, scientists, psychologists, economists and management theorists. While their work has led society forward, it has also led to our increasing disconnection from nature, each other and ourselves. Each step has furthered the industrialisation of our consciousness, which has become ingrained in our society. Our parents' consciousness was industrialised, and they helped industrialise our consciousness. The insights and ideas gained over centuries are taught to us in schools. This process is continued in the workplace, in institutions and reinforced by the media; it is all-pervasive. The industrialisation of our consciousness has become like what Yuval Noah Harari called in his book *Sapiens*, an 'imagined order'.[1] This is something most people believe, to the extent that it is perceived as a given reality, like gravity. But the imagined order is, as the name suggests, a product of people's collective imagination, past and present. It is a shared myth. Money is an imagined order. It has no value in reality. It only has value as long as we believe it does and that we trust others share that belief. Money is such a strong imagined order people are prepared to destroy our natural environment to get more of it.

By exploring the work of key influential people, this chapter maps out the path taken over the past 2,500 years, which has led us to the crises we face today. Creating this map, you will see where we are and how we got here. By understanding where we made mistakes, we can make wiser decisions in the future. With the crises we are facing in our environment, communities and our psychology, it would seem we have made great strides down the wrong path. You will see people were advocating different directions at various times. I am not suggesting we retrace our steps; we now need to take a new path. Identifying past paths may help find a better path in the future. However, first, we must develop our consciousness.

THE EVOLUTION OF OUR SEPARATION FROM NATURE

As discussed earlier, we can perceive nature in four different ways:

- **Spiritual ecologist:** Nature is psychologically alive, and humans are an integral part of nature.
- **Gaia theorist:** Nature is psychologically dead but interconnected as a complete system with humans as an integral part.

- **Earth steward:** Nature is psychologically alive, and humans are separate and above nature.
- **Utilitarianist:** Nature is psychologically dead, and humans are separate and above nature.

In western societies, our relationship with nature has transitioned from spiritual ecologist to utilitarianist. With this trend, we are increasingly becoming separated from nature.

Religions

Today's major religions have been around for 2,500–4,000 years. Before this, there was a myriad of primal religions. Many indigenous peoples continue to practise these primal religions, although their numbers are diminishing. Even though every primal religion has a unique character, they have many similarities in their relationship to and perspective on nature. Early primal religions and the indigenous religions of China and India, such as Taoism and Hinduism, share a 'spiritual ecology' connection with nature. For their followers, a line between human and nature is not easy to establish. In these religions, humans are deeply embedded in nature. They believe humans and nature belong to a single order that includes animate and inanimate entities. Consequently, the line between humans and inanimate entities such as rock is difficult to establish. For many, rocks are live spiritual beings, such as the sacred mountains in Tibet or Uluru in Australia. In primal religions, everything is alive, and each entity depends on the others.

Abrahamic religions, such as Judaism, Christianity and Islam generally teach an 'Earth stewardship' connection with nature. Man's role is to look after all of God's creations. Even so, some interpretations of scriptures in some Judeo-Christian traditions call for a 'utilitarian' connection with nature. There is the belief that God provided nature to sustain man and, therefore, it is a commodity that can be exploited.

Philosophy

For many centuries, religion, philosophy and science were one discipline, namely natural philosophy. Only recently, in historical terms, have they been separated into different areas of study and practice. It was not until 1833 that the term 'scientist' was first used by the philosopher and historian William Whewell (1794–1866).

Philosophical thought was initially grounded in spiritual ecology. For the early philosophers, nature was psychologically alive, and humans were a part of nature. This is seen in the work of Plato (428–347 BCE) and Aristotle (384–322 BCE) and was further developed by Thomas Aquinas (1225–1274) in the 13th century. Although their philosophies differed, in general, they saw a connectedness between the physical (nature) and metaphysical (spiritual) realms of existence. For them, nature had spirit, and everything was interconnected. It could be argued that they were the early 'idealists'. Idealism holds that the physical reality of matter is in some way indistinguishable or inseparable from consciousness. For idealists, everything is psychologically alive, and everything is interconnected. Idealism is very much aligned with spiritual ecology.

However, come the 16th century, everything changed. Idealism was gradually replaced, step by step, with materialism. Matter, rather than consciousness, became the fundamental substance in nature. From a materialist perspective, everything, including consciousness, is the result of the interaction between matter. René Descartes (1596–1650) created the Cartesian Divide, which separated consciousness from matter. Francis Bacon (1561–1626) advocated empiricism, which stated that knowledge could only be developed from observation of matter. He argued that a full understanding of a concept could only be attained through observing the particulars (specific parts) of nature and then inferring a general law. Hence, reductionism was born. Thomas Hobbes (1588–1679) viewed nature as if he were a mechanic, comparing all living things to automata or self-moving engines. All of these philosophers are viewed as the fathers of modern philosophy. Nevertheless, under their guidance, humans were separated from nature, which was to become psychologically dead. This paved the way for science to adopt a 'utilitarian' relationship with nature. This philosophical perspective allowed us to exploit nature for economic growth without considering the consequences.

Even though philosophy became increasingly materialist and utilitarian, philosophers, such as Benedict De Spinoza (1632–1677), continued with the idealism of the ancient Greeks and Thomas Aquinas. For materialists, matter is primary, and mind, spirit and ideas are secondary. For idealists, mind, spirit and ideas are primary, and matter is secondary. A leader in the idealism movement was Georg Friedrich Wilhelm Hegel (1770–1831). His work is thought to be the peak of German idealism. Hegel's work was influenced by his friend and contemporary, Friedrich Schelling (1775–1854), together with the work of both Immanuel Kant (1724–1804) and Johann Wolfgang von Goethe (1749–1832). Today, the work of these philosophers continues to be drawn upon by scientists trying to make sense of quantum mechanics.

From this review of the work of philosophers who have influenced our separation from nature, you can see that there has been a game of tug-of-war between materialism and idealism (see Figure 3.1).

Figure 3.1 Idealism–Materialism Continuum

Idealism
Nature is inseparable from consciousness
Materialism
Nature is objectively knowable, practical, measurable and governed by strict laws

Since the emergence and development of 'modern philosophy' in the 16th century, materialism has had the advantage. We will re-join the tug-of-war as we explore the influence science has had on our separation from nature.

Science

By building on the work of the materialist philosophers, scientists in the 17th and 18th centuries created what was called a New Science. This method of scientific inquiry was first practised by Galileo Galilei (1564–1642) and Sir Isaac Newton (1642–1727), both seen as leaders in the New Science movement. Within New Science, just like in modern philosophy, nature became a machine and was psychologically dead. Seeing nature as a machine put New Science at the heart of the Industrial Revolution. It encouraged people to take a utilitarian, exploitative perspective on nature.

However, the discovery of the quantum world has severely exposed the limitations of the New Science of the 17th and 18th centuries. Although no one fully understands quantum physics, scientists are increasingly embracing idealism to develop explanations. Quantum theory is a fundamental tenet of physics as it seeks to describe nature at an atomic and subatomic scale. The German theoretical physicist Max Planck (1848–1947) is seen as the father of quantum theory due to his work on black-body radiation. Quantum theory has then been developed by renowned physicists such as Niels Bohr (1885–1962), Richard Feynman (1918–1988), Werner Heisenberg (1901–1976), Erwin Schrödinger (1887–1961), Paul Dirac (1902–1984), Louis de Broglie (1892–1987), Wolfgang Pauli (1900–1958) and many others. The behaviour of nature at the atomic and subatomic scale often seems bizarre, difficult to understand and hard to believe. So much so that Bohr once stated, 'Anyone who is not shocked by quantum theory has not understood it,' and Feynman remarked, 'I think I can safely say that nobody understands quantum theory.'

In quantum theory, light waves act like particles and particles act like waves (particle–wave duality). To explain particle–wave duality, Bohr, Heisenberg and others developed the 'Copenhagen Interpretation', which is still the most accepted view in quantum physics. It states a particle does not exist in one state or another, but exists in all of its possible states at once, known as a wave of potentiality. It is only when we observe the wave that a quantum particle is forced to choose one probability, and that's the state we observe. Since it may be forced into a different observable state each time, this explains why a quantum particle behaves erratically. Consequently, it is the act of observation that determines the formation of matter at a quantum level. The Copenhagen Interpretation does not define what constitutes an 'observer' or 'observation'. In the 1960s, building on John Von Neumann's (1903–1957) work, Eugene Wigner (1902–1995) argued that it is the observer's consciousness that precipitates the collapse of the wave into a particle. His theory is known as the 'Von Neumann–Wigner Interpretation'. This interpretation of particle–wave duality is closely aligned with the George Berkeley (1685–1753) theory of immaterialism (also known as subjective idealism). Berkeley's theory states that objects do not exist as a material substance; instead, they only exist as ideas in the minds of the perceivers. Therefore, the Von Neumann–Wigner interpretation is a metaphysical interpretation that links matter and mind, putting idealism well and truly back into science.

By using idealism to understand quantum physics, scientists are breathing psychological life back into nature and reconnecting it with humanity. Nevertheless, the battle between idealism and materialism rages on. Materialism remains the dominant perspective in science, and those who dare introduce idealism into their work risk ridicule and ostracisation. Science continues to encourage a utilitarian relationship with nature.

This section has explored how western societies have been on a path of separation from nature. We once interacted with nature in a way that could be described as 'spiritual ecology'. We were an integral part of nature and did not overexploit it. Over centuries, as societies developed guided by religion, philosophy and science, we lost this connection and nature became psychologically dead to us. We lost our compassion for nature as it lost its soul. Nature became simply a resource for us to exploit for our needs and desires. It became a utilitarian means to an end (see Figure 3.2).

Figure 3.2 Triangle Model – Relationship with Nature

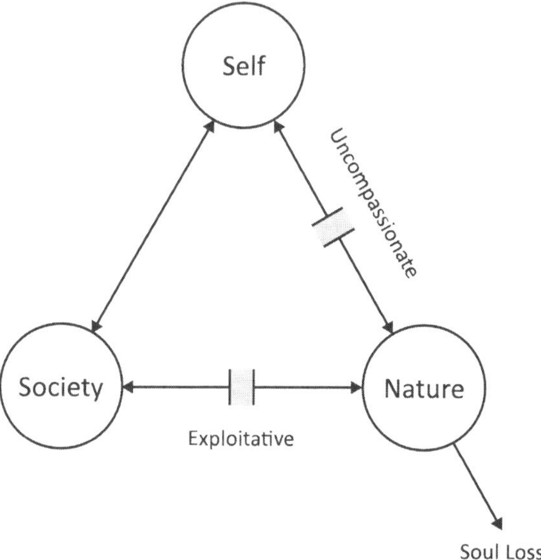

As we have journeyed along the path of separation from nature, the strongest influence has been the development of New Science. Its approach and methods valued materialism, reductionism, positivism and empiricism. It rejected idealism, which was open to nature being psychologically alive. Coupling New Science with an interpretation of scriptures that taught God created nature to sustain humans prompted an Industrial Revolution fuelled by nature's resources. Teachings from religion, philosophy and science separated us from nature, and society permitted us to exploit it for economic growth.

As we have seen, all is not lost. Reinterpretations of Biblical texts are encouraging followers of the Judeo-Christian traditions to take a less utilitarian approach to nature and become its stewards. This

'Earth stewardship' approach to nature has always been evident in Islam. There is also an increasing interest in following the primal and indigenous religions that have had a 'spiritual ecology' perspective on nature. In terms of philosophy and science, the theories being proposed to explain the quantum world are again drawing on idealism, which puts consciousness, soul and spirit back into nature. We still have hope.

THE EVOLUTION OF OUR SEPARATION FROM EACH OTHER

You will recall, from the previous chapter, the relationships between people in a community can be described in four ways:

- **Communitarian:** Collectivist and co-operative, communitarianism emphasises the connection between the individual and the community.
- **Social liberalism:** Individualist and co-operative, social liberalism emphasises the freedom of the individual within the context of collective rights.
- **Tribalism:** Collectivist and competitive, tribalism emphasises the solidarity within competing groups.
- **Neoliberalism:** Individualist and competitive, neoliberalism emphasises the freedom of the individual within the context of free-market competition.

Even though the nature of communities differs, it is the rise in neoliberalism around the globe, which is increasingly separating us from each other.

Philosophy

In the eastern world, societies tend to be communitarian in nature. The philosopher with the greatest influence on eastern societies was

Confucius (551 BCE–479 BCE). Confucianism is a moral and ethical system widely influential in countries such as China, Taiwan, Singapore, Vietnam, Korea and Japan. Although often classified as a religion, it is a humanist system of thought based on the belief that human nature can be improved through a systematic approach to self-cultivation. His philosophy advocated that people should practise altruism and benevolence and that the state should intervene in society to promote social relationships. The importance of the family and social harmony, rather than spiritual values, is at the core of Confucianism and is encapsulated in his well-known principle known as the Golden Rule: 'Do not do unto others what you do not want done to yourself.'

Societies in the Middle East tend to be social liberalist in nature. The philosopher who had the greatest influence on Middle Eastern societies was Abu Nasr Al-Farabi (872–950). Being known as the 'second teacher', after Aristotle, Al-Farabi had a significant influence on the development of societies in the Islamic world. For Al-Farabi, the ideal society is one that is directed towards true happiness, in which people co-operate to gain contentment. Societies that fell short were called vicious and were characterised by people pursuing wealth, sensual gratification or power rather than true happiness. In a virtuous society, Al-Farabi believed that each person in the state would take their place, according to their individual inclinations and abilities, and all contribute mutually towards achieving the overall goal of improving society.

Westernised societies tend to be social liberal or neoliberal in nature. The English philosopher John Locke (1632–1704) is known as the 'father of liberalism'. Locke was a firm believer in individual liberty, which he defined as being a natural law. He asserted that the role of the government is to protect this law. Locke generally viewed people as characterised by reason and tolerance and recognised that selfishness is part of human nature. If someone tried to restrict or take another person's labour, income or property, he believed this was against the natural law. It is thought Locke's conceptions of people's rights and the nature of government profoundly influenced the Declaration of Independence and the Constitution of the United States.

John Stuart Mill (1806–1873) was an English philosopher, economist and exponent of utilitarianism and classical liberalism who greatly influenced 19th-century British political and economic thinking. As well as being a utilitarian, Mill was a keen advocate of applying New Science techniques to moral and social issues to achieve unimpeachable proof for his conclusions. Mill believed the government's role was to establish social and economic policies that promote equality of opportunity. Even though he advocated equal opportunity, he was also an egalitarian and valued meritocracy achieved through competition. In later work, he became concerned about the spiritual and moral impact of industrialisation and began to advocate more socialist solutions.

This brief review of some key philosophers demonstrates how their work influenced cultures around the world. The teachings of Confucius appear to have led Far Eastern countries to be 'communitarian'. Al-Farabi's work helped Islamic countries become more socially liberal in nature. In western societies, especially the USA and UK, Locke and Mill's work enabled liberalism to establish and lay the foundations for neoliberalism. The greater the pull towards neoliberalism, the greater the separation we have from each other.

Psychology

Like other academic disciplines, psychology consists of several competing schools of thought. Each school researches, studies and practises psychology from their own perspective based on their beliefs and assumptions. Generally, each school of thought conceives the self in one of three ways:

- The individual self is what makes a person unique compared to others and, therefore, focuses on traits, characteristics and the defence of the ego (self-identity and self-esteem).

- The relational self is defined by the nature of the attachments a person has with significant others and, therefore, relies on the perception of and reflection on relationships.

- The collective self is defined by the person's inclusion in large social groups and, therefore, is based on identifying with people in the 'in-group' in differentiation with people in 'out-groups'.

Although there are many schools of psychology, I will contrast social psychology with positive psychology to explore how they view the self in relation to other people.

Social psychologists emphasise the conception of the self in terms of relational and group influences. Early social psychologists such as George Herbert Mead (1863–1931) and Lev Vygotsky (1896–1934) were the first to define the self as emerging from relationships. However, the Austrian philosopher Ludwig Wittgenstein (1889–1951) made the most significant contribution to defining the self relationally. You might like to think of yourself as being an autonomous, independent being with your own agency. Nevertheless, social psychologists believe much of what you think, feel and do has been heavily influenced by people around you, past, present and anticipated future. This school of psychology suggests we are all moulded by social influence, whether it be the one-to-one, family, group or culture.

Positive psychology conceives the self in terms of what makes a person unique. It focuses on how individuals can build a life of meaning and purpose so they can flourish rather than just survive. It is believed this is achieved through focusing on, and utilising, their individual strengths. Positive psychology became established as a school of psychological thought in 1998 when Martin Seligman chose it as the theme for his term as President of the American Psychological Association. While positive psychologists recognise happiness can come from social interactions, it places significant emphasis on developing positive self-esteem and self-identity. This is achieved by gaining a sense of personal efficacy and self-worth by using one's own talents and strengths to achieve a desired goal. However, this encourages individuals to compare their capabilities and achievements against those of others and, hence, encourages people to compete.

Positive psychology has become a dominant force in the western world. As a result, there is now a strong emphasis on seeing the self as individual and self-contained creating a clear distinction between self and other. Consequently, the social world is seen in terms of differences between us, which encourages competition and conflict. We increasingly become autonomous beings separated from each other and feel isolated and alone. In such a society, autonomy and winning become highly valued and celebrated. When others recognise this, our self-esteem and sense of self-worth increases. Conversely, it is seen as a weakness to be dependent on others or to need support, so we learn to take care of ourselves. Therefore, positive psychology encourages and supports our separation from each other. It reinforces competition between people rather than mutual support. Self-reliant individualism is the essence of neoliberalism.

Economists

Adam Smith (1723–1790), known as the 'father of economics' or the 'father of capitalism', produced two books *The Theory of Moral Sentiments*[2] and *An Inquiry into the Nature and Causes of the Wealth of Nations*.[3] Taken together, these books addressed the balance between morality and self-interest in economic activity and laid the foundations of the free-market economy. He argued that when individuals collectively pursue their self-interest, they unintentionally benefit society. Smith termed this concept 'the invisible hand'. His logic was that self-interested competition in a free market keeps prices low and encourages the offering of a wide variety of goods and services. To enable the 'invisible hand' to do its work and benefit society, governments should only interfere to ensure free-market competition and no further. This 'hands-off' relationship between government and business is termed laissez-faire economics or laissez-faire capitalism.

Friedrich Hayek (1899–1992), considered to be the 'father of neoliberalist economics', was also an advocate of free-market competition. He believed market prices were the result of the calculations of millions of competing market participants. Hayek argued that in a constantly changing world, free-market competition is the most efficient way for an economy to run and that no constructed system designed to manage the economy would be able to make the continual adjustments. He championed privatisation, deregulation and free competition in public services. Both the Republican American President Ronald Reagan and the Conservative British Prime Minister Margaret Thatcher were strong supporters of his ideas. Thus, neoliberal economic policies became mainstream in the US and UK societies and remained mostly in place even when more centrist governments followed.

Economist John Maynard Keynes (1883–1946) is known as the 'father of Keynesian economics' due to his substantial influence on the economics and government policies of the 20th century. A strong proponent of full employment, he argued it could be achieved by governments intervening in an economy to stimulate demand by increasing spending and lowering taxes, especially in the face of a recession. He argued that governments need to borrow money and invest to bring an economy out of recession, believing that demand, rather than supply, drives production and grows the economy. This approach sharply contrasts with the laissez-faire economics advocated by Smith and Hayek, and is known as adopting a 'fiscal policy'. Many governments adopt Keynesian policies during recessions.

Milton Friedman (1912–2006) was an American economist known for his opposition to Keynesian economics and his strong advocacy of free-market capitalism. He was seen as one of the second-generation leaders at the highly influential Chicago school of economics. Friedman argued for deregulation of the economy, leading to free-market competition. He believed free trade, smaller government and a slow, but steady, increase in money supply is the best way to grow the economy. An advisor to Ronald Reagan and Margaret Thatcher, his monetarist approach figured strongly in their leadership.

You can see from this short review, there has always been a strong emphasis on competitive individualism amongst influential economists. They advocated governments should intervene in the economy as little as possible. This led to deregulation and privatisation, as well as the curtailing of influence from trade unions. This focus on competitive individualism fuelled the development and spread of neoliberalism. Though they often refer to Adam Smith's work, neoliberal economists neglect to draw on his theory of morality. Consequently, neoliberalist economics has developed within a moral vacuum, treating people as self-interested agents, encouraging our separation from each other.

This section has outlined how, over the past few centuries, through the influence of philosophy, psychology and economics, westernised societies have been on a path towards competitive individualism. This has led to our society being characterised by neoliberalism, which has led to us becoming increasingly separated from each other. As the separation increases, we are losing our sense of community, the soul of our society (see Figure 3.3).

In the western world, neoliberalism has been the dominant force in economics since the 1970s. In other countries, especially in the east, they have been following a different path. Due to their religious and philosophical heritage, many countries have developed more collective and co-operative cultures and economies. Yet, due to globalisation and the influence of the IMF, neoliberal policies have spread.

Figure 3.3 Triangle Model – Relationship with Nature and Society

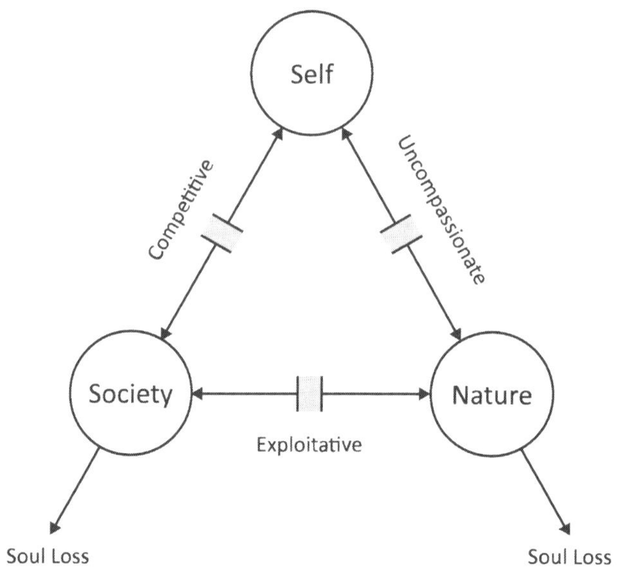

THE EVOLUTION OF OUR SEPARATION FROM OURSELVES

You will recall, from the previous chapter, the relationship we have with ourselves can be described in four ways:

- **Transcender:** This involves transcending your ego and compassionately connecting with your Self (soul), expanding your personal boundaries and considering yourself to be an integral part of a unifying whole.

- **Actualiser:** This involves focusing on your ego's growth towards achieving its full potential through self-fulfilment and self-acceptance.

- **Denier:** This involves connecting more with your Self than your ego and practising self-criticism more than self-compassion.

- **Esteemer:** This involves connecting more with your ego than your Self and being self-critical as a way of ensuring you continually maintain and strengthen your ego to build your self-esteem.

Within westernised societies, we have seen a rise in people focusing on building their self-esteem. With this trend, we are increasingly becoming separated from ourselves.

Religion, Philosophy and Science

To determine the path of separation from ourselves, through religion, philosophy and science, I will sometimes use the word 'soul' to mean the 'Self', which I defined in Chapter 2. This recognises that soul has been used across religions and philosophy for centuries, though its use in science is generally frowned upon.

In religion, the soul is alive and well. In Taoism, the soul consists of Hun and Po. They are not two aspects of one soul, and they are not two souls. Instead, they are mutually arising. The Hun is the ethereal consciousness that can exist after death and be reincarnated. In comparison, the Po is a more tangible consciousness that dissolves at the time of death. Some Hindu traditions believe in two aspects of the soul, being Jiva and Atman. Jiva is the individual's soul, while Atman is the soul connected to Brahman, the Godhead. In Judaism, it is believed God breathed life into Adam and, thereby, gave humans a soul. However, followers also distinguish five aspects of the soul: instinct (Nefesh), emotion and morality (Ruach), intellect (Neshamah), a part of God (Chayah) and singularity with God (Yechidah). The view that God gives people their soul follows through into Christianity, although there are subtle differences between various Christian traditions. In both religions, most followers believe God judges one's soul after death. Like Taoism, Islam also believes people have immortal and mortal elements. Rūḥ is a person's immortal and essential self as associated with the soul.

Whereas, Nafs is what we associate with the ego. It can be seen that these major religions all believe the human soul, or an aspect of the soul, has a spiritual basis in that it is immortal or connected to God. However, some include other elements of the psyche. This overlap between soul and psyche continues into the work of philosophers.

For Plato, the soul consists of three parts, reason, emotion and desire, equivalent to what we generally understand to be the psyche. He believed the soul was immortal and retained the power to think after death. His student, Aristotle believed the soul is united with the body, and its purpose is to develop the body. This understanding of the soul held until Descartes in the 17th century. He considered the soul as being separate to the body. This enabled Descartes to perceive the body to be very much like a machine. He believed the body moves of its own accord and the soul gives purpose and direction. How Descartes thought the soul and the body interact has never been clear and his work in this area attracted much criticism, especially from Spinoza. Instead, Spinoza argued that mind and matter are attributes of one substance (dual aspect theory) and that this is identified with God or nature. Descartes' reductionist and materialist approach paved the way for the New Science developed by Bacon, Hobbs, Locke and Hume. By the time New Science became a dominant force, the word 'soul' had been replaced by the word 'mind'. The focus of philosophical and scientific research was then to determine how the brain was able to think. Essentially asking, how does the brain produce the mind. Philosophers such as Hegel, Kant and Berkeley challenged dualism, reductionism and materialism by taking a position based on idealism. In general, idealism states it is the mind that creates the material. While philosophers working in the doctrine of idealism have challenged this materialist focus, it is still dominant today. The soul has been taken out of science, leaving it to the remit of religion. Consequently, we now have a divide between science and religion.

Since the emergence of New Science in the 17th and 18th centuries, the soul has not been considered a legitimate area of study. Yet, there has been interest in determining how the brain creates the mind and enables us to think. By using various brain imaging methods, neuroscientists have correlated the mind's processes with neural activity in the brain. These results suggest there is no need for the inclusion of a soul. Nonetheless, correlation does not infer causation and other unseen influences cannot be ruled out. What neuroscientists have not been able to find is the cause of consciousness. Until a materialist explanation for consciousness is proven, those who advocate positions taken from idealism will still be in the argument. Theories grounded in idealism are especially relevant in quantum mechanics, where the duality between mind and matter appears to be breaking down, and much remains unexplained. However, even in quantum physics, any talk of our soul can be still be viewed as being unscientific.

From this brief review, you can see how the perspective on our soul has developed through religion, philosophy and science. Apart from within religion, our soul has become our mind, which in turn has become the result of material functioning in the brain. According to much of philosophy and science, we do not have a soul. Without a soul, our psyche becomes dominated by our ego.

Psychology

Psychology has only been a separate discipline since around 1879 when, in Leipzig, Germany, Wilhelm Wundt (1832–1920) founded the first laboratory dedicated exclusively to psychological research. Since then, various schools of psychology have developed, two of which I briefly explored in the previous section. Each school has its own assumptions and methods of research and practice. The schools of thought are also considered to be part of a wider 'force' in psychology. Each force developing in reaction, and often opposition, to its predecessors. The four forces are psychodynamics, behaviourism, humanistic and transpersonal.

Psychodynamic psychology is an approach that emphasises the

dynamic psychological energy and forces that underlie and motivate our behaviour, emotions and cognitions. As many of these forces are unconscious, psychodynamics is particularly interested in the relationship between unconscious and conscious experiences and motivation. Sigmund Freud and his followers first developed the approach. Being an atheist, he was reluctant to use the word 'soul' and, instead, chose 'psyche' (the Greek word for soul). Carl Jung also used Self (with a capital S) in a way that is more akin to my definition of 'soul'. Jung believed we are born with a sense of wholeness and called this the 'Self'. It is evident that Jung believed that a separate ego crystallises out from the Self during the first half of our lives. During this time, psychological health was thought to be maintained by the ego periodically returning to this sense of Self. Once the ego has become fully formed, around midlife, further psychological growth is achieved by the ego reintegrating with the Self. Jung called this process 'individuation' and saw it as a way of people realising their full potential.

Behaviourism developed as a reaction to the assumptions and methods of psychodynamics. It was founded in 1913 by John Watson (1878–1958), who said 'consciousness' was not a definable or usable concept and was merely another word for 'soul'. He believed a kind of religious philosophy had previously dominated psychology. Watson wanted psychology to be a purely objective and experimental form of natural science. Consequently, he created behaviourism, which is only concerned with observable behaviour, its stimulus and reinforcement. The idea being that the desired behaviours can be encouraged with the right stimulus and reinforcement. The reinforcement can be rewards or punishment, depending on the behaviour observed.

Humanistic psychology was developed in the 1960s in opposition to both behaviourism and psychodynamics. Humanistic psychology treats people as unique individuals and focuses on their psychological growth. It is concerned with areas of growth such as increasing self-awareness, self-efficacy, self-worth, creativity, free will and wholeness.

Humanistic psychology emphasises a holistic perspective on the individual. Abraham Maslow (1908–1970) is considered to be the father of humanistic psychology and is best known for his 'Hierarchy of Needs', which sees 'self-actualisation' as the highest level of growth enabling people to realise their full potential. Consequently, in its purest form, humanistic psychology ignores the psyche's soul aspects and focuses on the potential of the ego. This focus of humanistic psychology developed into positive psychology.

Towards the end of his working life, Maslow became unsatisfied with his conception of self-actualisation, believing it did not reflect the highest level of psychological growth. Consequently, he further developed his theory and model to include transcendence levels. This extended version of his Hierarchy of Needs is not well known and has little influence. Nonetheless, it gave birth to transpersonal psychology, which Maslow described as the fourth force. Transpersonal psychology includes the transcendent and spiritual aspects of the human experience. It assumes the psychology of the individual extends beyond ego to include the soul and beyond to connect with a form of a collective soul (the spirit).

It can be seen that within the four forces in psychology, there has been a reluctance to use the word 'soul'. This was initially to ensure the separation of psychology from religion, even though many of the early models of the psyche developed within the psychodynamic school did include the soul, albeit under a different name. Psychology's separation from the soul happened in earnest with the development of behaviourism. Proponents of behaviourism wanted psychology to be viewed as a science and, therefore, adopted the methods of 'New Science', such as empiricism and reductionism. In just the same way as Descartes viewed the body, our psychology has come to be viewed as operating like a machine. The stimulus and response equating to cause and effect. For behaviourists, to quote Gilbert Ryle, there is no 'ghost in the machine' (no soul). In response to behaviourism, humanistic psychologists have tried to put the human back into psychology. However, the majority of their efforts have focused on developing and boosting the ego. As there is little mention of the soul in humanistic psychology, this has been rectified by transpersonal psychology. Yet, transpersonal psychology remains on the periphery. The 'New Science' perspective is still dominant and highly influential. Behaviourism is used extensively in counselling, psychotherapy and in the workplace. Overall, psychology has had a massive influence on our increasing separation from ourselves, our soul.

Management Theories

Connecting with our Self (our soul) can lead to finding greater purpose and meaning in our lives. Researchers have consistently found that meaningfulness is a motivating factor and more important than other factors such as pay and working conditions in the workplace. Consequently, for some people, work can literally give them their 'soul purpose'. Yet for others, work can be 'soul-destroying'. In research carried out by the Sloan School of Management at MIT, it was found that while employees could find meaning in their work, poor management destroyed it.[4] There are many different management and leadership theories, and each relates to the soul of the worker in a different way. The main theories are scientific management, bureaucracy, human relations, behaviourism, transformational leadership and servant leadership.

Frederick Taylor (1856–1915) is known as the founder of 'scientific management', a theory and practice designed to increase labour productivity by analysing workflows. It attempts to apply the science of engineering to the process of management. Taylor developed four principles: efficient workflows, workers attached to jobs according to their abilities and motivation, close supervision and employee training. Even though scientific management drove up efficiency, it de-emphasised teamwork, creative problem solving and autonomy.

Max Weber (1864–1920) believed a bureaucratic administration was the best way to manage the workplace. This involved division of labour with task specialisation, hierarchy, recruitment based on merit, rules and regulations and impersonal decision making. When Weber's bureaucracy is combined with Taylor's scientific management, organisations become machine-like, and people merely cogs. Management practices based on these approaches dehumanise employees. A cog does not need a soul or meaning and purpose. The human cog is simply a resource to be used and exploited.

To counter the influence of scientific management and bureaucracy, Elton Mayo (1880–1949) developed Human Relations Theory. He recognised that, alongside the formal organisation, there exists an informal one made up of relationships. His theory argues organisations should treat people as individuals with social needs rather than cogs in a machine. He believed productivity increases when people feel valued as part of a team, facilitating their development and growth.

The behaviourist school of psychology has a significant influence on how people are managed in the workplace. As outlined earlier, behaviourism suggests all managers need to do to encourage people to perform is to provide the right stimuli, such as clear structures and guidance, and the right reinforcements, such as rewards and punishments. This approach uses science to manage people as human machines. Consequently, management and leadership have become highly transactional. People are rewarded or punished according to their level of compliance.

Transformational leadership emerged as a reaction to this transactional way of leading and managing people. According to James MacGregor Burns (1918–2014), transformational leadership is seen when 'leaders and followers make each other advance to a higher level of morale and motivation'. Transformational leaders inspire followers to change expectations, perceptions and motivations to work towards common goals. Servant leadership could also be considered a transformational approach to leadership. Developed by Robert K. Greenleaf (1904–1990), servant leadership turns convention on its head. Rather than people serving the leader, the leader serves the people. A servant leader puts the needs of followers first and helps them develop and perform as highly as possible. The servant leader tries to develop other people to become wiser, freer and more autonomous servant leaders, allowing them to share power. As a result, people find greater meaning and purpose in their work. They become more committed to and engaged with both the organisation and the people they serve.

There is now an ongoing battle for the soul of employees. Those advocating more scientific approaches to management, such as scientific management, bureaucracy and behaviourism, encourage people to leave their soul at home and become a cog in the organisational machine. More transformational approaches, such as human relations, transformational leadership and servant leadership, urge people to bring their whole psyche, including their soul, to work. Which style will prevail? It depends on the industry, organisation and management, yet since most organisations are designed as machines, they tend to prefer cogs. Business leaders with the ability to accommodate the whole employee, soul and all, are few and far between. Most people's experience at work is one that increasingly separates them from their soul, stripping them of meaning and purpose. This inevitably impacts negatively on their psychological well-being.

This section has outlined how, over the past few centuries, we in western societies have been on a path of separation from our souls (our Self). Consequently, we are experiencing a loss of meaning and purpose in our lives. This adversely impacts our psychological health. Having separated from our soul, all that remains is our ego (see Figure 3.4).

Figure 3.4 Triangle Model – Relationship with Nature, Society and Ego

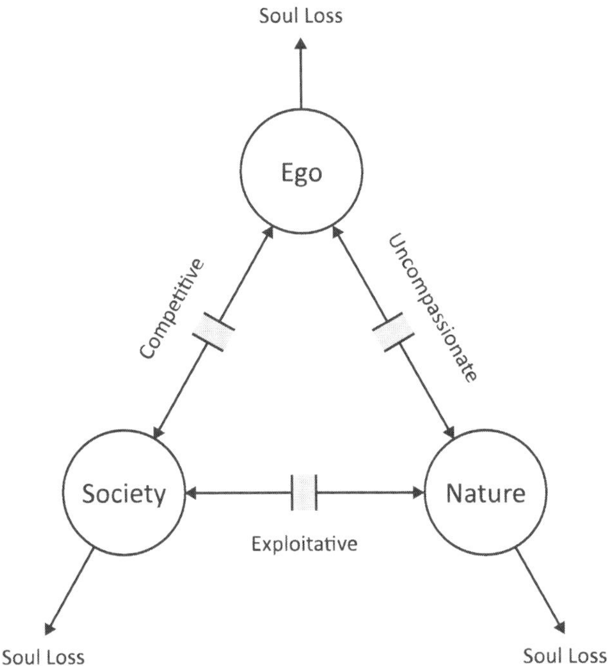

Although the psyche generally remains intact in major religions, the influence of the New Science revolution has removed the soul from it in much of philosophy, science, psychology and management. The mind has become a machine that can be easily be manipulated to achieve the desired outcomes.

There are philosophers, scientists, psychologists and management theorists working to reconnect us with our soul. Nevertheless, for fear of ridicule, many do not use the word soul. Instead, they use words such as 'Self', wisdom, meaning, purpose, transcendence, etc. Unfortunately, these philosophers, scientists, psychologists and management theorists work on the periphery with little influence. The all-pervading and dominant worldview remains that of the New Science of the 17th and 18th centuries, prioritising reductionism, materialism and empiricism.

The soul has little influence but clings on in religious or spiritual aspects of our lives.

SUMMARY AND CONCLUSION

Over the past 2,500 years, advances in philosophy, science, psychology, economics and management have resulted in us increasingly becoming separated from nature, each other and ourselves. As a result, nature has lost its soul and become psychologically dead, society has lost its soul with the loss of community and we have lost connection with our souls resulting in an over-reliance on our ego.

The development of New Science during the 16th, 17th and 18th centuries has been a significant influence. By valuing materialism, reductionism and empiricism, nature came to be viewed as a machine. Understanding the mechanics of nature fuelled the Industrial Revolution, which enabled societies worldwide to take significant steps forward and increased the standard of living for the majority. Nevertheless, stripped of its soul, nature has become a machine whose exploitation has caused the environmental crises we see today.

The teaching and methods of New Science have permeated into the theories and practices of psychology and management. The result being our own psychology and organisational relationships are viewed as being like a machine. People are cogs or resources to be exploited to grow business and the economy. New Science has stolen our soul just like it robbed nature of its soul.

Machines have no moral judgement. So, when New Science ideas were applied to economics, the system developed in a moral vacuum. There has been an emphasis on free markets, with minimum regulation or intervention from governments. Free markets need open competition. Consequently, people have become competitive individuals. This unregulated free-market economy based on individual competition is neoliberalism, the world's most dominant economic system.

Neoliberalism has taken away community, the soul of our society.

With the loss of soul from nature, society and our psyche, we have become increasingly separated from nature, each other and ourselves. These are the first three aspects of the industrialisation of our consciousness. When combined, these three separations have fixed our consciousness firmly in the Industrial Revolution. While our industrialised consciousness supported the Industrial Revolution, increasing the standard of living for many people, we now need to move on if we are to address the environmental, social and psychological crises we are facing today.

These three separations have also had a considerable impact on our psyche, as they have left us with an extremely isolated, fragile and competitive ego. Our ego now feels incredibly vulnerable and needs constant reinforcement and defence. Having a vulnerable ego makes us highly susceptible to the fourth and final aspect of the industrialisation of our consciousness, being conditioned into being consumers.

CHAPTER 4

OUR CONDITIONING INTO CONSUMERS

Eventually, Sophia reached the rugged peak of the mountain. Here, high above the mists that had enveloped her earlier, the heat was intense and burned into her skull. Though tired to the point of near collapse, she was too hot to rest and immediately started her descent down the far side. Entering the cooling mist once more, she could just make out enough of the path to maintain a slow and dogged descent. At the foot of the mountain, four paths met. To the left lay the Way of Nature, and to the right, the Way of the People. Directly in front of her, a path led off into what looked like a street market.

Trucks came along the Way of Nature, laden with products, and turned left towards the street market. Once unloaded, they returned along the same route back into the desert, heading towards the dense forest. People were running on the path that was the Way of the People. There was a distinct finish line at the end where it met her path, and Sophia could see some people were being lauded as race winners. They were rewarded with bags of money and ran off to the market, while the 'losers' were sent back, presumably to run again.

Sophia was relieved that by taking the Way of Self, she had been able to bypass all those tiresome races. Clearly, she was far more intelligent than those people still running, she thought to herself. As she passed a man handing out the winners' money, she shouted, 'I won, and I didn't even need to run your stupid race.' The man ignored her. With that, Sophia saw some wonderfully colourful products on the back of one of the passing trucks, and she fell in behind it as it trundled slowly towards the market.

The market was bustling and the air full of the smell of sweet spices and rich perfume. The sound of individual stallholders' voices blended into a chorus of sound which rose and fell like the call from a flock of gulls circling and swooping overhead ahead of a storm. Deals were being done, here, there and everywhere. People jostled each other and fought over the most desirable products. It was all very exciting. One stallholder grabbed Sophia.

'Want a sun hat?' he asked in a deep husky voice, 'Looks like you need a good sun hat.' Sophia had to agree it was a lovely hat. 'You could cross any desert in this,' the stallholder said, looking her straight in the eyes. Sophia had to admit to herself that would have come in handy along the Way of Nature. She rummaged in her bag, found some money and gave it to the stallholder.

Seeing that she was buying, another stallholder grabbed hold of her and whispered, 'You look like the type of woman who would appreciate a good pair of running shoes.' Without a second thought, Sophia bought the running shoes.

A little further along, another stallholder held up a colourful summer dress to Sophia, 'This dress looks like it was made for you.' She bought the dress.

By the time Sophia had come to the end of the street, she was laden down with all sorts of goods, including sunglasses, dresses, shirts, jewellery, shoes and even some crockery. She had to buy some cotton bags to carry her new possessions. Even though they were all highly desirable, she needed none of the products to fight a three-headed dragon or to be a tailor to that mind. The feelings of joy she had when buying each of the products soon wore off. She was left feeling exhausted from the day and from carrying all her new purchases. She was also very, very hungry. It was then it hit her. She hadn't any more food, and she'd spent all her money on the goods she was now lugging around. What was she going to do now? Sophia felt as though she had been tricked by the stallholders into buying all this stuff. They had taken advantage of her knowing she was tired from her journey.

Sophia felt like an empty shell. Even though all the products she had bought made her feel good at the time, nothing filled the hole within. She felt hungry, not just for food but also for psychological sustenance.

If only I had some more money, Sophia thought, I could go back into the Street Market buy some food and maybe a little something to cheer me up.

How can I get some more money?

I know, Sophia said to herself, I'll put on my new running shoes and go and join the races. That way I'll be able to win some money.

As she started lacing the new shoes, she heard a familiar voice whisper in her ear. 'The dragon, Sophia. Don't forget the three-headed dragon.' Startled by hearing Mimir's voice again, Sophia threw away the running shoes.

'What am I doing?' she shouted. 'I'm here to fight the dragon. That's why I'm here. That's my purpose.'

It was starting to get dark. To ward off the hunger pains, Sophia decided she should make camp for the night and get some sleep.

INTRODUCTION

> But industrial civilization is only possible when there's no self-denial. Self-indulgence up to the very limits imposed by hygiene and economics. Otherwise the wheels stop turning.
>
> Mustapha Mond, Resident Controller for Western Europe
>
> Aldous Huxley, Brave New World

When you last purchased something significant, how did it make you feel? I remember the last car I bought. It was second hand but only a couple of years old. I felt so proud, driving it back from the showroom. As soon as I got home, I took my family out for a ride. For months afterwards, each weekend, I would be out on my drive washing, polishing and hoovering my new car. I felt proud to own such a vehicle. My neighbour's admiring comments heightened these feelings of pride. It was self-indulgence up to the limits – of my time and finances. Owning this car made me feel good. Why? It was only a lump of metal and plastic. It was what the car represented that made me feel happy. It was the boost to my ego which made me feel good. The more I kept the car in pristine condition, the longer the ego boost would last. Of course, gradually, the feeling wore off, and I found other, more enriching things to do with my weekends. Over time the car became dented and dirty. The more it declined, the less I looked after it. A battered old car is not a great boost to the ego. I suspect you have had similar experiences in your life.

So far, in this book, I have explored how, through the industrialisation of our consciousness, we have increasingly become separated from nature, each other and ourselves. Our industrialised consciousness has enabled industry to capture the commons (things freely available to all of society for the benefit of all) of our natural resources, community relationships and psychology. The loss of our connection with nature, each other and ourselves is having a detrimental impact on our psychological well-being. As a substitute for this loss, industry converts our commons into products and services to sell back to us. Yet, these products and services never really satisfy us in the long term.

This chapter will demonstrate that consuming products, rather than improving our well-being, leaves us still feeling empty inside. Our emptiness is the result of our separation from nature, each other and ourselves. This separation creates a psychological hole within us, which forms the foundation of our consumerist economy. No matter how much we consume, we can never fill the hole. We are stuck on what Philip Brickman and Donald Campbell have called the hedonistic treadmill.[1] Despite how much we consume, we never feel happy in the long term.

Our separation from nature, each other and ourselves also leaves us with an isolated, fragile and competitive ego. Each of us has been left with such a vulnerable ego that we need to prop up and defend it continually. Businesses use techniques to manipulate our vulnerable ego so that we consume more products and services. These techniques work at a psychological level, fuelling consumerism.

Continuous economic growth is a goal of the leaders of industrialised societies, and they seek to achieve this through continually increasing productivity and consumerism. For continual economic growth, our industrialised consciousness must be conditioned so that we develop the consciousness of consumerism. As a society, we have now become addicted to consuming.

THE IMPACT OF SEPARATION

This section summarises the impact our increasing separation from nature, each other and ourselves has had on our consciousness. I recognise that I may take things to the extreme in doing so and, therefore, you might not entirely recognise yourself in these characteristics of the industrialised mind. If this is the case, stop and reflect for a while. As I said in the Introduction to this book, we have become 'subject' to the industrialisation of our consciousness. You may not be aware of the extent of the impact separation has had on your mind. While these descriptions may appear to be extreme, there are plenty of people in westernised societies who demonstrate these characteristics. Research indicates these characteristics are increasingly becoming the norm.

The Hole in Our Psyche

Our increasing separation from nature, each other and ourselves has left a massive hole in our psyche. Throughout this chapter, I will demonstrate how businesses sell us products and services on the promise these will fill the hole and leave us satisfied. Before I get into all of that, let us just take a little look inside the hole.

While our separation from nature has allowed industry to exploit it for profit and economic growth, it has also had a detrimental impact on our psychology. In his book *Last Child in the Woods*, Richard Louv coined the phrase 'nature deficit disorder'.[2] It was never meant to be a medical diagnosis but, instead, to serve as a description of the human costs of alienation from the natural world. Louv stated that the rapid disengagement between children and direct experiences in nature has profound implications, not only for the health of future generations but for the health of Earth itself. He believes children who do not get to spend time in nature are more prone to anxiety, depression and attention-deficit problems.

Although Louv's work was not a scientific study, there have since been several studies that have provided evidence that a greater connection with nature makes us healthier and happier. One study, published in 2020, was carried out by the University of Derby and The Wildlife Trusts to measure the impact of the '30 Days Wild' campaign.[3] The campaign asked people to engage with nature every day for a month.

An estimated 18,500 people took part, resulting in around 300,000 engagements with nature by the participants. It was found that those taking part demonstrated significant and sustained increases in health and happiness from the change in their relationship to nature. Another study, published in 2019, was carried out by the University of Exeter Medical School.[4] It found, based on 20,000 interviews with people in England, that the likelihood of reporting good health or high well-being became significantly increased with contact with nature greater than or equal to 120 min per week. Positive associations peaked between 200 and 300 min per week with no further gain after that. These studies suggest that our separation from nature leaves a hole in our psychology, which negatively impacts our mental health and well-being.

As we increasingly separate from each other, we still feel lonely despite getting 'likes' on social media. It is reported we are experiencing high levels of loneliness in our society. The statistics on loneliness are hard to nail down. Some people speak of a global epidemic of loneliness. Others agree there are problems associated with loneliness, but they do not believe it has reached epidemic proportions. These disagreements are probably due to how loneliness is measured. Social scientists define loneliness as the emotional state created when people have fewer social contacts and meaningful relationships than they would like. Therefore, if you feel lonely, you are deemed to be lonely.

In the USA, a study carried by the health insurance company Cigna found that 61% of respondents reported in 2020 that they often felt lonely or left out.[5] This percentage has increased year by year, and by 7% since 2018. In 2017, after recognising pervasive loneliness as a public health crisis, the UK Government set up the Jo Cox Commission on Loneliness and in 2018 became the first country to appoint a Minister for Loneliness. The 2020 'Looking Further with Ford Trends Report', authored by Sheryl Connelly (Ford's Global Consumer Trends and Futuring Manager), stated that loneliness has become an epidemic of global proportions in young people, citing 62% of Generation Z reporting that they feel lonely on a regular basis.[6] Even though loneliness is not a mental health problem per se, it is clearly linked to the increased risk of certain mental health problems, including self-harm, depression, anxiety, low self-esteem, sleep problems and increased stress.

As we increasingly separate from ourselves, we lose our own sense of meaning and purpose. 'Purpose' is a stable and generalised intention to accomplish something that is personally meaningful and, at the same time, leads to productive engagement with some aspect of the world beyond the ego. The psychiatrist Viktor Frankl (1905–1997), following his experience in Auschwitz concentration camp, concluded that having meaning and purpose in our lives can lead to us developing greater resilience, which improves our psychological health. In his book, *Man's Search for Meaning*, Frankl identified three main ways of realising meaning and purpose in life.[7] These were making a difference in the world through our work, encountering love and adopting a courageous attitude in situations of unavoidable suffering.

To be effective, these ways of finding meaning and purpose must be aligned with our personal values, not other people's values. Our personal values do not derive from our ego; they derive from somewhere deeper in our psyche. They derive from our Self (our soul). By separating from our Self, we are increasingly losing our sense of what is meaningful in our lives and, therefore, what gives our life purpose. In 2008, the Centers for Disease Control and Prevention (CDC) in the USA carried out research which found that about 4 out of 10 Americans had not yet discovered a satisfying life purpose.[8] It is likely to be the same ratio in other westernised societies. Without meaning and purpose, we lose our resilience and become susceptible to mental illness. Research increasingly shows that people with a strong sense of purpose in life tend to demonstrate higher mental health, well-being and cognitive functioning. As the philosopher Friedrich Nietzsche (1844–1900) said, 'He who has a why to live for can bear with almost any how.'

So, the hole in our psyche is what remains after taking away our connection with nature, other people and ourselves. We are experiencing this hole as increasing mental health problems. In the absence of reconnection, we try to fill this psychological hole with consumption. Fortunately, businesses are all too eager to help us consume. But does consumption really fill the hole? Are we really totally satisfied? If we were, would it be good for business? We need to self-indulge up to limits; otherwise, the wheels of the economy will stop turning.

Our Individual Competitiveness

As a result of our increasing separation from each other, we have become a society of individuals who are highly competitive with each other. In neoliberal societies, competitive individualism has become the accepted norm. We increasingly believe achievement and non-achievement are down to individual merit and are not a function of societal systems. Ability, motivation and effort are seen as the prerequisites of success. Consequently, it is thought competition enables people to perform at their best. Neoliberalism, therefore, creates systems that encourage competition, resulting in winners and losers. These systems support the inequality people experience as a result of winning or losing.

When we constantly compare ourselves to others, we frequently develop feelings of inadequacy. Clearly, we cannot be the best at everything and, therefore, we sometimes come off second best. However, constantly trying to be the best can lead to perfectionism. When we take individual competitiveness to the extreme, this is known as 'hyper-competitiveness'. The German psychoanalyst Karen Horney (1885–1952) defined this as an indiscriminate need to compete and succeed at any cost as a means of maintaining or enhancing one's self-worth. In 2011, Andrew Luchner and his team at Rollins College in the USA found that people who score high on hyper-competitiveness are more narcissistic and less psychologically healthy than those who score low.[9]

Our Vulnerable Ego

As we increasingly separate from ourselves, with our Self (our soul) leaving our psyche, our ego becomes isolated and vulnerable. To protect our ego, we need to maintain our self-esteem continually. However, due to individual competitiveness, we are trying more and more to increase our self-esteem by comparing ourselves to other people. Our efforts are leading to, as discussed, an increase in perfectionism. When perfectionism is combined with a vulnerable ego, an unhealthy type of self-esteem is the inevitable result. This type of self-esteem is called 'threatened egotism' or 'fragile high self-esteem' and is on the narcissism spectrum.

Narcissism is defined as an exceptional interest in, or admiration of, oneself. It lies on a continuum from healthy to pathological. Healthy narcissism is self-love and confidence gained through increasing self-esteem. It becomes a problem when a person becomes preoccupied with themselves and needs excessive admiration from other people. Some researchers point to an increase in narcissism in westernised society. For example, Jean Twenge, Professor of Psychology at San Diego University, compared the results of students completing the Narcissistic Personality Inventory (NPI) from 1979 with those of 2006.[10] She found NPI scores were 30% higher in the most recent cohort compared with the first. Other research studies have found an increase in narcissistic language in books, songs and media. Recent research has even shown that activities like posting 'selfies' on social media can increase narcissism. Although a lot of this research is rigorously debated in academia, overall, there does appear to be an increase in narcissism in western societies.

In increasingly neoliberal societies, the rise in narcissism is associated with the shift away from being part of a collective to focusing on being an individual. This individualism has led to a decline in the social support mechanism people can draw upon in society, such as family or friends who live nearby or a trusted local community. Instead of having social support networks, we need to be more psychologically self-reliant. It seems many of us are not good at this. Consequently, the increase in perfectionism and narcissism in society is associated with a global rise in depression, anxiety and substance abuse.[11]

Our consciousness has now been industrialised to the extent that all we have left is our isolated, fragile and competitive ego. I recognise I may have taken this to the extreme. However, we are all on this path to some degree. The more our consciousness becomes industrialised, the further along the path we travel.

Having an increasingly vulnerable ego allows businesses to create and sell us products and services to prop it up and make us feel good. Even though they may boost our ego in the short term, these products and services do not make us happy long term. They do not provide the deeper meaning and purpose in our lives that is essential for our well-being. The products and services we buy, despite the promises, also never fill the hole within our psyche. Consequently, many people are now struggling with their psychological well-being. Again, this allows industry to capture the commons of our psychology and sell us even more products and services designed to improve our mental health. Although these products may treat the symptoms, they rarely address the cause: our increasing separation from nature, each other and ourselves.

Our vulnerable ego has made us susceptible to the final aspect of the industrialisation process – to be conditioned into consumers.

THE BIRTH OF CONSUMERISM

You and I are both consumers. We consume to meet our basic needs, such as food and shelter. Consumerism is different. It is about consuming things that make us feel good. Therefore, it is more about consuming goods and services that help us build relationships and increase our self-esteem. While there are many definitions of consumerism, we can consider it to be the increasing consumption of goods and services purchased in the market to increase well-being and happiness.

Consumerism is not a new phenomenon. It goes back to colonialism when exotic goods such as tobacco, tea, sugar and spices were traded worldwide to be consumed by the wealthy. The Industrial Revolution saw consumerism begin to spread to the general population. However, it was not until the 1920s and then again in the 1950s (following world wars), when the world saw mass production leading to overproduction, that consumerism became an important part of the economy. Today, many people say we are in a consumer-led economy. When we go into an economic recession, you will often hear politicians encouraging people to spend as a way of fuelling economic growth. They talk of a consumer-led recovery.

But what is an economic recession? The accepted definition is a significant decline in general economic activity, typically recognised as two consecutive quarters of economic decline as reflected by gross domestic product (GDP). So, politicians encourage consumerism as a way to boost economic growth and avoid a recession. Clearly, politicians believe continual growth is essential.

ECONOMIC GROWTH

This section explores economic growth in terms of its purpose, measurement and how it is generated. In doing so, I challenge whether it is necessary at all. As you will see, continuous growth is dependent on consumerism, which is destroying our planet. In turn, as we found in the previous section, consumerism is dependent on the industrialisation of our consciousness, which is also destroying our communities and causing an increase in mental health problems. All of this is an incredibly high price to pay for economic growth. Is it really worth it?

GDP

Adam Smith advocated measuring the wealth of nations by their economic activity rather than by the amount of silver and gold they held. This measure came to be known as gross domestic product (GDP), a measure that has had an enormous impact on our lives ever since. Though the concept was first developed by William Petty (1623–1687), it was not until 1944 that GDP became the primary tool for measuring a country's economy. It was formulated at a conference of 44 allied nations, brought together to regulate the international monetary and financial order after the conclusion of World War II. GDP is the total monetary or market value of all the finished goods and services produced by a country within a year. It is a measure of economic growth or recession.

There have been many criticisms of GDP, mainly because it measures the quantity and not the quality of the economic activity. In 1968, 2 days after he had declared his candidacy for the Democratic nomination in the US Presidential Race, Robert F. Kennedy (1925–1968) gave a speech in which he questioned whether GDP (gross national product as it was then called) was a legitimate measure of national well-being. He said, 'it measures everything in short, except that which makes life worthwhile'. What he meant by this is explained in this excerpt from his speech:

> It counts air pollution and cigarette advertising, and ambulances to clear our highways of carnage. It counts special locks for our doors and the jails for the people who break them. It counts the destruction of the redwood and the loss of our natural wonder in chaotic sprawl. It counts napalm and counts nuclear warheads and armored cars for the police to fight the riots in our cities. It counts Whitman's rifle and Speck's knife, and the television programs which glorify violence in order to sell toys to our children.

> Yet the Gross National Product does not allow for the health of our children, the quality of their education or the joy of their play. It does not include the beauty of our poetry or the strength of our marriages, the intelligence of our public debate or the integrity of our public officials. It measures neither our wit nor our courage, neither our wisdom nor our learning, neither our compassion nor our devotion to our country.[12]

Despite these types of criticisms, GDP remains the method countries worldwide use to measure their economies.

Why Do We Need Economic Growth?

Take a few moments to consider your answer to this question before reading on. Why do economies need to grow beyond population growth?

I have been asking people this question for the past 30 years. Most people initially look at me with a blank stare as they struggle to find an answer. People believe they should know the answer and then become embarrassed when they struggle to find it. The usual answer is 'It is just what they need to do'. It is as though I have just asked them, 'Why does a child need to grow?' Environmentalist David Fleming (1940–2010) said, 'Market economies, like bicycles, are only stable when they are moving forward – and that, for an economy, means growth.'[13] To some degree, Fleming is right. We have all seen the financial and social destruction wreaked when an economy stops moving forward and falls over. Millions of people lose their jobs, homes are repossessed, shares lose their value and people see a fall in the value of their pensions. But why do economies fall over when they stop moving forward?

Another answer I often hear is the economy needs to grow so that each generation has a better standard of living than its predecessor. It is called progress. We have this view that society needs to continue to progress forward. Measuring the economy using GDP can help ensure society moves forward in terms of quantity and the amount people consume, but not necessarily quality. Working long hours to earn money to consume lots of goods may grow the economy, but it does nothing to sustain good mental health, relationships or the environment. If economic growth does continually improve the standard of living in each successive generation, this is not reflected in the statistics on life expectancy. As Wilkinson and Pickett found, while GDP growth does initially increase life expectancy, it soon reaches a plateau.[14]

Financially astute people often state that economic growth is a fundamental component of our financial system. They point to 'cost of capital', which is the term for money costing money. So, when we borrow money, the institution or person we borrow from can no longer benefit from using the money themselves. Therefore, we have to compensate them for this loss of benefit. In the case of a loan, this is called 'interest', and in the case of equity, it is called a dividend or rise in share price (combined, they create total shareholder value). So, if we borrow money to invest in a business, we need to grow the business to pay for the cost of capital. For example, in very simplistic terms, if you borrow £100k to set up a business at 10% interest to be paid after 1 year, if you then sell the business at the end of the year it will need to be worth at least £110k to pay off the loan and the interest. The business will need to have grown by at least 10%. Of course, the reality of business is far more complex than this simple example, but it demonstrates the underlying principle. Collectively, as we have lots of businesses in an economy funded by debt or equity, as most capitalist economies do, the economy will grow in line with the growth in the businesses. A lot of this business growth is then reflected in increases in shareholder value, a lot of which eventually feeds through into paying the pensions of the elderly. As a financial system, it seems to work, but as we know, we cannot have continued economic growth on a finite planet. A financial system cannot work in isolation from the environmental system.

Of course, economic growth could be the result of good old-fashioned greed. Business owners who want more profit will generally try to grow their business and produce more. In doing so, they may increase the profit margin in their business by gaining economies of scale, assuming they can keep the business under control and continually find greater efficiencies. There is also self-esteem to be considered. Many business leaders want to be associated with a successful business, often measured in the sales as well as the profit of a business. Therefore, in the eyes of many business leaders, bigger is better for their self-esteem. So, growing a business may just be the psychologically natural thing to do if you are a business leader. If all leaders are doing this, then the economy will naturally grow.

Reflecting on my own thoughts on why economies need to grow, I have come to a conclusion that, for governments, it is about power and influence. In the past, countries with the most wealth could build the biggest and best-equipped armies, which allowed them to invade other countries and capture their natural resources. They could then use these captured natural resources to grow their economies even further and generate more wealth, which could be invested back into their armies. It is basic competitiveness at the level of survival of the fittest. Today, people often accuse the western world's involvement in Middle Eastern conflicts of being a way to control access to oil. We also see this power and influence expressed in other ways through the Group of Twenty (G20) and Group of Eight (G8). The G20 is an international forum, founded in 1999, for the governments of 19 countries and the European Union to discuss issues pertaining to international financial security. As, collectively, the G20 economies account for around 90% of the gross world product (GWP), having a sizeable growing economy is clearly a way to get a seat at the table at the summits of this influential group. The G8 is a similar forum formed in 1975 and includes seven highly industrialised nations in the world (Russia suspended at the time of writing). The G8 aims to foster consensus on global issues such as economic growth, global security, food supply, terrorism and energy.

So, it can be seen that if a country is highly industrialised and wealthy, gained through economic growth, it can have a tremendous influence on how the world is run. To gain and maintain this influence, governments will inevitably encourage business leaders to continually grow their production, which will increase employment and, overall, grow the economy.

Productivity

When politicians in government talk about economic growth, they often talk about increasing productivity. So, what is the connection?

Productivity is a measure of efficiency. The more efficient business is, the more productive it is. It is really about how a business can produce more with fewer resources, including labour. If a business can produce and sell more with fewer employees, then, in theory, the people who remain in work have the potential to earn more money. So, at a national level, if the country can produce and sell more, then, in theory, its population will have more money to spend, which in turn will grow the economy. Of course, this all depends on the balance of trade. For a favourable balance of trade, a country needs to sell more to overseas markets than it imports. Therefore, its products and services need to be competitive in global markets. As a competitive advantage is gained through increasing the quality in relation to the price or reducing the price in relation to the quality, it once again comes down to productivity, producing more with less. Therefore, increasing the productivity of businesses increases the competitiveness of a nation, which in turn attracts investment and grows the economy. Consequently, productivity and economic growth are intertwined in lots of different ways.

The Austrian-American political economist Joseph Schumpeter called this process 'creative destruction'. He argued that innovations in the manufacturing process increase productivity by outcompeting and destroying old practices. Schumpeter believed that entrepreneurial innovations in old markets were the disruptive force that sustained economic growth. Consumers would buy more of the innovative product because of its increased quality/functionality or reduction in cost. Consequently, manufacturers committed to older technology would soon go out of business.

Today's destructive technology is automation. Machines can produce more, work longer, work faster and with a more consistent quality than people. Therefore, when businesses have access to additional capital, they like to invest it in automation. While automation mainly occurred in the manufacturing sector, we now increasingly see automation in the service sector through the use of artificial intelligence. In the new post Covid-19 economy, there is likely to be significant investment in automation. Machines do not get sick or need to isolate. Also, for economies to recover, interest rates will be low for a long time, allowing many businesses to borrow the money needed to invest in automation.

The problem with increasing productivity through investing in automation is that people will lose their jobs. However, governments prefer the economy to function with virtually full employment. People who are not working are not good consumers. In a consumer-led economy, if too many people are unemployed, the economy goes into recession. Therefore, while governments encourage businesses to improve their productivity so that the nation is competitive in world markets, they also encourage businesses to produce more to keep more people employed. To employ people who have lost their jobs due to productivity increases, governments encourage new start-up businesses. These new businesses then produce more products.

As a consequence of productivity increases, our society is continuously swamped with new products. For businesses to constantly produce more, we have to be encouraged to keep buying more. 'Built-in obsolescence' is commonly used by companies to artificially limit the life of the product, such as ensuring goods break down after a period of time or become too old to function correctly, e.g. when new software does not run on an old system. Other methods include stopping the provision of spare parts or maintenance. As a result, many societies have developed a 'throw-away culture'. Another way businesses encourage us to buy more products is to appeal to our greed through public relations and advertising.

In business, there is a saying, 'If you cannot measure it, you cannot manage it.' Governments measure the economy using GDP so they can manage it. However, it follows that if you choose a poor measure, then poor management will ensue. It is evident that GDP is a poor measure of an economy that should be serving society. Consequently, economies around the world have been mismanaged to the extent they are not serving their societies. For economic growth to continue, according to GDP, we must continue to consume our planet, our relationships and our own psychology.

PUBLIC RELATIONS

This section explores the public relations (PR) profession's techniques used to encourage us to buy more products, so productivity can continually increase and the economy can continually grow. In doing so, I outline the methods developed and employed by the earliest pioneer of PR and then explore how they are used today across our modern media.

Edward Bernays – The Father of PR

After World War I, industry had a substantial problem. Productivity had increased production significantly to provide armaments and equipment to supply the war effort. In peacetime, this high level of productivity led to an oversupply of products in the market. Up until that time, people bought products based on their needs. Although the manufacture of products had increased, people's needs had not. Returning from the war,

Edward Bernays (1891–1995) believed he had the solution. Bernays was Sigmund Freud's nephew, and he had learned a lot from his uncle about the workings of the mind, especially the unconscious. He applied this learning to his work in the military during the war and in business during peacetime.

As the US entered World War I, Bernays was hired by the 'Committee on Public Information' to build support for the war both at home in America and abroad. While, at the time, most people referred to his work as 'propaganda', he often referred to it as 'psychological warfare'. He was the first person to use this term. Seeing the problem of oversupply following the war, Bernays realised he could use psychological warfare techniques to help businesses sell more products. He knew he could not call his techniques psychological warfare or even propaganda, so he invented the term 'public relations'.

Rather than selling to people's needs, as had been previously the case, Bernays taught businesses how to sell to people's greed. He found that greed to be engendered by using psychological techniques to manipulate people's egos. By this time, people's egos were becoming increasingly isolated, fragile and competitive. Bernays saw that, through becoming increasingly separated from nature, each other and ourselves, people were ready to be conditioned into becoming consumers. To do so, he needed to appeal to people's unconscious mind rather than their rational thought. He later called this approach the 'engineering of consent'. It involved engendering fear or, its close relative, desire. Products would then be sold on the basis of their ability to allay fears or feed desires. In his book *Propaganda*, he said:

> If we understand the mechanism and motives of the group mind, is it not possible to control and regiment the masses according to our will without their knowing about it? The recent practice of propaganda has proved that it is possible, at least up to a certain point and within certain limits.[15]

Bernays worked with a wide range of major corporations, including Procter & Gamble, the American Tobacco Company, Cartier Inc., CBS, the United Fruit Company and General Electric, in his career. The following case study demonstrates the approach he used.

> In 1927, though it was common for men to smoke cigarettes, it was frowned upon for women to smoke. Cigarette manufacturer Lucky Strike realised they could potentially double their market if they could sell to women. They hired Bernays, who decided to link smoking with a fear of becoming overweight. Not only did he promote 'thinness' as an ideal in the media at the time, but he also encouraged doctors to recommend smoking cigarettes rather than eating sweets. His campaign worked to some extent, but it was still frowned upon for women to smoke publicly. Therefore, he switched his focus onto linking equality for women with smoking in public. By calling cigarettes 'Torches of Freedom' and encouraging 'Women's Party' members to smoke at the 1929 Easter Sunday parade in New York, he increased sales further. The colour of the packaging was the final stumbling block. Green was not a fashionable colour. So, in 1934 he promoted green as the colour of the year with fashion designers and magazines as well as organising a 'Green Ball' at the Waldorf-Astoria. Amongst the attendees were many famous society women and everyone had to wear green. Even before the ball took place, the colour green had become the height of fashion.

To support his campaigns, Bernays would also enlist the help of the celebrities of the day, many of whom were his clients. Bernays would ensure the newspapers printed stories about the celebrities, including a photograph of the celebrity with a new product. This way, he could combine the promotion of the celebrity and the products. Today we refer to this as product placement, and it is such a valuable marketing tool that laws and guidelines have been introduced around the world to restrict its use.

Bernays did not solely focus on selling more products; instead, he focused on changing people's views to make selling to them easier. A skilled PR professional connects with and manipulates our most basic emotions. They often do this through third parties, not directly, using popular leaders and influencers in society. Bernays is reported to have said, 'If you can influence the leaders, either with or without their conscious co-operation, you automatically influence the group which they sway.'

PR Today

Bernays' techniques continue to be used today. PR firms are paid to get positive media coverage for their clients, which they do through pitching creative stories to editors and journalists through press releases and direct contact. Many journalists depend on PR firms to provide them with stories and give them access to the people in the news. It is a symbiotic relationship. Given that many newspapers are struggling financially due to the rise of online news reporting, online advertising and social media, they cannot afford to employ hordes of journalists hunting down their own news stories. So, the few journalists who remain are increasingly relying on the news stories being fed to them by PR firms to keep them on top of the breaking news and fill column inches. It makes you wonder how much of the news we consume is actually publicity and, therefore, a continuation of our psychological conditioning as consumers.

Given that the way we view media (i.e. via traditional press or broadcasting) is declining, PR firms are increasingly turning to the 'influencers' on social media. These are people who have built up a significant following on various social media platforms due to their reputation, knowledge, expertise or views. Consequently, they can engage and influence a significantly large population of consumers. For this reason, businesses love social media influencers and increasingly engage them to help create new trends and promote new products. The significant effect these influencers have on consumers has led many governments to ensure they declare to their followers when they are being paid by a business or PR firm to promote a particular point of view or product.

So, although as consumers, we are aware of advertising on television, radio, billboards, in newspapers and social media feeds, few of us are aware of how we are continually being manipulated to buy more products via the news, entertainment and social media influencers. Through these techniques, businesses are manipulating our isolated, fragile and competitive egos and conditioning us to be consumers.

THE PSYCHOLOGY OF CONSUMING

What is it about our isolated, fragile and competitive ego that makes us susceptible to being conditioned into becoming consumers by businesses? It is the vulnerability of our ego, which means we need to defend it. Businesses emphasise the threat to our ego and then provide the product or service that reinforces our defence. Basically, businesses tell us we have a headache before selling us the pill to numb it. They are creating the demand for us to consume the overproduction caused by increases in productivity. This section outlines the psychology behind how this is done in different ways: social comparison, conspicuous consumption, social dominance and addiction.

Social Comparison Theory

We determine our own social worth and self-worth through social comparisons based on how we believe we compare to other people. Social comparison theory was first developed in 1954 by the American social psychologist Leon Festinger (1919–1989) and has been the basis of many research studies ever since. We make upwards comparisons with those we believe have a higher social standing, motivating us to improve. Conversely, we make downwards comparisons with those we believe have a lower social standing, enhancing our self-esteem. Essentially, we use social comparisons to determine what is normal in our social group and then our relative standing against this norm. In neoliberal societies, characterised by competitive individualism, these social comparisons feed people's desire to increase, or at least maintain, their social standing to avoid feelings of inadequacy. Our social comparisons thus encourage us to compete with each other.

The most important comparisons we make are those associated with our self-image, our ego. Through PR and advertising, we are constantly bombarded with the 'ideal image', against which we are encouraged to compare our own self-image. Unfavourable comparisons are a threat to our ego and, therefore, need to be rectified. We feel most threatened when we believe our peers compare more favourably to the 'ideal image'. Businesses then reassure us, through PR and advertising, that if we buy their product or service, we will compare more favourably with the ideal image and our peers. They do this by selling the 'lifestyle' associated with the product or service rather than its utility. This way, they sell to our ego desire rather than our functional need. When we feel inadequate, a product or service always has a solution. The products and services we consume, therefore, protect and boost our vulnerable ego. Gradually, our material possessions can start to define our identity, or at least who we want to be or how we want other people to see us. With our increasing loss of soul and reliance on our ego, our material possessions can come to define who we are in our entirety. To maintain our sense of self and self-esteem in competition with others, we must keep buying and consuming products and services.

I will give you an example of how powerful social comparisons can be. I once worked for a company that was struggling financially. To rectify the situation, the Board of Directors decided to give everyone a pay cut and downgrade their company cars. While no one was happy with the situation, most people saw the need, accepted cost-cutting was necessary and were grateful to keep their jobs. However, some people were really unhappy with the downgrade of their company car and protested quite vocally. I asked my manager why people were protesting about their cars and not their pay. His reply was, 'Your neighbours can see your car on your drive; they cannot see your salary.'

Conspicuous Consumption

For many, the car we drive is an example of conspicuous consumption. This term was coined by the American sociologist and economist Thorstein Veblen (1857–1929). Conspicuous consumption is the practice of purchasing luxury goods or services to display wealth and status. Luxury can be defined in terms of acquiring goods at a higher quantity or quality than practically needed. The purchase of these goods and services then helps us to compare favourably against our peers. So, with my example, the downgraded company car still met the practical need, but it took away the 'conspicuous' value from its user. For some people, this created greater psychological pain than the financial loss caused by the reduction in salary. For Veblen, conspicuous consumption explains the psychological dynamics at play in a consumer society and the increase in the number of different goods and services people now seem to need in their lives.

Conspicuous consumption, consuming more than is practically needed, appears to increase with wealth. The wealthier we become, the more we have to lose in the social comparisons with the people in our peer groups. According to the World Bank, in 2005, the wealthiest 20% of the world's people accounted for 76.6% of total private consumption while the poorest 20% accounted for just 1.5%.[16]

Social Dominance Theory

Why do we have such inequality in consumption? One explanation may be found in 'social dominance theory' developed in the 1990s by Jim Sidanious and Felicia Pratto. It proposes that people with power will always seek to get more of what they desire in life at their subordinates' expense. It is underpinned by the observation that most modern human systems have a tendency to be organised as group-based hierarchies, with one small group at the top and a variety of groups at the bottom. Consequently, as humans, we tend to organise ourselves in social systems, which results in inequality. However, the degree to which we accept this social dominance does differ. To measure these differences, Sidanious and Pratto designed a scoring system called the 'social dominance orientation' (SDO).[17] Using this measure in a large-scale study (2017) of 5,400 participants in 25 countries, they found that people accepting social inequality (high SDO scores) are less likely to take pro-environmental actions. When we accept social dominance, we accept conspicuous consumption. Consequently, we willingly allow the richest people in our society to consume more of the common natural resources than they need.

Most people accept this inequality of consumption because we are encouraged to believe that we will one day be in the socially dominant group if we work hard. Then we will be able to enjoy all the luxuries associated with conspicuous consumption. It is the American Dream, and it is spreading worldwide with the rise of neoliberalism. Further research carried out by the University of Wellington in New Zealand looked at the link between social and environmental attitudes at the national level.[18] The results showed there is more of a focus on addressing environmental issues in countries with less social inequality. Conversely, studies from the universities of Freiburg, Kiel and Berlin have found that people placed less value on the natural environment in more unequal societies. These findings are not a surprise to Sidanius, who says they fit with the notion that social dominance measures a short- and medium-term desire to gather as much social power and resources as possible, with little concern for the long-term consequences. These studies demonstrate that our acceptance of inequality leads us to tolerate people consuming the planet's resources to reinforce their social dominance.

Addiction

We also consume in isolation as a means to increase our well-being. As I outlined at the beginning of this chapter, due to our increasing separation from nature, each other and ourselves we have been left with an empty hole within our psychology. We try to fill our emptiness inside with various addictions, such as alcohol, drugs, sex, work, junk food, sport and consuming products. You have probably heard that, when feeling down, people often go out for some 'retail therapy'. Even though we initially feel good as a result of our purchases, unfortunately, this feeling does not last for long. We soon need our next fix. Gradually, we can become addicted to consuming.

So, in neoliberal consumerist societies, we are constantly comparing ourselves to the 'ideal norm' communicated to us through PR and advertising as well as with people in our own social groups. This comparison is threatening to our isolated, fragile and competitive ego. If we compare unfavourably, then our self-esteem is negatively impacted. To protect against this threat, businesses tell us, through their advertising, that if we buy this product or that service, we will impress our peers and we will feel good. We buy the products and services, and gradually our identity can become defined by what we purchase. As we have also been conditioned to compete with other people, we can often aspire to be seen as being in a higher group in our community. When this happens, the purchases we make increasingly become conspicuous in terms of their quality or quantity. Even though our purchases make us feel good in the short term, they never fully satisfy us in the long term. While the products we purchase can boost and protect our vulnerable ego, they can never fill the hole in our psyche left by our soul, relationships and nature. Before too long, we need to get our next consumer fix. It is at this point that we have become addicted to consumerism.

SUMMARY AND CONCLUSION

It is evident that governments encourage economic growth to increase their country's competitiveness in the global markets and increase their power and influence within the world. This is achieved through increasing productivity. To maintain full employment while increasing productivity means there is a danger of an oversupply of goods and services. For the economy to continue to function, this oversupply must be consumed. For this to happen, our consciousness needs to be industrialised and we need to be conditioned into becoming consumers.

The first three aspects of the industrialisation of our consciousness are our increasing separation from nature, each other and ourselves. As a result, we are left with an isolated, fragile and competitive ego, which constantly needs boosting and reinforcing to maintain our well-being. It is our vulnerable ego that makes us susceptible to being conditioned into becoming consumers. This conditioning is the fourth and final aspect of the industrialisation of our consciousness.

Businesses exploit our psychological tendency to compare ourselves against an ideal norm presented to us in advertising to encourage us to consume more than we need. Inevitably, we do not compare favourably. Our isolated, fragile and competitive ego then feels threatened, and our well-being declines. When we see others in our social groups comparing more favourably against this ideal norm, we experience a 'social comparison threat'. Businesses tell us that if we buy their goods and services, other people, especially our peers, will admire us and we will feel good. As a consequence, we buy products and services to protect our isolated, fragile and competitive ego.

We also tend to try to raise our social standing in comparison to our peers. The higher we rise, the more we tend to believe we are entitled to consume. It is seen as a reward for our success and signals to others that we are successful and have power and influence. We have gained greater social dominance. Our consumption then becomes conspicuous. Although all this consumption can boost and protect our isolated, fragile and competitive ego, it never really fills the hole in our psyche left behind from our increasing separation from nature, each other and ourselves. Nonetheless, we are still told consuming will make us feel better, but these good feelings never last for long. So, we have to keep consuming. Gradually we can become addicted to consuming, and the industrialisation of our consciousness is complete.

Is the industrialisation of your consciousness complete? Are you addicted to consuming? Do you like to keep up with the latest fashions, decorate your home in the style of those you see in magazines, keep up to date with the latest technology or have a nice car sitting on your drive? Do you wrestle with other consumers to get the best bargains during the sales? Do you queue outside shops for hours waiting for them to open so you can be one of the first to get the latest version of your favourite product? Despite all this consumption, do you still feel empty inside? Are you reliant on alcohol, even if it is just one or two glasses of wine each evening? Do you rely on social media to manage your social life? Are you oblivious to nature's pain? If you have answered yes to some of these questions, then you are in tune with the vast majority of people in westernised societies. We have all had our consciousness industrialised to some degree through our education, family upbringing, work and the media. It is what drives our economy.

The completed Triangle Model demonstrates how the industrialisation of our consciousness is perfectly aligned with the needs of a consumer-led economy (see Figure 4.1). It works as a highly effective system, but it cannot continue. As I have argued, while the economy continues to grow, providing income and pensions, we are in the process of consuming our planet, our relationships and our psychology. While we have created a perfectly self-reinforcing system over the centuries, we now know that it is not sustainable.

Figure 4.1 Triangle Model – Complete

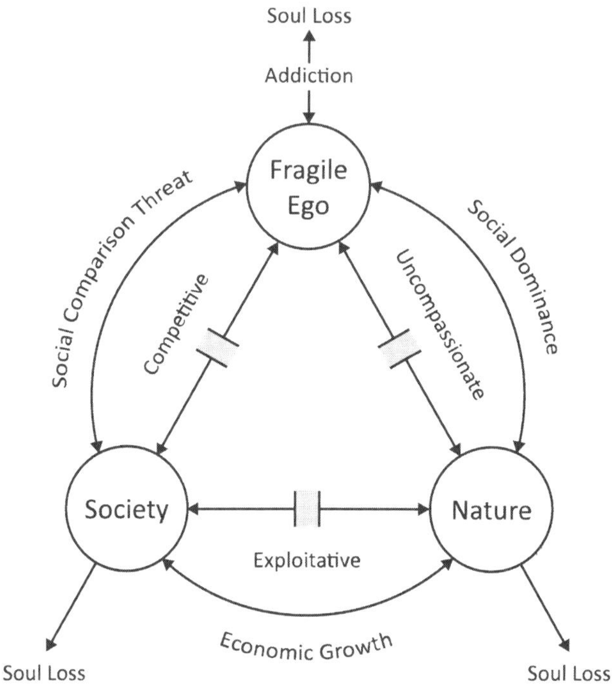

If humans are to survive on this planet long term and continue to enjoy the standard of living we have become accustomed to, we need a new type of economy. For that, we will need a new type of society.

The problem is, the system we have created, while leading to our demise, does not seem to stop long enough for us to create a change. It is like a merry-go-round that turns faster and faster, and we cannot get off. Occasionally, it slows down, such as in recessions, but it never stops. The closest we have come to the merry-go-round stopping is the Covid-19 pandemic. If any good can come from this global crisis, it will be an opportunity to build a new economy and society. If we do not, the pain of the environmental crisis, inequality and mental illness will increase to the extent that change becomes inevitable. Many people will suffer and perish as we try to resist the change.

In this way, our society is like our own psychological growth. As we go through life, we all experience periods of psychological growth and periods when we plateau. Before each growth period, we experience tension, discomfort and, if we do not change, pain and distress. In the discomfort phase, our current way of viewing and dealing with the world no longer works. During this time, things increasingly go wrong. Eventually, a new way of viewing and dealing with the world develops, and we enter a new period of psychological growth. Our society is currently in the discomfort phase, rapidly heading towards pain and distress. Unless we collectively develop a new way of viewing and dealing with the world, we will suffer more pain and distress like pandemics, climate change, unsustainable migration, social problems, mental illness, conflicts, etc.

To collectively view and deal with the world in a new way, we need to develop our consciousness beyond consumerism. There are plenty of ideas for creating a new, more sustainable economy and society. We do not lack solutions. We need to develop a new collective level of consciousness to allow them to unfold.

CHAPTER 5

THE MARRIAGE OF ECONOMICS AND CONSCIOUSNESS

As day broke and Sophia awoke, she realised she must keep focused on her purpose. She needed to deal with the dragon one way or another. Sophia remembered Mimir had said each of the three paths would lead her to the dragon, but she has taken all of them and has not found it. Can Mimir be trusted? Sophia thought to herself. But what else was she to do? 'I will keep going,' Sophia said out loud as if giving herself a good talking to. Then, still hungry, she broke camp and headed down the path away from the street market.

Soon Sophia came to a small stream. She sat down and replenished her water bottles and drank the cool water. As she sat, she noticed some regular puffs of grey smoke rising from behind a small hill to the south. 'There's the dragon!' Sophia cried out loud. Today she would see the dragon.

As a peaceful person by nature, the idea of fighting the dragon wasn't sitting well with Sophia. She didn't want to inflict violence upon the poor creature and hurt it. Nor did she relish being burned to a crisp herself. So, she set about devising three plans:

Plan A: She would try to reason with it to persuade it to

> *change its ways. This would convince the dragon there was no need to go plundering different towns. A dragon could be a force for good. It could help the towns and, in return, receive food and shelter.*
>
> *Plan B: Sophia would use the rope her mother had given her and divide it into three lengths. She would use each piece to lasso one of the dragon's three heads. She would then knot the three lengths of rope together and tie them around a tree. Just like restraining a dangerous dog, the dragon would be incapacitated, and people could train it to behave better.*
>
> *Plan C: This was the plan Sophia least preferred. She would use the axe her mother had given her to chop off two of the dragon's heads. The logic being, this would reduce the dragon's capacity to inflict damage on towns and villages by two thirds. Perhaps, this reduction would enable people and the dragon to live together harmoniously.*

Sophia decided she would try each plan in succession. She packed away all her new purchases into bags. Holding one in each hand, and with one on her back, she waded across the stream and headed towards the smoke. As she came over the crest of the hill, she spotted it, sleeping amongst some rocks only a few yards away. Her heart jumped into her mouth. It was a fine and fearsome beast! Sophia suddenly realised how scared she was. Every muscle and nerve in her body wanted her to run away. Yet, she was able to keep herself walking forward. As she approached, the dragon slowly opened one of its six eyes and raised one head. The other two heads continued to sleep.

'What do you want?' the dragon enquired in a deep rumbling voice, which vibrated the ground and made small stones dance around her feet. The noise woke the other heads, who were now regarding her with an air of irritation.

'I've come to talk with you about the devastation you are causing to our towns,' whimpered Sophia.

'What about it?' replied the dragon eyeing her suspiciously.

'You have to stop,' said Sophia, with all the determination she could muster.

With that, all three of the dragon's heads roared with laughter. 'You can't be serious young lady. Devastating towns is what we do. It's our purpose,' boomed each of the three heads in unison.

The stones danced up and down, scratching her legs as Sophia realised that reasoning with a dragon would not work. It will have to be Plan B.

She reached into her bag and pulled out the three pieces of rope she had already fashioned into lassoes. While the dragon looked on in mild amusement, she swung the first one around her head a few times and then launched it off towards one of the dragon's heads.

'Yes!' she shouted.

To her utter amazement, she had caught one of the heads in the loop of rope. She pulled it tight, and as she was looking for somewhere to tie it off, she felt the rope go slack. She turned around to see the rope was on fire. Ah, she thought, rookie error.

'Nothing else for it,' she muttered as she rummaged around in her bag for her axe.

With new confidence that she was at least a good shot, she threw the axe at one of the dragon's necks. It hit some scales and rebounded, having slightly nicked some exposed skin. Sophia ran forward to grab the axe, which had landed close to one of the enormous feet. The axe had blood on it, and as she gathered it up, she cried out in pain. She didn't know the blood of a dragon is toxic. Grabbing her bags, and not looking back, she didn't stop running until she reached the stream, where she tried to wash off the blood and soothe her hand.

Nothing had worked. All three of Sophia's plans to change or restrain the dragon had failed. Sophia felt like an utter failure. Lying there on the bank nursing her injury, tired, alone and very hungry, she sobbed, 'Father was right, there is nothing to be done with the dragon, I should have stayed at home.'

INTRODUCTION

> Until they become conscious they will never rebel, and until after they have rebelled they cannot become conscious.
>
> George Orwell
>
> Nineteen Eighty-Four

You will have heard the clichéd conundrum 'What came first, the chicken or the egg?' It is the same when we explore the relationship between economic systems and the collective consciousness of society. So far, this book has explored how, over the centuries, our consciousness has been industrialised. First, through our increasing separation from nature, each other and ourselves causing our ego to become isolated, fragile and competitive; and, second, by businesses exploiting and manipulating our isolated, competitive and fragile ego to condition us into becoming addicted to consuming. At a societal level, our individual consciousnesses combine to create our collective consciousness, allowing us to see and understand the world in a way we can all share. Our 'collective industrialised consciousness' supports and maintains our neoliberal, capitalist and consumer-led economic system. Which came first? Did our collective consciousness create our economic system, or did the system create our collective consciousness?

This chapter explores the relationship between economic systems and collective consciousness and how they have both developed. It aims to demonstrate that through individual psychological growth, we can shift our collective consciousness. However, it will take a critical mass of people to develop their consciousness sufficiently to allow society to create a new economic system that regenerates the environment, reduces inequality and supports mental health. If enough people develop their individual consciousness and reject consumerism, a new economy can start to unfold, which, in turn, will support the emergence of a new level of collective consciousness.

ECONOMIC SYSTEMS

The economy is typically defined as the production, use and management of scarce resources. These resources are often referred to as scarce because they are finite compared to demand, which is thought to be infinite. The economy determines how scarce resources are distributed in the production, consumption, and trade of goods and services that are used to fulfil the needs of the people living in a defined region. Consequently, the purpose of the economy is to serve the people by enabling the distribution of resources. In economics, money is not considered to be a resource. It is seen as being a facilitator in the trade of resources, including natural materials, labour and intellectual property. How these resources are distributed depends on the type of economic system being employed. This section outlines the types of economic systems used in different societies.

Agrarian

The most basic form of economy is often found in 'agrarian' societies, where small groups of people collaborate to provide food, build their houses, make clothes, etc. As a community, they are likely to produce all they need for themselves without trading. Therefore, there is no need for money to facilitate trade. Instead, resources are shared within the community according to people's needs. However, there may be some division of labour within the community based on people's skills, talents and abilities. People's labour will be rewarded through reciprocal exchange.

Feudal

As communities become larger, people start to organise themselves according to social dominance and class systems emerge. In these communities, a more 'feudal' economic system often arises. This is where the dominant classes may own the resources, and the lower classes provide the labour to grow the food, build houses, make clothes, etc., for the whole community in exchange for security and safety. The dominant classes would manage and organise production and security. Hence, a ruling class becomes established. If these feudal societies trade with other communities, then some form of medium of exchange is required, such as money. Once money enters into a feudal system, land becomes leased by the ruling classes, resources and products are bought and sold, and security is paid for by taxes. Once trade is enabled, a market is soon established.

Free Markets

Pure market economies enable the free flow of goods and services through trade facilitated by a medium of exchange, such as money. Money is essentially an 'I owe you' to allow for the exchange of goods and services to be managed over a time period. For example, I may agree to build you a house on the basis you provide my family with food for a year. To seal this deal, we agree on the value of the house and the amount of food in terms of an equivalent amount of money. This is known as the price. I build the house, and you give me the money, which I gradually pay back to you in return for food.

Consequently, money facilitates the division of labour. In market economies, the price of goods and services is set in the market according to supply and demand. If few people have the skills or tools to build houses, and the demand for houses is high, a builder could ask a high price to build a house, which would keep their family fed for many years.

In market economies, supply and demand tend to naturally balance out, allowing prices to remain stable in the long term. For example, if people realise there is a good living to be made from building houses, supply will increase, and more builders will compete for less work. To survive, they must build the best-quality houses, lower their prices or do both. If there is an oversupply of houses in the market, house prices will fall, builders will not make a sufficient living and they would be forced to apply their skills to other markets, allowing the price to recover.

Capitalism

At the onset of industrialisation, capitalist economies developed as a hybrid combining both the feudal system and free markets. Capitalism essentially separates the ownership of goods and services from the people producing them. In this economic system, the dominant classes became owners of business and tools that produce the goods and services. Consequently, they own the goods and services produced until they are sold to the consumer. The owners of the business then retain the profit from the sale. The people producing the goods and services do not own what they produce and are, instead, paid money for their labour. Capitalism is based on the accumulation of the profit retained, which is then distributed amongst the business owners or reinvested into the assets of the business needed to increase the means of production. With capital reinvested, the business produces more products that need to be consumed. If all businesses are doing this, then the economy will inevitably continue to grow. Capitalism and continual economic growth are inseparable. Capital is defined as wealth in the form of money or other assets owned by the business. With capitalism, it is believed the purpose of the business is to build up capital. The capitalist economic system relies heavily on free markets to distribute goods and services and to set the price.

The purest form of capitalism is called laissez-faire or free-market capitalism. This is where there is no intervention by governments or other organisations to provide regulation and control. In this economic system, only the market determines which goods and services are provided and the price. However, most economies have regulated markets and are called mixed economies. In these economies, governments provide the essential services that are not sufficiently supplied by the market and bring in regulations to ensure fairness, health, safety and ethical practices.

Planned

The opposite of free-market capitalism is a centrally planned economy. There is not a market to determine the supply and demand of goods and services and their price. Communism is an example of this type of controlled and planned economy. In communism, there is no private ownership of businesses or means of production. Instead, these are owned by the people and managed, on their behalf, by the central planner (the State). Socialism differs from communism in that, while the businesses and means of production are still owned by the people, the goods and services are still bought and sold in the market place. The business ownership can come through the nationalisation of the industries (owned by the State on behalf of the people) or through co-operatives, where the workers collectively own the business.

While the purpose of an economic system is to distribute scarce resources, it also becomes an integral part of political and social systems. Economics is a fundamental aspect of how we organise, interact and live together. Consequently, economics has a significant impact on the conditioning of our consciousness. As Margaret Thatcher said, ‘Economics are the method; the object is to change the heart and soul.’

ECONOMIC ERAS

All of these types of economies exist, to a lesser or greater extent, in societies worldwide. As societies have developed over time, so too have their types of economies. The development of the economies across Europe can provide a good example of these economic eras.

Before the 5th century, European societies went through what can best be described as an agricultural revolution. Rather than hunting and gathering, communities settled down and grew their own food crops and raised animals. Consequently, an 'agrarian economy' was established. With the rise of agriculture, a larger population could be maintained. Larger communities needed to be organised and protected, giving rise to the feudal economic systems in the medieval period between the 5th and 18th centuries. Feudalism is more than an economic system; it is also a social and political system. As feudalism developed, so did the system of serfdom. Peasants worked for feudal lords through indentured servitude or debt bondage. As technology advanced and travel across and between nations became easier, trade between feudal systems was enabled. This led to the development of free markets.

The period between the 15th and 18th centuries is often called the mercantile era. It was the start of substantial trade between nations. Governments, usually royal families, controlled most foreign trade during this period. The Industrial Revolution of the 18th to 20th centuries, fuelled by advances in 'New Science', led to capitalism's development. There was a need for large investments of capital in machinery and factories. When capitalism combined with liberalism, the emphasis on equal opportunities began. Unlike in feudalism, the new mantra was that anyone could become wealthy with enough hard work and entrepreneurialism. However, the reality of capitalism was that rather than lots of people sharing the wealth, it was concentrated in a few families. Although there may have been some equality of opportunity, there was not equality of outcome or reward. Due to the inequality inherent in capitalism, alternative 'planned' systems such as communism and socialism took root in some countries in the early 20th century to provide and manage the capital required for the ongoing Industrial Revolution.

THE RISE AND FALL OF CAPITALISM

Many people argue capitalism has its foundations in the mercantile period of the 16th and 17th centuries. However, it was not until the Industrial Revolution that it became established as the economic system we see today. Vast amounts of money from mercantile trade were invested in factories and machinery. Landlords became the capital owners, and the indentured peasants became the wage-labourers. Products previously produced by artisans and craftsmen gave way to mass production. Cottage industries could not compete with mass production, and capitalism soon spread across the nations and internationally during the mercantile period. Small producers went out of business and highly skilled labour increasingly become commodified as machinery operators. By the mid-19th century, capitalism had become the dominant economic system in the developed world.

You will recall that at the beginning of this chapter, I stated the purpose of an economic system is to distribute scarce resources. All the economic systems I have outlined do this in different ways and with varying levels of efficiency. What makes them different is how this is achieved, such as through collaboration, division of labour, power, control or free-market competition. Capitalism distributes scarce resources through free-market competition or mixed economies with some regulation. Capitalism is also defined by characteristics such as ownership of private property, capital accumulation and reinvestment. As capitalism has developed, these characteristics have increasingly overshadowed its core purpose as an economic system to fulfil the people's needs. Rather than prioritising the distribution of resources, capitalism now prioritises the accumulation of wealth. Money has become core to the purpose of capitalism, whereas it was originally seen as a facilitator of trade.

In a capitalist system, the force driving all economic activity is the desire for profit. Capitalists see profit as a motivator for people to work hard, innovate and find ways to beat the competition in the free market. To increase profit, there is a strong incentive to keep the workers' wages as low as possible and automate, thus eliminating or further reducing the overall cost of labour. The profit gained is then distributed amongst the owners of the business, with some retained for reinvestment. This reinvestment increases productivity, and more profit is made. Hence, through this process, capital is accumulated within the business and, subsequently, by its owners. This extraction and accumulation of wealth enable business owners to use their wealth to capture and take ownership of the commons of our natural resources, our relationships and our psychology. By capturing more commons, they are able to generate more wealth. The end result of capitalism is that the owners of the means of production get richer while the workers become relatively poorer. Increased inequality is, therefore, the inevitable result of capitalism.

Advocates of capitalism tend to believe inequality is a good and necessary aspect of capitalism. They believe it is a strong motivator to work hard, innovate and compete. The social comparison and social dominance theories we explored in the previous chapter would support this view. Through hard work, innovation and competition, advocates argue that the overall national economy becomes more competitive in the global markets, enabling the wealth of the nation to be increased. This wealth is then thought to trickle down through all the layers in society so everyone benefits. While this may have been true in the early days of capitalism, when living standards increased substantially, it is no longer the case. Rather than everyone's standard of living increasing, levels of inequality are increasing. Why is this happening?

One of the reasons is that businesses are designed to behave like psychopaths. Although psychopathy is not an official psychiatric diagnosis, the term is generally used to describe people who suffer from a condition where they demonstrate socially irresponsible behaviour, disregard or violate others' rights, have an inability to distinguish between right and wrong, and have difficulty with showing remorse or empathy. Businesses get this diagnosis because they are designed to pursue just one aim, profit, with no regard for the impact this has on people or the planet. Therefore, if left to their own devices, businesses would behave like psychopaths. So, they need rules to govern their behaviour and protect people and the planet. This tendency towards psychopathy has increased over the past few decades with neoliberal deregulation and more businesses floating on stock exchanges. Big businesses tend to be owned by shareholders rather than by their founding entrepreneurs or families. The problem with companies on a stock exchange is that the managers and executives are the legal agents of the shareholders, its owners. In our society, many people, and organisations, hold shares in companies purely as a financial investment. All they are interested in is getting a return on their investment. They want to see the company's executives and managers ensure it makes good profits to increase shareholder value. When all that matters is profit, then moral or value-based decision making can get lost.

Private companies have more of an opportunity to use business to serve society, which was seen with the Quakers in the UK in the 19th century. After being barred from many professions due to their non-conformist faith, they set up many companies that survive today. They are perhaps best known for establishing several well-known brands such as Cadbury, Fry's and Rowntree. The founders were able to bring Quaker ethics such as truth, honesty and fairness into business. Workers were paid above-average wages, and the company was used to serve people in the local community by providing good-quality houses in a healthy environment at an affordable price. An example was Cadbury creating a new village called Bournville. Inhabitants were not tied to Cadbury.

In fact, fewer than half the village inhabitants had direct links with the factory.

Some companies are beginning to see the harm pure capitalism is doing to our society and are making their purpose to serve society, with profit as a reward for this service. These more ethical businesses believe their long-term success and survival depends on maintaining their social licence to operate. Many shareholders also see the importance and benefit of ethical business, demonstrated by the fact that many ethical funds (portfolios of shareholdings) are now matching or outperforming traditional funds in terms of return on investment.

For the vast majority of capitalist businesses, people are seen as a resource to be exploited to ensure a maximum return on the capital employed. Hence 'Human Resources' is the most common name given to the department that looks after people in a business. People are the fuel for the capitalist machine; they provide the labour and consume the goods and services. Through our conditioning to be good workers and good consumers, we have come to serve a capitalist economy rather than the economy serving us. As a result of its focus on accumulating wealth, the capitalist economic system has lost sight of an economy's purpose, which is to distribute scarce resources to fulfil the people's needs. It has forgotten that money is the 'means' and not the 'objective' of an economy. Capitalism has forgotten how to serve society and is, instead, destroying it.

Many commentators predict the demise of capitalism. To establish public attitudes to the capitalist system, in 2015, the Legatum Institute commissioned YouGov to ask ten questions of populations in seven nations: the UK, the USA and Germany (from the developed world) and Brazil, India, Indonesia and Thailand (from the fast-growing emerging world).[1] In six of the seven populations surveyed, most people agreed the rich get richer, and the poor get poorer in capitalist societies (the exception being Indonesia). In Germany, Brazil, India and China the figure was over 70%, while it was 64% and 55% in the UK and USA, respectively. They also found over 70% of people in the UK, Germany, India and Thailand believe the world's biggest businesses have cheated and polluted their way to success.

While Karl Marx (1818–1883) believed the workers would eventually overthrow capitalism through violent revolution, the economist Schumpeter believed capitalism's success would lead to its demise. Schumpeter surmised that, through capitalism's success, some corporates would become so large they would start to control States. They would then adopt values and practices that would make 'intellectuals' hostile towards capitalism. These practices would include high rates of unemployment and a lack of fulfilling work. The intellectuals' critique of capitalism would lead to discontent and protests. In response, he believed governments would vote to restrict capitalism and increase industrial democracy. Through 'creative destruction', new forms of working relationships and processes would ultimately undermine and destroy capitalism's structures. Was Schumpeter right? We are certainly seeing the intellectuals critiquing capitalism.

Overall, when combined with neoliberalism and a desire for continued economic growth, capitalism is accused of causing high levels of inequality, environmental destruction and poor mental health. People are increasingly calling for a new and different economic system that distributes scarce resources more equitably and sustainably. Even though there are many ideas for a new economy, there is no one replacement waiting in the wings. Instead, it appears that we are entering into a transition period where capitalism is trying to remould itself so as not to be destroyed.

NEW ECONOMIC SYSTEMS

As people are becoming disenchanted with capitalism due to its increasing destruction of the environment, association with inequality and mental illness, there is a move towards developing alternatives. This section outlines some of the alternatives that have gained support in our societies. These include moving away from continuous economic growth as measured by GDP, developing more balanced economies, becoming more ethical in business and prioritising local economies.

Buddhist Economics

Buddhist economics applies the teachings of the Noble Eightfold Path. In particular, it emphasises 'Right Livelihood', which teaches people to make their living in a way that does no harm and is ethically positive. It sees people as interdependent with each other and with nature rather than as being separated and independent. Consequently, Buddhist economics emphasises co-operation, harmony and doing no harm.

Ernst Friedrich Schumacher (1911–1977), a German economist, first coined the phrase 'Buddhist economics' in 1955 when he travelled to Burma. He used the phrase as a title for an essay published in 1966 and then again in 1973 in his book *Small Is Beautiful*.[3] Schumacher's work has since been expanded upon by Clair Brown, Professor of Economics at the University of California in her book *Buddhist Economics: An Enlightened Approach to the Dismal Science*.[4]

In Buddhist economics, work has three functions: to give people the opportunity to develop and utilise their abilities, to enable people to overcome their ego-centredness by joining with others in a common task, and to bring forward the goods and services needed for a better existence. Hence, the development of people is at the centre of Buddhist economics, and people are not to be replaced by automation as a way of increasing productivity. In fact, it believes there is no need to increase productivity because there is no need for increased consumption. Traditional economics believes the person who consumes more is better off than the person who consumes less. Buddhist economics turns this on its head, stating the aim should be to achieve maximum well-being with minimum consumption, thus providing a better return on investment.

Consequently, the measure of economic success is well-being rather than production.

The focus on increasing well-being while minimising consumption allows people to live without putting undue pressure and strain on the environment. Buddhist economics believes that to use non-renewable resources is an act of violence, which is contrary to the teaching of 'Right Livelihood'. Non-renewable resources must only be used if it is absolutely necessary, and then only with the greatest effort for conservation. It believes that living on non-renewable resources is a parasitic existence.

Gross National Happiness

The Kingdom of Bhutan has adopted Buddhist economics as a way of managing its economy. Since its foundation, spirituality and compassion have been integrated with its governance. As Bhutan developed, spirituality and compassion became more explicit and articulated. One expression of this development is the gross national happiness (GNH) index. The phrase 'gross national happiness' was first coined by the fourth king of Bhutan, King Jigme Singye Wangchuck, in 1972. Since then, it has come to replace the gross domestic product (GDP) as the most important measure of economic success. The GNH index includes traditional socio-economic measures such as standards of living, health and education, as well as more non-traditional measures such as culture and psychological well-being. Consequently, it is a holistic reflection of people's well-being rather than a survey of their happiness.

In 2008, GNH became instituted in Bhutan's Constitution as the goal of the government. Since then, there has been wide international interest in GNH. In 2011, the United Nations urged other nations to follow Bhutan's example. However, without the underlying Buddhist economics philosophy and practices, GNH simply becomes another measure alongside GDP. Without the underlying philosophy, nations continue to inflict violence upon the environment and businesses put people out of work to increase productivity and profit. Meanwhile, governments employ other means to try to make people happy, such as cognitive behavioural therapy (CBT). GNH will not make a significant difference in capitalist societies while businesses, and their owners, are addicted to accumulating wealth, and their customers are addicted to consuming.

Economy for the Common Good

An index to replace a single measure of economic performance is also at the heart of a new economic model called 'Economy for the Common Good' (ECG) developed by the Austrian historian, entrepreneur and university lecturer Christian Felber. It advocates a good healthy life on a healthy planet should be the primary purpose of an economy. Felber believes the profit-oriented and competitive nature of business leads to greed and uncontrolled growth. He advocates businesses should co-operate in providing the common good for society. The ECG has now become a movement that encourages businesses to be values-driven and committed to human dignity, social justice, environmental sustainability, co-determination and transparency. The ECG movement has created a balanced scorecard to measure progress against these goals. They aim to make the scorecard mandatory for every business and thereby bring about systemic economic change. So far, around 1,750 businesses, mainly from Germany, Austria and Switzerland, have signed up to using the scorecard and are actively trying to improve their scores.

Prosperity Without Growth

In 2009 Professor Tim Jackson, an economist from the University of Surrey in the UK, published a study for the 'Sustainable Development Commission', an advisory body to the UK Government. The study was controversial because it explored whether a society could be prosperous without economic growth. This study was later published as a book called *Prosperity without Growth: Economics for a Finite Planet.*[4] In 2016, Jackson set up the 'Centre for the Understanding of Sustainable Prosperity' (CUSP) to continue his research work. Based on his findings, Jackson has proposed a route to a sustainable economy by redefining 'prosperity' in light of the evidence of what contributes to people's well-being.

In his report, Jackson describes our current economic era as the 'age of irresponsibility'. He argues that the focus on ever-increasing profits and economic growth is leading to human exploitation and environmental destruction. Jackson advocates an economy should increase prosperity, which he defines as necessary material sustenance. He also includes social and psychological dimensions. In doing so, he recognises there is a basic need for material consumption, but this needs to be contained within sustainable boundaries. He also recognises that above this basic material need, continued growth does not increase well-being. Consequently, Jackson argues prosperity is more about quality than quantity.

Jackson also recognises that, while continued economic growth is unsustainable, degrowth is unstable. As previously discussed, due to productivity increases, the economy needs to keep growing to provide employment. When economies shrink, people lose their jobs. Jackson's solution is to decouple economic growth from material consumption. For this to happen, there needs to be an end to consumerism brought about by people finding their self-identity and happiness in other areas. There needs to be greater investment in building and protecting the assets on which future prosperity depends. Forging 'post-growth' economics continues to be central to Jackson's and CUSP's work.

Doughnut Economics

Doughnut Economics, formulated by the economist Kate Raworth from the University of Oxford in the UK, further develops the idea that humans need a certain level of material sustenance, but not to the extent of destroying the environment. Raworth took the planetary boundaries developed by Stockholm University (see Chapter 1) and combined them with the complementary concept of social boundaries. This creates a ring, like a doughnut or a lifebelt, within which is a safe and just space for humanity to live. The hole in the middle represents a space where people do not have the resources to live with access to life's essentials, such as sufficient food, shelter, healthcare, education, etc. Outside of the ring is where human activity is harming the environment and causing unsustainability. Since Raworth's book, *Doughnut Economics: Seven Ways to Think Like a 21st-century Economist,* was published in 2018, local governments are increasingly using the model in several different countries worldwide.[5] Most notably by the city of Amsterdam to assist in the economic recovery following the Covid-19 pandemic.

Transition Movement

The final economic system I explore in this section is the idea of localism. Most notable in this approach is the Transition Movement formed in 2007 in the UK by the permaculture educator Rob Hopkins along with Peter Lipman and Ben Brangwyn. The movement supports grassroots community projects that aim to increase self-sufficiency and community resilience to reduce the potential effects of climate destruction and economic instability. In doing so, they seek to reclaim the economy for their local area through networking, entrepreneurship, regenerating local assets, creating local circular economies and implementing local complementary currencies. Projects include local food production and community energy groups. Since its formation, the Transition Movement has spread to over 50 countries. Given the collapse of many international supply chains at the beginning of the Covid-19 pandemic, it is likely many governments around the world will look at ways to increase local community economic resilience.

Clearly, we are not short of ideas for developing a new economic system should capitalism come to the end of its useful life, as many commentators predict. What we are short of is the will to make the change. Due to the industrialisation of our minds, the vast majority of the population have the consciousness that supports the ongoing turning of the capitalist machine. If we are to avoid the destruction our neoliberalist, capitalist and consumerist economic system is doing to our environment, our society and our psychology, we need one or a combination of these solutions to become mainstream in the near future. However, this will require a change in the collective consciousness of the population. We need to develop consciousness beyond consumerism.

ERAS IN COLLECTIVE CONSCIOUSNESS

An economic system is very much aligned with the collective consciousness of the people. They reinforce and maintain each other. The collective consciousness conditions our individual consciousness. This conditioning has increasingly separated us from nature, each other and ourselves. These separations have served industry and are now supporting our neoliberal, consumer-led, capitalist economic system. For a new economic system to emerge, a new type of collective consciousness needs to emerge. However, this cannot happen instantaneously. It will be a gradual transition, starting with a few people breaking away from the norm in terms of the qualities of their consciousness. These people may be viewed as eccentrics because they see the world differently compared to other people. They will no longer feel part of mainstream society and, therefore, will not be subject to it. Instead, they will able to see society from an objective perspective. This objectivity will allow them to see structural faults within the dominant economic system and predict future problems. Gradually, people who have developed this different type of consciousness will collaborate, forming a critical mass sufficient to make visible changes to the economic system. Other people will see these changes and join them. Gradually, through small changes, the economic system will start to shift, and a new economy will emerge, which will condition other people's consciousness. Gradually, a new collective consciousness in society will emerge.

It is likely this process has already begun, but we have not reached the critical mass of people with the consciousness required to enable a new economic era to unfold. Before we actively work on creating a new economic system, we need to focus first on seeding a new era of collective consciousness. The two go hand-in-hand.

To describe the different eras in collective consciousness, I will use terms frequently used by philosophers and sociologists to describe 'cultural movements'. These are pre-modernism, modernism, postmodernism and metamodernism. In his book, *The Listening Society*, Hanzi Freinacht (believed to be a pseudonym for the sociologist Daniel Görtz and philosopher Emil Esper Friis) argues that these terms do not really describe cultural movements.[6] To describe cultural movements he uses the term 'memes', which the psychologist Susan Blackmore says are evolving stories, songs, habits, skills, inventions and ways of doing things that we copy from person to person by imitation. Instead, Freinacht argues that pre-modernism, modernism, postmodernism and metamodernism are more like different code systems that people download and install according to their psychological capability. Consequently, these code systems allow our consciousness to be programmed in a new way. Each era is denoted by the qualities of the consciousness of the majority of people in the population. For example, as you will see below, we are likely to be coming to the end of the modernism era. Through the industrialisation of our minds, the vast majority of people have had their consciousness programmed by modernism, which in turn, supports industrialisation and our neoliberal, consumer-led, capitalist economic system. Yet, there will also be people in the population whose consciousness is more aligned with pre-modernism, postmodernism or metamodernism programming due to psychological capability and life experiences.

Pre-modernism

Around 2,000–2,500 years ago, there was a major development in people's consciousness around the world. It was a golden era for Greek philosophy, with Socrates, Plato and Aristotle laying the foundations for our understanding of the world. Taoism, Buddhism and Confucianism became established as the three pillars of Chinese culture in the eastern world. In the western world, the birth of Christ led to the formation of Christianity. The teachings of Islam were soon to follow. These religions and philosophies established a 'universal truth' or the 'word of God', which provided a guide for morality, behaviour and thought, which typifies pre-modernism. Before then, collective consciousness was typified by power and control.

Throughout the agricultural revolution, people had learned to have power and control over nature. However, the arbitrary use and abuse of power and control, including war, slavery and oppression, had become commonplace. For society to continue to develop, people needed unifying standards of behaviour. The newly formed religions of the pre-modernist era provided these standards. As God was beyond most people's full comprehension, the word of God was something to which people needed to surrender. Kings and emperors could only lead with a mandate from God. Consequently, religion provided the means for the mass socialisation of people's consciousness. Those who conformed were honoured with visible titles and medals. For the non-conformists, there was shame, pillory and often death. Consequently, the nature of consciousness within this era was characterised by seeking to gain acceptance by controlling one's own behaviour. In return, people gained a greater sense of inclusion and were able to form morally bonded relationships.

The norms of the accepted behaviour are internalised without question and conditioned through all aspects of society, through parenting, education, law and religion. People, from other religions, with different versions of the 'universal truth' were often seen as threatening. Either one's own 'universal truth' is wrong or the other people are wrong. It was believed that God provided the universal truth and also our souls. If the universal truth is questioned, then we must also question our soul. How much safer is it to say other people are wrong than to question the universal truth or your own soul? This is the nature of consciousness that fuelled the Christian crusades and, more recently, gave rise to ISIS (also known as Daesh). This type of collective consciousness believes people with different views of the universal truth need to be converted or even killed. The pre-modernist era of collective consciousness supported the development of the feudal and market economies right through to the Industrial Revolution. Its focus was on 'dependence'; being dependent on the 'universal truth' for moral guidance.

Modernism

With the development of 'New Science' in the 17th, 18th and 19th centuries, people started to think differently. Even though the 'universal truth' was not necessarily questioned, at least at first, it was believed it could be verified using the methods of New Science, such as materialism, positivism, determinism and reductionism. This new way of thinking ushered in the modernist era of collective consciousness, which became dominant in the late 19th and early 20th centuries. With New Science, it was believed the 'universal truth' could be verified by everyone.

Therefore, verifiability depends on each person having an

independent, rational and objective perspective on the truth. If everyone agrees, this means the truth is verified. Modernist collective consciousness, therefore, assumes everyone can be the author of their own mind and be independent of any external influences. It assumes we are not slaves to other people's views or conditioned by our social context. With a modernist collective consciousness, the person is self-contained, self-created and self-defined. Independence gives people the motivation to achieve on their own and to be different from other people in their own authenticity. This difference gives value to the verifiability of the truth. With everyone striving to achieve, society can progress forward. Consequently, the modernist collective consciousness enabled science to understand the natural world rationally and objectively so society can exploit it in order to progress the human endeavour and increase our well-being.

Modernist collective consciousness helped fuel industrial and scientific revolutions and supported our capitalist, consumer-led and neoliberal economy. Rather than focusing on 'dependence', modernism focuses on 'independence'. It is about being an individual, with your own perspective and thoughts, while at the same time being rational and objective to ensure the 'universal truth' can be perceived and agreed by everyone using the scientific method.

Postmodernism

Since the 1960s, there has been a growing backlash against the modernist collective consciousness, especially from within universities. Philosophers have described this as the 'postmodernist' era, which is essentially a critique of modernism. Postmodernist collective consciousness questions whether people are truly independent and, therefore, whether the truth can be verified. It is characterised by scepticism, which critiques the generally accepted notions of objective reality, morality, truth, reason and social progress.

Rather than accepting there is an objective truth, postmodernist collective consciousness believes there are multiple perspectives on the truth, with each perspective being grounded in the perceiver's social context. In this way, people with postmodernist consciousness point to, and challenge, the industrialisation of our minds, which mainly occurred during the modernist era. Rather than the truth being verified, it is believed to be the result of 'groupthink'. For people with postmodernist consciousness, a verifiable truth does not exist. Instead, all truths are valid. Accepting multiple truths is often described as relativism. Consequently, the postmodernist collective consciousness creates and accepts a pluralistic society, giving space for us each to perceive and understand the world in different ways according to our own diverse social conditioning.

Without a shared perspective on the world uniting us and creating a cohesive society, we are now fragmenting in sub-groups and we see the rise of 'identity politics'. We are increasingly attaching our identity to the beliefs and values we share with similar people in our society. These groups may be aligned with our politics, sexuality, gender, religion, ethnicity, etc. We are experiencing the rise of tribalism. Examples include the alt-right, the Occupy Movement, Extinction Rebellion, etc. As we are turning away from modernism, due to its association with the Industrial Revolution and capitalism, societies are becoming increasingly postmodern in nature. So, while our society is facing a sustainability crisis, in the postmodernist era we are busy arguing amongst ourselves.

Metamodernism

Do not despair; hope is on the horizon. Philosophers are now discussing metamodernist collective consciousness and its emergence as a reaction to postmodernism. While the term has been around since the 1970s, it has gained ground since the economic crisis of 2008. As a description of collective consciousness, metamodernism values acceptance and thrives in our society's paradoxical and self-contradictory nature. It takes a 'both–and' rather than an 'either–or' perspective on life. Therefore, it accepts both modernist and postmodernist perspectives and unites them.

Metamodernist collective consciousness enables people to oscillate back and forth between different and often opposing views. Hence, it employs concepts such as 'sincere irony', 'informed naivety' and 'pragmatic romanticism'. It values left and right politics, objectivity and subjectivity, co-operation and competition, secularism and spirituality, etc. Metamodernist consciousness can hold paradoxical views without conflict. With it, rather than being separated by arguing for or against or deciding who is right or wrong, people can use the energy of difference to stimulate and create change. It believes that difference creates the opportunity for listening and dialogue. Rather than focusing on the negative and what divides us, metamodernist consciousness enables us to focus on the positive and what can unfold in the space between us as we come together. It transcends differences by creating something new, which unites people. Rather than focusing on 'independence', metamodernist consciousness focuses on 'interdependence'. It is a type of consciousness that enables co-creation. A metamodernist collective consciousness has the potential to allow us to create a new, more sustainable economic system. It represents our collective consciousness beyond consumerism.

Does the metamodernist collective consciousness sound a bit far-fetched? Is it just an excuse to flip-flop in our decision making? Maybe so, but remember, the emergence of a collective metamodernist collective consciousness is dependent on a critical mass of people having the psychological capability to allow this programming to be downloaded and installed. It is dependent on psychological growth. Only at the highest stages of individual psychological growth are we able to hold paradoxical views without conflict. Only when we have developed to this level of consciousness, as an individual, will we be able to see its need and its value. Until then, we are likely to regard it as far-fetched and flip-flopping. If we are to avoid the environmental, societal and psychological crises caused by our modernist collective consciousness supporting industry and our capitalist, consumer-led and neoliberal economy, we need to focus on our individual psychological growth. As individuals, we each need to develop our own consciousness. It is only then that we will be able to co-create a new economic system to replace capitalism and create greater levels of sustainability, equality and mental health.

SUMMARY AND CONCLUSION

Different economic systems have been, and are being, utilised to distribute scarce resources and money is a facilitator of these transactions. As societies developed, they progressed through agrarian, feudal, mercantile and free-market economic systems. These systems often did more than manage the economy; they also shaped social and political interactions. In westernised societies today, the most dominant free-market economic system is capitalist, consumer-led and neoliberal.

Capitalism was needed to support the Industrial Revolution when huge amounts of money were required for machinery and factories. As individuals generally could not afford the investment required, businesses were created to attract this investment in the form of debt and equity. This led to the separation of labour from the means of production. The businesses owned the premises, machinery tools, products and the resulting profit, and workers were paid a wage for their labour. Profits were retained by the businesses and reinvested to improve productivity, which led to more profits. Businesses became wealth accumulators. Some family-owned businesses used the profits for the common good of society. However, most large companies are now owned by shareholders, who are primarily interested in a financial return. Consequently, in the capitalist system, businesses have been set up to behave like psychopaths, in that they focus only on earning profits, to the detriment of the environment and people. The capitalist system has forgotten that its purpose is to distribute scarce resources and that money is just the facilitator. Instead, money has now become the focus of economics.

Many westernised societies are increasingly concerned with the damage the capitalist economic system causes. Capitalism stands accused of destroying the environment, increasing inequality and causing poor mental health. Consequently, many people are seeking alternatives to capitalism. Many replacements have been proposed, including Buddhist economics, ECG, Doughnut Economics and localism. Nevertheless, none of these is taking hold and being seen by the majority as a viable alternative to capitalism. Instead, despite the damage being caused, our collective consciousness continues to support and maintain capitalism. To create and implement a new economic system, we need to develop a new level of collective consciousness.

In the past, different economic systems have been supported and maintained by different eras of collective consciousness. Our capitalist, consumer-led and neoliberal economy has been, and still is, supported and maintained by the modernist collective consciousness, which values the progress, objectivity, reductionism, materialism and empiricism of New Science and the Industrial Revolution. Modernism has programmed our individual consciousness. However, more and more people have recently downloaded and installed postmodernist consciousness, a critic of capitalism. This type of consciousness does not see an objective truth and instead allows people to hold relative views of reality according to their own social condition. This relativism has led to the growth of 'identity politics' where people align themselves with others who share their views (tribalism). It seems that while our environment continues to be destroyed, we continue to fight amongst ourselves.

If society is to find, develop and implement a replacement for our capitalist, consumer-led and neoliberal economy, we need to move beyond both modernism and postmodernism in our collective consciousness. Philosophers have seen the emergence of a new collective consciousness called metamodernism since the financial crisis of 2008. As metamodernism allows people to hold paradoxical views without conflict, it has the potential to reunite people. We now need metamodernism to programme our consciousness beyond consumerism.

Consciousness development is part of our ongoing human evolution. Consciousness beyond consumerism will evolve naturally. But it takes time for the consciousness of individuals to evolve. Do we have the time?

Figure 5.1 Consciousness and Economic Reinforcement

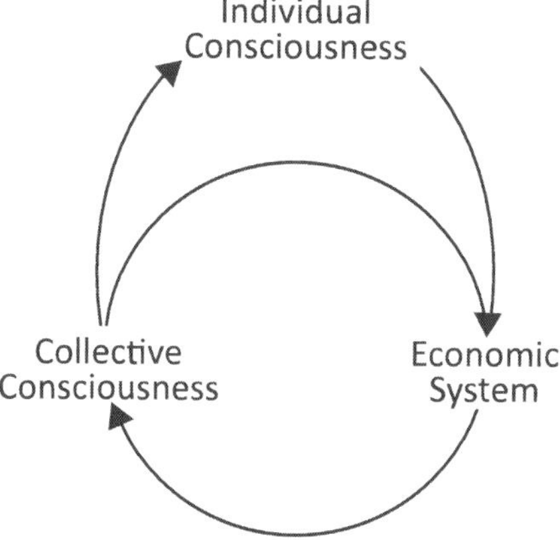

Given the destruction our industrialised, capitalist, consumer-led and neoliberal economy is doing to our environment, communities and our psychology, we now need to take deliberate and purposeful actions to develop our individual consciousness and accelerate our progress as a society. As economic systems and eras of consciousness reinforce each other, society needs a critical mass of people to develop consciousness beyond consumerism (see Figure 5.1). This critical mass needs to be sufficient to enable a new economic system to take hold long enough for metamodernism to become the new collective consciousness era. This will require purposeful psychological growth to enable people to develop the psychological capability to be receptive to metamodernist programming. Otherwise, we will become stuck in the modernist era that will continue to programme our consciousness in a way that maintains our current destructive economic system.

PART 2

HOW TO DEVELOP CONSCIOUSNESS BEYOND CONSUMERISM

CHAPTER 6

CONSCIOUSNESS EXPLAINED

Sophia picked up her bags and walked back towards the street market, feeling utterly dejected. On the path, she saw an old man walking towards her. It was Mimir. How embarrassing, she thought to herself. Of all the people to meet, what could she to say to him?

Approaching the old man, she blurted out 'I'm so sorry, I couldn't do it. I couldn't stop the dragon.' Mimir beckoned Sophia to sit down, and he listened to the tale of her encounter with the dragon. 'In the end, I just wasn't good enough,' Sophia sobbed. None of this was news to Mimir. He had been with her the whole time, ever since she had left their camp early the day before. He had been observing her every action. Being an objective observer, Mimir could see exactly where Sophia had gone wrong.

'What am I to do, Mimir? How can I return to Halkeld now that I failed? But I can't stay here either. I've got no money and no food. I am so hungry, what am I to do?'

'There is one thing you can do. You can work towards your purpose.'

'What do you mean?' Mimir said nothing; he just looked at her. 'You don't mean go back and face that dragon? Surely not.' Again, Mimir

didn't say a word. They both sat in silence for a good ten minutes. 'If I must go back and face the dragon again, will you help me?'

'I do help you.'

'No, I mean really help. Help me get new weapons and fight it together.'

'I told you, Sophia, I'm too old for fighting dragons.' With that, Mimir had brought the discussion to a close, and he got up to leave.

'Wait! There must be something I can do to beat the dragon.'

'In your current state, there is nothing you can do that will beat the dragon. You are just giving the dragon more energy. It will waste you, just like it has laid to waste all those towns.'

Sophia, shocked by what she had heard, asked, 'What do you mean?'

'To beat the dragon, you must change your state and, for that, you must look within.'

With that, Mimir walked away. He walked within scorching distance of the dragon without giving it one glance. The dragon didn't even look at Mimir. It was as if neither of them existed in the physical realm.

INTRODUCTION

> The key to growth is the introduction of higher dimensions of consciousness into our awareness.
>
> Lao Tzu

Despite this book being about consciousness, I have not yet defined or explored what it is. Why is this? One answer could be that we all know what consciousness is. As it is a word we frequently use in our everyday language, surely we all know what it is and, therefore, it does not need definition. Another answer is the opposite: no one knows what consciousness is. Both of these answers have merit. Consciousness is a word we use all the time, even though we do not really know what it is. However, the time has now come to tackle this 'hard problem'. It is time to explore what we mean when we say 'consciousness'. Developing our consciousness is fundamental to creating a more sustainable economy. If we are to develop it, we first need to understand it.

If we are to understand consciousness, we will inevitably be using our own consciousness to investigate it, leading to the strange idea of consciousness investigating itself. While this can cause objectivity problems in scientific investigations, it does mean that each of us can study our own consciousness through introspection. As a result, we can all have our own theories of consciousness. Scientists are not immune to this. When new scientific findings emerge from consciousness research, they are interpreted differently according to each scientist's or philosopher's preferred theory. Consequently, we have many contrasting and opposing theories of consciousness, each supported by scientific evidence. What are we to do? All we can do is make up our own minds based on our studies, the research and our introspective experience. As you read through this chapter, and the remainder of the book, you will see that I have included my own model of consciousness. This model should not be seen as the truth or the right answer. It is just my current understanding based on my reading of different theories, interpretation of the research evidence, experience working as a psychologist and my own introspection. I hope this is useful.

Before we dive in, I would like you to spend some time considering your answers to these questions:

- What is consciousness?
- Why do we have consciousness?
- How is consciousness generated within us?

These are not easy questions to answer. They have kept philosophers and psychologists busy for decades and caused many arguments. The dictionary definition, on the other hand, is quite straightforward. Consciousness is often defined as 'the state of being aware of and responsive to one's surroundings' (source: Oxford Languages). This chapter goes beyond this simple definition to explore more of the what, why and how of consciousness. It will examine consciousness related to our psyche and then in terms of states, lines, and stages. First, however, we should investigate why consciousness is considered to be a 'hard problem'.

In 1994, the Australian philosopher David Chalmers presented a paper to the first Tucson conference on consciousness.[1] During his presentation, he stated consciousness could be divided into 'easy problems' and the truly 'hard problem'. Easy problems he defined as those that could be solved by the standard methods of science. These would include how we focus our attention, control our behaviour, respond to stimuli, and the difference between waking and sleeping. Even though we may not yet have all the answers in these areas, we generally know how to go about finding them. The truly hard question is how the physical processes in the brain give rise to subjective experience. This division of consciousness into easy problems and a truly hard problem resonated with people and, despite much debating, has been adopted ever since.

WHAT IS CONSCIOUSNESS?

This section explores the nature of consciousness from its most basic qualities (sentience) to its most complex (self-consciousness). You will see as consciousness becomes more complex, we do not lose the basic qualities. Instead, they are retained and built upon.

Sentience

We know from the dictionary definition that consciousness is about being aware and responsive. Let's unpack this a little more. From Chapter 1, we know that trees are aware and responsive. For example, deciduous trees are 'aware' of when seasons change and 'respond' by growing and shedding their leaves. Are trees, therefore, conscious? Worms and slugs are aware and responsive, but is their consciousness the same as that of humans? Probably not. By considering these questions, we quickly come to the conclusion that consciousness differs in nature and quality between species.

The most fundamental aspect of consciousness is 'sentience', which is an organism's capacity to perceive and feel things. All animals are sentient and, therefore, are deemed to be conscious. An organism is able to perceive and feel through its sense organs. As plants and trees are considered not to have sense organs, they are deemed not sentient. You may disagree. I suspect Peter Wohlleben, the author of *The Hidden Life of Trees* whom we met in Chapter 1, would disagree.

Wakefulness

The next level in consciousness hierarchy is the ability to be awake or asleep. Most animals and all humans have this ability. However, it is not as simple as two different states of being. Psychologists have shown that we go through several different modes of sleep. It is considered that there are two main modes of sleep, rapid eye movement (REM), which is generally when we dream, and non-REM when we are in a deep sleep. These are considered to be different states of consciousness. So, even when we are asleep, we still have consciousnesses. Our dreams feel very real to us at the time. Some people have lucid dreams where their minds can control their behaviour within the dream. So, the distinction between being conscious and unconscious, even though we use these terms in everyday language, is probably not accurate. Even when a person is seen to be unconscious from the outside, on the inside their consciousness may still be really active. Just as we have different states of sleep consciousness, we can also have different states of wakefulness. You may have experienced being highly alert when you feel in danger. Conversely, when you feel safe and relaxed, you may become inattentive.

Self-consciousness

If we go up a level, we see another type of consciousness emerge called self-consciousness. This is where an entity is not only sentient but is aware it is sentient. The entity is aware it is aware and can observe and witness itself. It is aware of its own thoughts and emotions, rather than just being them. This awareness gives an entity the ability to reflect on past behaviours and plan for the future. It was once believed self-awareness was the demarcation between humans and animals. I was taught this at school and it is what I believed until I got Dylan. He was a collie cross who loved to eat the mail when it was posted through the door. To stop him from destroying our post, he was rewarded with a carrot if he was able to bring us intact letters without chewing them. Dylan was soon greeting the postman at the front gate and carefully carrying in the precious post. This process worked well for a few months. Then, one day, we noticed he was giving us letters one at a time all through the day. Each time he presented a letter to a family member, he got a carrot as a reward. Dylan was planning for the future. He was hiding letters in the garden and bringing them to us one at a time throughout the day to maximise his carrot intake. Nowadays, it is considered that most animals and young children do not have self-consciousness, but I will leave it to you to decide.

Self-consciousness allows us to manage our consciousness. We can direct our conscious awareness to focus on one thing, which happens when we concentrate. Alternatively, we can allow ourselves to be easily distracted by becoming aware of things as they enter our consciousness and then letting them go again, which happens when we let our mind wander. Managing consciousness can be outward, such as focusing on a picture we are painting or the words we are writing. It can also be inward, such as focusing on our thoughts or our emotions. When we are managing our consciousness, we are simply directing our attention. Of course, it does not always work. When we want to concentrate, we can still easily get distracted. I am sure you will have experienced trying to work in front of the television or reading in a room full of people chatting. Managing our consciousness is a skill that can be practised and developed. It is like a muscle: the more you practise, the stronger it gets.

Differences in Consciousness

So, we can see the nature of consciousness is likely to differ between species. However, it is also likely to differ between people. We have already seen we can have different states of consciousness and how our consciousness can be managed or not. It is also believed consciousness can vary across people due to our education, psychological growth, social conditioning and the influence of the environment. All of this influences how we perceive and respond to the world, our basic sentience. In 1974 Thomas Nagel, an American philosopher, famously argued that while a human might be able to imagine what it is like to be a bat by taking the bat's point of view, it would still be impossible to know what it is like for a bat to be a bat. In doing so, he was saying that consciousness is subjective and, therefore, cannot be understood objectively. So, while I might be able to imagine what things are like from your point of view, the basis of empathy, I will never know what it is like for you being you.

Our consciousness continually changes due to how we are feeling and what is happening. It also changes as we go through life, as we are educated and learn from experience. Our experiences change our consciousness and, as a result, we perceive and respond to the world in new and different ways. However, to allow us to understand each other and build relationships, we have a collective consciousness, which is the commonality in our consciousness. It is the overlap in our consciousness with others and it can make us compatible in relationships. It can bring us together as a society or nation. As we have seen in the last chapter, this collective consciousness can support our economic system and can gradually change over time.

So, from this quick run-through of what is consciousness, we see the dictionary definition, 'the state of being aware of and responsive to one's surroundings', is far too simple. Levels of consciousness differ between species and within species, such as humans, due to psychological growth. We can have different states of consciousness and direct our consciousness in different ways. Yet, amongst all this difference, we still have elements of our consciousness that bring us together and unite us. But this does not mean we cannot have a consciousness that is different from the norm and create change. As individuals, we can have consciousness beyond consumerism when most people in society are walking around addicted to consuming.

WHY DO WE HAVE CONSCIOUSNESS?

This section tries to answer the question why do we have consciousness? Computers do not have consciousness, yet in 2014 one was able to convince judges it was human. A computer program called Eugene Goostman simulated a 13-year-old Ukrainian boy and successfully passed the Turing test at an event organised by the University of Reading in the UK. The Turing test, developed by Alan Turing (1912–1954), is a test of a machine's ability to exhibit intelligent behaviour equivalent to or indistinguishable from a human. The test is conducted by judging whether the language being used in conversation is natural and human-like. If a computer without consciousness can perform as well as a human, then why do we have it? For consciousness to evolve in humans, it must give us some sort of advantage in our environment.

Evolution

As humans evolved from fish through early mammals and primates, the quality of consciousness would have changed. Initially, the fish may have simply been sentient. The early mammals then developed different states of consciousness. Gradually, they may have developed the ability to direct their attention and gain a degree of self-consciousness. This ability may have continued through the evolution of primates, allowing them to reflect back and plan ahead. Gradually, we developed empathy and were able to form relationships. All of these developments in consciousness had to provide a benefit for evolution to retain them. The development in consciousness would have enabled a better fit with the environment and, therefore, better survival. Offspring would inherit the more developed consciousness and had it conditioned into them by their parents. Gradually, the more advanced level of consciousness would have become a characteristic of the species. Taking this evolutionary perspective on consciousness, we can hypothesise that consciousness is still developing in modern humans. As our environment changes, our consciousness will need to change to fit our environment and thrive.

Flexibility and Adaptability

Even though we have evolved self-consciousness and can direct our attention, we still have basic sentient consciousness, which allows us to perceive and respond almost unconsciously, without much thought or with full conscious awareness. Many of our skills, such as riding a bike or driving a car, are done unconsciously, without conscious thought. You perceive and respond naturally, without thinking about it, which is different from learning a skill when you need to concentrate on every action. However, even though you can cycle or drive pretty much unconsciously, when something unexcepted happens, such as someone stepping out in front of you, all your attention is focused on avoiding a collision. You become highly self-aware, manage your conscious attention and quickly decide your next course of action. Higher developments in consciousness give us this flexibility and adaptability to cope with the unusual or unexpected.

Collaboration

One theorised reason for Neanderthals dying out was that they lacked the social coordination and collaboration skills necessary to survive. This theory is unlikely to be the whole story, and recent DNA tests have found many people today have some Neanderthal genes. So, clearly, there was some degree of interbreeding with *Homo sapiens*. However, the development of self-consciousness enables us to recognise our own behaviours, emotions, thoughts, motives, perceptions and intentions. By recognising our own, we can then recognise them in others. This recognition allows us to empathise and co-ordinate our social interaction. By collaborating, we can divide up labour and respond more effectively to changes or emergencies.

Integrating Information

Consciousness also allows us to integrate information from our senses. In simple environments, creatures with sentient consciousness (perceive and respond) can thrive without a problem. However, the more complex the environment, the more complex the consciousness needs to be for the creature to be able to thrive. A more developed consciousness enables us to integrate all the information accumulated from our senses and build a bigger picture. As a part of this integration, we can see relationships between bits of information inferring association or cause and effect. Gradually, we begin to see how these relationships come together to form a system. With even more complex consciousness, we can see how multiple systems come together to form a bigger picture. Again, this development of consciousness allows us to adapt and fit with our increasingly complex environment.

Free Will

Finally, some people argue consciousness gives us free will. Rather than merely perceiving and responding, we can choose how we respond. Others believe, though, free will is simply an illusion and we are only responding to stimulus in the environment. To have free will implies we have an intrinsic motivation to respond in a way that is independent of our environment, which could be something that gives us greater meaning or purpose for which we have a plan. If this is true, we would need a greater level of consciousness to allow us to choose between different options and select the one that gives us a greater chance of implementing our plan. Again, being able to plan ahead and have a choice over options would give us greater adaptability. It would also give us greater capability to create our future rather than merely respond to the present. By creating our future, we are less exposed to perceived dangers. For example, planning and creating a shelter from the most suitable materials to protect us from the weather or wild animals would enable us to survive longer, pass on our genes and raise future generations.

These reasons why we have consciousness demonstrate that it enables us to maintain our alignment with our environment. Greater alignment gives us more chance of thriving, passing on our genes and raising future generations. In doing so, consciousness develops and evolves through generations. Also, consciousness gives us the opportunity to create our future to some degree. As we have transitioned from an agricultural society, through the Industrial Revolution, to today's increasingly digital society, our environment has become increasingly complex. Even though we have created this increased complexity, if we are to thrive, our consciousness needs to develop to maintain alignment with the complexity we have created; otherwise, we may perish. One of the reasons we are struggling to deal with multiple crises of sustainability today is that our collective consciousness has not yet developed to the necessary level of complexity to deal with them. Our consciousness, as a collective, appears still to be aligned with creating the Industrial Revolution, not dealing with its aftermath.

THEORIES OF HOW

We have now reached the truly hard problem: how does our brain produce consciousness? Even though there are many theories, no one really knows. In asking this question, I have already made one assumption: that our brain produces consciousness. This may not be the case. Theories of how consciousness is produced generally fall into one of two camps, monism and dualism. In monism, there is no separation between mind and matter. However, monism is split into materialism and idealism. Materialists believe the workings of physical structures in the brain produce consciousness. Idealists believe consciousness is already an integral part of the physical structures. In the dualism camp, philosophers and scientists deem that at least some aspects of consciousness fall outside the brain's physical structures. This section outlines the main theories from these two camps and introduces you to some of their major proponents.

Materialism

The vast majority of western philosophers and scientists researching consciousness are monists and adhere to materialist and reductionist theories. The purest and most fundamental materialist theory is 'eliminative materialism', which I briefly mentioned in Chapter 2. This theory holds that consciousness does not exist and what we believe to be consciousness is an illusion. They view consciousness as a convenient label for something we do not yet understand. The American philosopher Patricia Churchland is a proponent of eliminative materialism and argues that once a framework for understanding consciousness has evolved, there will no longer be a practical use for the term. Nevertheless, other materialist theorists tend to believe in consciousness, or aspects thereof, and contend consciousness must be identical to the processes in the brain. These types of theories are often called functionalist, as they hold there is a link between certain activities or functions in the brain and certain experiences of consciousness. Although consciousness has not yet been reduced to brain functions, most materialist philosophers and scientists believe it is only a matter of time.

Idealism

Panpsychism, which we explored in Chapter 1, is an example of an idealist theory of consciousness. It contends that all material contains a form of consciousness. Consequently, consciousness is seen as being the primary presence in the universe. Therefore, rather than matter producing consciousness, consciousness produces matter. In Chapter 1, we met many philosophers championing the idealism cause in the face of the New Science's relentless materialism. These included Benedict Spinoza, Georg Friedrich Wilhelm Hegel, Friedrich Schelling, Immanuel Kant,

Johann Wolfgang von Goethe and George Berkeley. Recent proponents of idealist theories of consciousness have included the American philosopher Thomas Nagel and the British philosopher Galen Strawson.

Dualism

We have already met the founding father of dualism, the French philosopher René Descartes in Chapter 2. In dualist theories, consciousness and the brain are completely different but, somehow, they manage to interact. Building on Descartes' theory, the Australian neurophysiologist John Eccles (1903–1997) and the Austrian-born British philosopher Karl Popper developed a theory called 'interactionist dualism'. This theory contends that physical states will cause phenomenal states, and phenomenal states cause physical states. Therefore, corresponding psycho-physical laws will run in both directions. The Australian philosopher David Chalmers believes this theory explains how, in quantum physics, consciousness may collapse the wave of potentiality to create particles. Hence, this is in line with the 'Von Neumann–Wigner Interpretation' of particle–wave duality, which we briefly considered in Chapter 3.

Interactionist dualism is supported by recent findings in neuroscience that our conscious experience really does change the physiology of our brain. The process is called neuroplasticity, the brain's ability to form new neural connections throughout life to respond to new challenges in the environment. In a Seattle study carried out by Washington University, researchers tested the cognitive abilities of 500 adults every 7 years from 1956.[2] The results show that middle-aged adults performed better on four out of six cognitive tests than they did as young adults. One explanation for this increase in ability is that the amount of white matter in the brain, which forms connections amongst nerve cells, appears to increase until around age 40–50 and then begins to decrease. The new brain connections grow to correspond with our conscious experience.

Near-death Experiences

Before leaving this section, I would like to introduce one more theory that has not been put forward by a philosopher or scientist. Instead, it is promoted by a Dutch medical doctor, Dr Pim van Lommel, who, during his 25 years working as a cardiologist, has witnessed many people having 'near-death experiences' (NDEs). From his observations and research, he believes he has found consciousness can exist during brain functioning loss.[3] He concludes that this discounts the materialist and dualist theories and supports idealist theories such as panpsychism. People who have experienced NDEs frequently report experiencing enhanced consciousness detached from the body. Van Lommel hypothesises that the brain may merely be a receiver of consciousness and acts as a relay station. In this way, the brain could be compared to a television or radio, which receives programmes over the airwaves. Even though these programmes exist on airwaves, we cannot experience them unless we have a television or radio. It may be the same with consciousness. In van Lommel's theory, consciousness exists non-locally, but we experience it through our brain while we are alive. It is only through death, or NDEs, that we can experience consciousness directly in an enhanced way, which we remember when the brain starts to function again.

So, by briefly outlining these main theories as to how consciousness is produced, we have three possible answers:

- Physical interactions in the brain produce consciousness.
- Consciousness already exists and creates the brain (and all other matter).
- The brain and consciousness are mutually independent.

All of these may be wrong; the brain may be merely a receiver for consciousness. We may only experience our own 'local' piece of consciousness. What we experience as our own consciousness could be the equivalent of being one wave on a vast sea of consciousness.

CONSCIOUSNESS AND THE PSYCHE

In Chapter 3, I briefly considered models of the psyche, developed by psychologists such as Freud, Jung and Assagioli, and decided they were too confusing. Instead, I used a simplified model that included the Self, ego and witness. However, in doing so, I missed out layers of our unconscious. When considering how consciousness relates to our psyche, it is useful to use the light spectrum as a metaphor. You will be aware we can see a range of colours in the visible light spectrum and outside of this is infrared light at a lower frequency and ultraviolet light at a higher frequency, both of which are not visible to us. It is the same with consciousness. We have a personal consciousness, our witness consciousness, which we can see and outside of this, we have our lower unconscious and a higher unconscious, both of which we cannot see. To make things slightly more complicated, there is also the collective unconscious. To further explain all these concepts, I will draw on Assagioli's model of the psyche.[4]

Collective Unconscious

The collective unconscious, a term coined by Jung, refers to structures of the mind that are shared amongst beings of the same species. Consequently, as I have suggested, it is similar to a sea of consciousness, and individuals are the waves. Even though we have a separate identity, we are all connected and a part of the same thing. This connectivity may explain how people can have the same insights or create the same inventions separately, at the same time, without knowing of the existence of the other. For example, the principles of differential calculus were determined by Newton in England and Gottfried Wilhelm (von) Leibniz

(1646–1716) in Germany at about the same time in 1669. Darwin had to accelerate his plans for publishing *On the Origins of Species* in 1859 because Alfred Russel Wallace (1823–1913) had just published an essay that laid out the principles of Darwin's ideas. On 14 February 1876, Elisha Gray filed for a patent for the telephone just a few hours before Alexander Graham Bell registered his patent. These are a few of many examples throughout history. It appears that when we have an idea, the thought may travel through our collective unconscious to someone else who develops the same idea. You may have experienced thinking about someone, and then they call you a few seconds later, or you think about having a drink, and someone offers you a cup of tea. Of course, all of these could be mere coincidence, and the synchronicity of inventions may be the inevitable and logical progression of science, but these experiences do make you wonder whether Jung was right, in that we are all connected by an unconscious field. The closer people are to us, the more connected we become and the greater the synchronicity of our thinking.

This idea of the collective unconscious is similar to Rupert Sheldrake's theory of a 'morphic field', which he describes as the inherent memory in nature.[5] To explain the morphic field, Sheldrake tells the story of rolling sheep. The story goes something like this. Each morning a shepherd found that one of his sheep had escaped its field. Having inspected the fences, he was bemused as to how this had happened. For the next few nights, more and more sheep were escaping. Unable to work out how this could happen, the shepherd stayed up one night to observe the sheep. He found that the sheep had learnt to roll across the cattle grid. Clearly, one sheep had the idea, and the others had copied. What makes this story so fascinating is that other shepherds in the local area began to report that their sheep had started rolling over the cattle grids. Gradually, reports of rolling sheep were coming in from across the country. It appears the learning had gone into the morphic field, the collective unconscious, of sheep. Sheldrake also uses his concept of the morphic field to explain how birds instinctively know how to migrate, even without learning from other birds, in terms of when, where and how. Due to these examples and many others, the collective unconscious is thought to contain the collective memory of the species, such as our natural instincts.

Personal Unconscious

As well as being connected to the collective unconscious, we also have our own personal unconscious. You will be aware you do things semi-consciously, such as skills we frequently practise. You will also be aware our bodies function without conscious thought when we breathe or when our heart beats. You may also be aware our memories never entirely disappear and can come flooding back when triggered. These are just some examples that demonstrate we have an unconscious element to our psyche. Assagioli divided the personal unconscious into three areas: lower, middle and higher.

The lower unconscious contains the psychological activities that control our bodily functions, our fundamental and primitive drives and urges (survival and sexual). It includes things we do not like about ourselves, disturbing memories that we have suppressed or repressed, our phobias and delusions, etc. It is thought healing and psychological growth can be gained through accessing and recovering some of the psychological material we have suppressed and repressed in our childhood and reprocessing it. The reason being that even though this material is in our unconscious, it still influences our conscious psychology, behaviour and, hence, our well-being. This material was filed into our unconscious when we did not have the psychological capability required to process it effectively. However, as adults with greater psychological capability, we are able to reprocess the material, so it no longer has an influence. For example, we may have needed to stay alone in a hospital as a child. Although the psychological suffering caused by the experience may having been suppressed, being separated from our parents could have caused attachment issues that last into adulthood. Going back and dealing with the separation as an adult can resolve the attachment issues so they have less of an influence.

The middle unconscious is the space where we put memories, skills and, to some degree, perceptions, etc., which are not currently within our field of conscious awareness. Yet by directing our attention, we can make conscious the contents of our middle unconscious. Consequently, our field of conscious awareness resides within our middle unconscious. The witness consciousness or 'I' then operates within this field of consciousness and can become aware of everything that enters into it (from the middle unconscious), such as thoughts, emotions, sensations and perceptions. These are the contents of our psychology. The ego, our self-image and self-esteem, is also thought to reside in the middle unconscious. Some of this will be in our field of consciousness, generally who we think we are, but a large proportion will be unconscious, such as our ego defences. Nevertheless, with psychological development work, most of the ego can be made conscious. We can expand our field of conscious awareness and become more aware of what is in the middle unconscious. You may have experienced this when you felt in danger. At these times, we can become acutely aware of what is happening both within and around us.

The higher unconscious is the opposite of our lower unconscious. It is the space that contains the positive aspects of our psychology, such as inspiration, intuition, altruism, spiritual energy, etc. It is where our flashes of brilliance and genius come from. You may have experienced working on a difficult problem, with your conscious awareness, all day and not being able to find a suitable solution. Then, in the middle of the night, you suddenly wake with the answer. Your higher unconscious, or intuition, has been working on the problem without your conscious awareness. Once a solution is found, it somehow flashes into conscious awareness. This flash of insight can also happen during the day.

Researchers at Carnegie Mellon University found that the brain regions responsible for making decisions continue to be active even when the conscious brain is distracted with a different task.[6] Their study, published in the journal *Social Cognitive and Affective Neuroscience*, provides some of the first evidence on how the brain unconsciously solves a problem while being distracted by working on another task. They found that this period of distraction actually improves decision making. As the soul, as I defined in Chapter 3, is thought also to reside in the higher unconscious, it can also be where we can find the meaning and purpose for our lives.

So, if we go back to the metaphor that our personal consciousness is the wave on a sea of the collective unconscious, you can imagine our soul as being what pulls the wave out of the surface of the sea. Our soul is what makes us a separate identity while being connected to everyone and everything else through our collective unconscious (see Figure 6.1).

Figure 6.1 Wave of Personal Consciousness

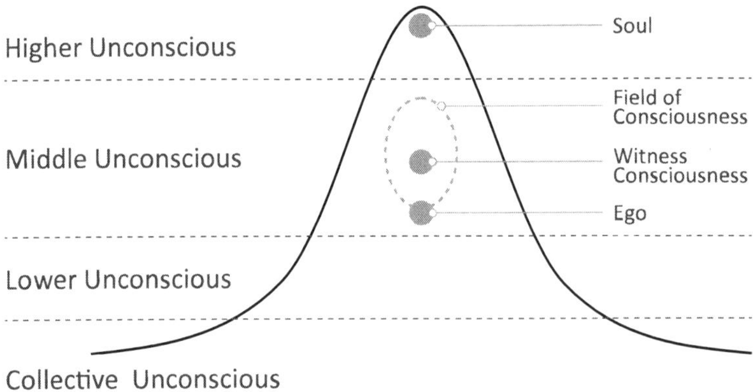

You can see that when I talk about our personal consciousness, I include both our conscious awareness and our unconscious. The lines between them are purely arbitrary. Content and influences regularly pass between them, hence the dotted lines in the diagram.

STATES, LINES AND STAGES OF CONSCIOUSNESS

Ken Wilber, an American writer on transpersonal psychology, has identified that consciousness can be described in terms of states, lines and stages.[7] He also calls them states, streams and waves. Wilber is a controversial figure and has caused much debate in the world of transpersonal psychology. He has been accused of simply placing eastern spiritual states of consciousness on the top of western science's stages of consciousness. Although the accusation may be accurate to some degree, it is a little unjust since western science on its own has, so far, struggled to make much headway in understanding consciousness.

States of Consciousness

We are all aware of different states of consciousness, such as waking, sleeping and dreaming. Yet there are many more 'altered states of consciousness' (ASCs). You may have experienced an ASC through consuming alcohol, taking medication or being deprived of sleep. ASCs can be brought on by techniques such as being in nature and the wilderness, meditation, hypnosis, sensory deprivation, dance, yoga, etc. They can also emerge spontaneously, which people often describe as a spiritual experience. One type of ASC is what Maslow called a 'peak experience'.[8] This is when we experience intensity of perception, depth of feeling or a sense of profound significance, to such a degree that it significantly stands out from everyday events. Most peak experiences occur during athletic, artistic, religious or nature experiences, or intimate moments with friends or family members. During a peak experience, we tend to have a heightened sense of wonder and awe. A peak experience can also be deemed as inhabiting a higher stage of consciousness for a short period of time.

Lines of Consciousness

Lines of consciousness are generally different aspects of our psychology, such as cognition, emotion, values, moral reasoning, motives etc. All of these can develop at different rates throughout our lives. When I say develop, I mean they become more sophisticated or provide the ability to operate in more complex situations. For example, most adults are able to solve problems using linear, cause-and-effect type of thinking. However, some people, who have developed their cognition, are able to use systems thinking to solve problems. Although these lines of consciousness can develop at different rates, their combination often indicates a person's current stage in the development of their consciousness.

Stages of Consciousness

Recent advances in neuroscience have found our brain continually changes throughout our adult life. This would not have surprised many psychologists who theorised, many decades ago, we continually change and develop throughout our life. These psychologists viewed adult growth in terms of periods of transition, followed by plateaux of stability. This combination of plateaux and transitions is the basis of most stage models of adult psychological growth and development. One of the first psychologists to create a theory of adult development was Maslow. In 1943 Maslow first proposed, in a paper called 'A theory of human motivation', that we all have a 'Hierarchy of Needs'. His theory was further developed and fully expressed in his 1954 book *Motivation and Personality*.[9] Taught in business schools worldwide, his theory is often positioned as a management model and used to teach leaders how to motivate people. In fact, as previously mentioned, Maslow was one of the founding fathers of both humanistic and transpersonal psychology, and it can be argued his theory is more about stages in the development of our consciousness.

It is believed the changes neuroscientists see in the physiology of the brain are due to neuroplasticity. The brain is actually changing as a result of our conscious experience. Consequently, if our environment becomes more complex, in time, our brains adapt to cope with greater complexity. This new brain physiology leads to our consciousness becoming more complex and we transition to a higher stage giving us a new way of perceiving, understanding and acting in the world.

In this section, we have seen that our conscious experiences change the structures in our brain. These changes, in turn, change the nature of our consciousness. This aligns with an 'interactionist dualist' theory of how consciousness is produced. If the changes in our consciousness are produced by facing greater complexity in our environment, we can develop new and higher consciousness stages. However, if we are fortunate, we can temporarily visit these higher consciousness stages by having peak experiences. We can also facilitate our progression to these higher stages of consciousness by developing our lines of consciousness, such as our cognition, emotion, motivation and moral reasoning.

SUMMARY AND CONCLUSION

From this exploration of the what, why and how of consciousness, you can see it is truly a hard problem. No one knows the answers to questions about consciousness and, while many philosophers, scientists and psychologists have theories, they tend not to agree with each other. The use of the scientific method does not help. Scientists can only observe, measure and record either what they believe produces consciousness or the results of consciousness in action. From the results of scientific research, scientists can only hypothesise what consciousness is. Researching consciousness directly is currently beyond the scope of science. Perhaps this is why some philosophers and scientists prefer to believe consciousness does not exist. This lack of understanding and agreement as to the nature of consciousness inevitably leaves the layperson bemused and confused. Nonetheless, for our purposes, it is important we have some degree of understanding as to the nature of consciousness.

Our collective consciousness is keeping our current economic system in place. Our industrialised minds and our destructive economy are perfectly aligned and reinforcing each other. If we continue with our current level of collective consciousness, we will not be able to prevent our economy from destroying our environment, ourselves and, probably, most other life on Earth. To create, develop and implement a new, more sustainable economy, we first need a critical mass of people who have developed a new level of consciousness. A consciousness beyond consumerism. Are you one of these people?

In the following two chapters, I will outline how you can develop consciousness beyond consumerism. Before that, I would like to summarise my own understanding of consciousness. To make sense of consciousness theories, I have used the metaphor that our personal consciousness is a wave on a sea of collective unconsciousness. Our soul is what pulls the wave out of the surface of the sea to create our separate personal consciousness while still enabling us to be connected to everyone and everything through the collective unconscious. Even though our personal consciousness consists mainly of unconsciousness elements, it is only through our brain that parts of our unconscious can become conscious. The more complex the structures of the brain, the more complex our consciousness and the higher the stage of consciousness we can attain. If we can expand our consciousness, we can access more of our psyche, which was previously unconscious.

Through evolution, consciousness develops to ensure a species maintains alignment with their environment. The more complex and demanding a species' environment, the more complex the consciousness needs to be. Consequently, the nature of consciousness varies across species. However, it can also be argued that, as humans, our environment is changing and becoming increasingly complex and, therefore, we need also to evolve our consciousness continually. Our collective consciousness needs to evolve to become more complex and thereby transition to the next stage.

The evolution of our consciousness may be occurring through neuroplasticity, as brain imaging shows structural changes resulting from our conscious experiences. This interpretation is in line with interactionists' dualist theories of consciousness, which suggest the brain produces consciousness and consciousness produces the brain. Therefore, we can purposely develop our consciousness by choosing to have specific experiences. If we frequently experience a more complex environment, the nature of our consciousness may become more complex in turn. In doing so, we can develop to a new, higher stage of consciousness. If enough people actively try to raise their consciousness to the next stage, collectively, we can encourage the evolution of human consciousness.

Raising our consciousness to the next stage may also be facilitated by having ASCs, such as a peak experience. When we have a peak experience, it appears that we visit a higher stage of consciousness for a short amount of time. The more we visit our next stage, the more comfortable we become and, hence, the easier it will be to develop to that stage. We may also be able to prepare ourselves for the transition to the next stage of consciousness by developing our lines of consciousness. This preparation would entail developing greater complexity in how we think, feel and behave.

So, even though consciousness is a truly hard problem, I believe there is sufficient understanding to suggest we can purposely develop a higher level of consciousness. By developing our consciousness beyond consumerism, together, we can create a more sustainable economy.

CHAPTER 7

OUR JOURNEY OF CONSCIOUSNESS DEVELOPMENT

Sophia found a tree, sat down and rested her back against its wide trunk. It was an extremely old tree. She thought to herself; it had probably seen many battles with dragons in its time. If the tree could talk, it could tell her how to beat the dragon.

As she sat, Sophia realised all her possessions were strewn around her and the tree where she had dropped her bags. Even though they had given her joy and pleasure earlier, carrying them around was exhausting. She sat for what seemed like a few hours, preparing herself to die from exhaustion or hunger. Drifting in and out of consciousness, all of a sudden, she heard Mimir's voice in her head.

'You must change your state and, for that, you must look within,' he told her.

'What do you mean?' Sophia said out loud. There was no reply.

'That's it!' Sophia shouted out loud. 'I will stay here, under this tree, until you tell me what you mean or until I die.'

Night came. Sophia was barely conscious. She was no longer sure what was real or dreams, nor did she care. She felt sad she wasn't going to be able to say goodbye to her parents or her friends. During the night, the racers came to visit. With all their might, they tried to persuade Sophia to put on her new running shoes and join them in a race. Sophia resisted. People came with axes and tried to move her so they could chop down the tree, feed into their machine and convert it into products. Sophia refused to be moved. Some of the market stallholders tried to trick her into buying more goods, but Sophia sent them away. As dawn broke a thick mist descended and Sophia felt really cold and alone. But still, she didn't move.

Looking at her scattered possessions gathering dew, she wondered why she had ever bought them. But she had no answer. Then she realised they had inhibited her when she was fighting the dragon. How could she persuade the dragon not to plunder when she held all these products stolen from nature? To defeat the dragon, she had to let go of her desire to possess all these things.

INTRODUCTION

> When we quit thinking primarily about ourselves and our own self-preservation, we undergo a truly heroic transformation of consciousness.
>
> Joseph Campbell

Before we go any further, it might be useful to take a brief pause and reflect on the journey we have taken together so far. We have found that, in westernised societies, we have increasingly become separated from nature, each other and ourselves. These separations have led to our ego, for most people, becoming isolated, fragile and competitive. Our ego has become vulnerable. Businesses have exploited our vulnerable ego to sell us products and services on the promise they will make us feel good and bring us admiration. We have been conditioned to be consumers to serve the economy. The industrialisation of our consciousness is complete.

As a population, our industrialised minds create a collective consciousness, which is highly aligned with the modernist era of consciousness. Our modernist collective consciousness creates, supports and maintains our capitalist, consumerist and neoliberal economic system, which, in turn, continues to condition our consciousness, so we continue to consume. We are trapped in a vicious cycle, a destructive spiral. In the early days, this economic system did increase the standard of living for many. Today this same system has become unsustainable and causes us ever-increasing pain. It is significantly responsible for climate change, mass extinction, growing inequality, high levels of mental illness and epidemics. Yet, even as we try to cope with these existential threats, we continue with business as usual.

We are not short of solutions to the threats facing us today. But the collective consciousness in our society will not let us implement them. To implement any solutions, we first need to develop our consciousness beyond consumerism. This will be achieved by developing our psychological capability, which will enable us to download the programming from the emerging metamodernist collective consciousness. We may be on the evolutionary path to this new level of collective consciousness, and the current pain may be part of this natural process of growth. But how much more pain can we take? We must accelerate the process of developing a new level of consciousness before the damage to our planet goes beyond human repair.

We need a critical mass of people to break away from the norm and develop their consciousness. The idea that we can develop our consciousness might seem bizarre and preposterous to many. It has long been held that once we become fully grown adults, our brain does not change. At that point, our psychological growth was believed to come to an end. However, now that neuroscientists have discovered neuroplasticity, we know that our brain does change throughout our lives. It changes as a direct result of our experience. So, if we purposely manage our experience, we can deliberately manage the changes in our brain and, as a consequence, manage the development of our consciousness. Even if we do not purposefully manage our experience, our consciousness can still develop and grow naturally, but we can get stuck. Our psychological growth can become stunted and be halted altogether by our experience. Today, collectively, the growth of our consciousness has got stuck due to our experience industrialising of our minds.

This chapter will demonstrate that while the continued development of our consciousness is a relatively new concept for neuroscientists, it has been a long-held belief in the mystical traditions of the major global religions and for many psychologists. With insights gained from mystics and psychologists, we can plot the development of our consciousness from our past and into the future. Reviewing our progress on this path allows us to manage the development of our own consciousness.

There is a common view in mystical traditions and psychological theories that some people begin to let go of their ego at some point in their life. They do not lose their ego but let go of their attachment to it. In doing so, the ego quietens down and becomes less demanding. We can transcend its constraints and be less defensive. At this point, we begin to venture into the higher stages of adult development of consciousness. Development into these stages is aligned with consciousness beyond consumerism. If enough people purposely manage the development of their consciousness, we will create the critical mass needed to enable a new collective consciousness to unfold; our next step in human evolution.

MYSTICAL JOURNEYS

Have you ever had a mystical experience? It is a type of altered state of consciousness, or peak experience, where you transcend the everyday reality to experience enlightenment or a spiritual union. The philosopher William James (1842–1910) popularised the term in his book *The Varieties of Religious Experience.*[1] He described the experience as having four characteristics:

- Transient – the experience is fleeting, and normality soon returns.
- Ineffable – the experience is difficult to describe to other people.
- Noetic – something really valuable is learned from the experience, which is normally hidden in the everyday reality.
- Passive – the experience happens without conscious control.

Most of the world's religions have their own form of mysticism. In her book *Green Spirit*, Marian Van Eyk McCain uses a giant cartwheel as a metaphor to describe how religions and their mystical traditions relate to each other.[2] She describes each separate religion being on the rim of the cartwheel, with the spokes being their mystical tradition connecting them all to a common hub. She says this hub is what Aldous Huxley referred to as 'The Perennial Philosophy', which is common to all religions and cultures.

Each mystical tradition employs its own range of practices designed to enable a person to experience a mystical state of consciousness or develop to a mystical stage of consciousness. So, even though neuroscience has only recently recognised that consciousness can be developed over a lifetime, most religions have been employing practices to achieve the same for centuries.

This section will briefly outline how the mystical traditions of the major religions conceive consciousness and how it can be developed to enable transcendence.

Hinduism

The main aim of Hinduism is to enable people to have what they want. To be satisfied. The question is, do we know what we want? For some, it is sensual pleasure, and Hinduism sees this as a legitimate goal. However, for most people, there comes a point when sensual pleasure is not enough. It becomes too trivial to satisfy fully and too private to engender social recognition. When this realisation hits, people often look for success. This can come in terms of wealth, fame and power. Again, Hinduism sees success as a legitimate life goal. But does success really satisfy? Once you have experienced success, you feel good briefly, but the feeling goes leaving a craving for more. Yet, not everyone can be successful all the time. Success generally requires competition, and sometimes you win, sometimes you lose. For some people, there comes a time when even the combination of sensual pleasure and success is not enough. They are left with a sense there must be more to life. Eventually, they realise sensual pleasure and success have simply been serving their ego. It is at this point in life when a duty to serve others emerges. Serving others can attract people's gratitude and lead to a sense of self-respect. But these rewards never truly satisfy some people, and they contemplate whether there is more to life. They then find Hindu mysticism.

Where Hinduism provided advice and guidance on how pleasure, success and service could be achieved, it now offers liberation. Freedom from the finite experiences of joy gained from sensual pleasure, success and service. With liberation comes access to an infinite being, infinite awareness and infinite bliss. It is unlimited and unrestricted consciousness. It is the ultimate freedom. Hinduism believes all of these are not only within everyone's reach but that we all already possess them. Within us all is a hidden being with infinite consciousness and bliss. In Hinduism, it is called 'Atman', our soul, a part of Brahman, the Godhead.

Consequently, Hinduism believes we can tread two paths in life. The 'Path of Desire', leading to sensual pleasure and success, and the 'Path of Renunciation', leading to service and liberation. It is believed we need to have completed the Path of Desire before we embark on the Path of Renunciation. Yet, we do not have to complete either path. We can stop at any time if we feel we are satisfied in this lifetime. Hindus believe in reincarnation, so it is believed we can continue our journey over many lifetimes. Consequently, Hinduism differentiates between chronological age and psychological age. A person can be young and yet psychologically mature or vice-versa.

Buddhism

According to Buddhism, it is our attachment to our ego that prevents us from realising happiness. Therefore, if we let go of our ego, we can access our true self, which has infinite consciousness and is called our Buddha-nature. Buddhism recognises that we experience suffering in our lives caused by our attachment to things that are not permanent. Everything is impermanent, but we want to retain the things which give us pleasure. When they change or leave, we experience loss and suffering. To protect ourselves from this, we retreat into behaviour patterns that either avoid full contact or give us comfort. These patterns create our self-identity and maintain our self-esteem. They create our ego. Although the ego protects us, it essentially gets in the way of us experiencing life directly. It becomes a defensive structure that needs to be continually maintained like a high wall around a castle.

Over centuries Buddhism has developed nine consciousness levels to describe how the ego is formed and how we can let it go. The lowest five levels are our sentient consciousness, which consists of our five senses (touch, taste, sight, hearing and smell). It is through our senses that we perceive the world, attaching to things that give us pleasure and avoiding things that give us pain. The sixth consciousness, also classed as a sense, is our mind's eye. It learns to understand what we perceive through our senses. It uses our imagination to integrate information gathered by our senses into a meaningful whole; it is our thoughts. The seventh level of consciousness allows us to step back and observe our mental life. Once we attain this level, we are aware of ourselves and have the ability to attach to things that give us pleasure and detach from those that give us pain. It controls our mental life. Being controlled by this level of consciousness leads to insecurity and the development of our ego. The eighth level of consciousness is considered to be the 'storehouse'. It contains all our thoughts, words and actions throughout our lifetime, as well as their impacts, known as karmic energy. Unlike the first seven levels of consciousness, which cease when we die, Buddhism believes this one continues after death and is reincarnated with our soul in the next life. The ninth and final level of consciousness is known as our 'Buddha-nature'. It is the purest of all the levels of consciousness and cannot be affected by the other eight. It is always within us, provides the foundation of our psychology, and serves as the source of our mental and spiritual activity. But it gets smothered by our ego as we develop through life. Buddhism believes the cure for suffering is to attain this ninth level of consciousness, thereby rising above the ego in our psychological development.

The way to attain our Buddha-nature is not through desire or renunciation but through a middle way, called the 'Noble Eightfold

Path'. The eight practices can be categorised as:

- Ethics – Right Speech, Right Action and Right Livelihood.
- Meditation – Right Effort, Right Mindfulness and Right Concentration.
- Wisdom – Right View and Right Intention.

While these can be considered to be eight steps along a path, this would be a misconception. The practice and development of one can facilitate the development of others.

Three Abrahamic Religions

Kabbalah, the mystical tradition within Judaism, describes five ascending levels of awareness that bring people closer to communion with God. The first level is awareness of the physical body and the physical world. However, it is more than awareness; it is also the life force God breathes into our body. Through divine service and proper action, it is possible to develop to the second plane of awareness. This level is awareness of emotions, which allows for the love and awe of God to be aroused. With greater effort, the third plane of awareness can be realised, which is the conceptual grasp of the intellect. This level allows for the contemplation of God's divine energy, which enables continuous creation and sustenance of life and existence. With purification, the fourth plane of awareness can be reached where the soul nullifies the ego. With no ego, there is no self-seeking and no self-identity outside of communion with God. Kabbalah believes this enables people to love God with all one's being. Through further dedication, the fifth level of awareness can be reached where the soul transcends all worlds and is bound to God.

Gnosticism, a Christian mystical tradition, describes four ascending states of consciousness. The first state is ignorance and a profound lack of awareness. It is instinctive and can be brutal and cruel. The second state of consciousness is an awareness of opinions and beliefs. From this, the 'Truth' can be distorted into prejudice, sectarianism and fanaticism. Gnosticism believes this is the level of consciousness for most of humanity. The third state of consciousness enables the intellectual revision of one's own opinions and beliefs for the purpose of using them to establish clear and fair laws. The fourth state is the perfectly awakened consciousness, called our 'Essence'. It is a state of profound inner illumination that enables thought and to be intuitive, clear, uncontaminated and objective. Those who have reached this level have no ego and, therefore, their perception and reasoning are not contaminated by emotions such as pride, lust, anger, envy or fear.

Sufism, considered to be the mystical tradition within Islam, describes how a Sufi experiences sequential stages, or stations, in their spiritual life. While the stages differ between sects, here are the main ones. The first is repentance of sins and worldly life, which requires remorse for the violations committed, the immediate abandonment of the sin and a promise never to return to sin. The second is abstinence from the desires of the world, which requires the Sufi to be watchful in the grey area between what is prohibited and permitted, for anything that concerns sin and anything that distracts from God. The third is the renunciation of all desire. The objective of this state is to feel no joy in worldly goods, not to grieve for what is lost, take no pleasure in praise from others and give up hope of heavenly reward or fear of hell. The fourth is poverty and involves giving up the desire for wealth and not asking anyone for anything. To receive something would create gratitude towards the giver and not towards God. The fifth is patience, which requires the Sufi to exhibit self-control to bear the burden of hardship for the sake of God. The sixth stage is trust, which is complete trust in God and surrender to His will. This state is not one of fatalism but an active and persistent work on oneself through pious practice. The final stage is acceptance of God. The Sufi must silence their anxiety and not look for God's acceptance of them; instead, they must accept that God has preordained all of His creations. In Sufism, reaching a new stage does not destroy the previous; they continually build on each other.

From this brief review of the mystical traditions of the world's major religions, it can be seen that there are many similarities. In one form or another, each of these traditions suggests that a 'higher consciousness' is already contained within us when we are born. This higher consciousness contains our soul (our Self) and connects to a wider spiritual entity. According to these different religious beliefs, our higher consciousness goes by various terms, such as Essence, Buddha-nature or Atman. It can also be described in terms of communion with, or acceptance of, God.

While this higher consciousness is within us, it soon becomes smothered by the development of our ego-consciousness. As we go through life, our higher consciousness becomes invisible to us, being submerged within our psyche under the weight of our ego. We become disconnected from our soul. Eventually, there comes a stage when life governed by our ego no longer satisfies, and we look for a more meaningful way of living. The mystical traditions suggest greater meaning in life comes from gradually letting go of our ego. In doing so, we can access our higher consciousness and experience increasing levels of purity in perception, clarity in thinking and bliss. Within our higher consciousness, we can reconnect with our soul (our Self) and then find a greater spiritual connection.

This journey of consciousness development is represented in Figure 7.1.

Few people will complete this journey in their lifetime. According to Hindu and Buddhist teachings, it may take many lifetimes. Most people in westernised societies get stuck halfway along the path when the ego is most dominant because our minds have been industrialised. To create a more sustainable economy, we need to turn the corner in our consciousness development. Turning the corner will set us free from the industrialisation of our minds and allow us to access the hidden qualities within us, which lay dormant under the weight of our ego.

Figure 7.1 *Journey of Consciousness Development*

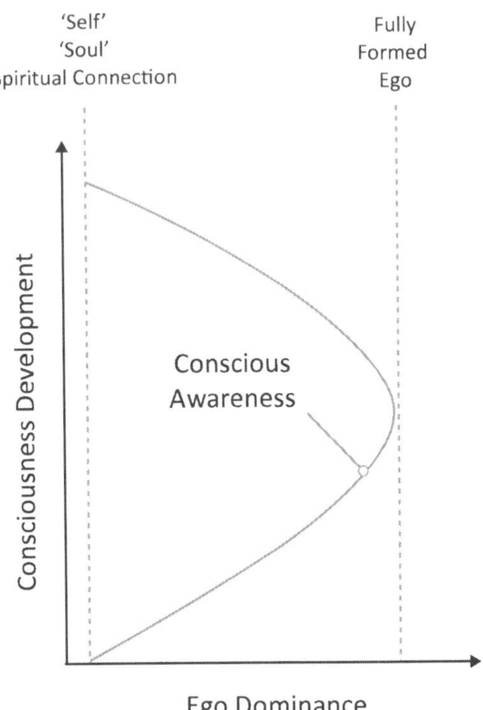

PSYCHOLOGICAL JOURNEYS

Many psychologists have been influenced by these mystical traditions and have incorporated them into their work. Carl Jung wrote numerous books and articles about eastern religions and extensively researched Gnosticism. Consequently, these mystical traditions influenced the development of his theories. He came to believe everyone could contact the divine through the collective unconscious and that it is our natural instinct to strive towards a relationship with a higher force or being that transcends the human ego. These beliefs informed his theory of 'individuation', which I briefly introduced in Chapter 2, which is the core of his work.

Jung saw individuation as a process whereby the person becomes whole in the course of self-realisation. In the first half of our lives, he believed we attempt to establish ourselves within our society. We essentially try to conform and succeed. In the process, we create our ego. This contains all the psychological attributes we like about ourselves. Inevitably, this means we have to dump all the traits we do not like. According to Jung, we store these in the 'shadow' part of our psyche. Consequently, our ego grows strong and powerful and helps us succeed. But there comes a time, usually around midlife, when our ego starts to lose its hold over us. This change is often triggered by recognising a higher force or being, which transcends our ego. During the second part of our life, the mask of ego is stripped away to reveal the true self. The traits we dumped in the shadow are recovered and reintegrated. We become whole once again. This process of discovery allows us to find greater meaning in our lives.

As one of the founders of psychology, Jung's theory of individuation has informed numerous adult psychological development models. Although each of the models focuses on a different line of consciousness, they are all structured in terms of development stages. Consequently, they can be combined to create a holistic model of the 'stages of consciousness development'.

Here are the main models of consciousness development (details of each can be found in Appendix 2):

- Abraham Maslow's 'Hierarchy of Needs' focused on the development of motivation.[3]
- Clare Graves' 'Emergent Cyclical Levels of Existence Theory' focused on the development of personal values.[4]
- Lawrence Kohlberg's 'stages of moral development'.[5]
- Robert Kegan's 'subject–object theory of development' focused on cognition.[6]

- Jane Loevinger's 'theory of ego development' focused on personality.[7]

Table 7.1 *Models of Lines of Consciousness*

Stage of Development	Kohlberg 'Morals'	Maslow 'Motivation'	Graves 'Values'	Kegan 'Cognition'	Loevinger 'Personality'	Seven Stages of Leadership
	Pre-conventional		Purple	1st Order Impulsive Mind	Impulsive	
1		Safety	Red	2nd Order Imperial Mind	Opportunistic	Power & Control
2	Conventional	Love/Belonging	Blue	3rd Order Socialised Mind	Conformist	Inclusion
3		Esteem	Orange	3rd/4th Order		Competence
4		Self-actualisation		4th Order Self-authoring Mind	Conscientious	Delivery
5	Post-conventional		Green	4th/5th Order		Clarity
6			Yellow	5th Order Self-transforming Mind	Autonomous	Service
7			Turquoise		Integrated	Luminary

Although focused on a different aspect of our psychology, each of them is built upon research that shows adult psychological development proceeds through periods of transitions and plateaux. Therefore, they align with each other relatively closely. Consequently, it is possible to map them all on to a generic model of adult consciousness stages of development (see Table 7.1).

The 'Seven Stages of Adult Consciousness Development', outlined below, are an amalgam of the stage theories developed by the psychologists included above and are detailed in Appendix 2.

Stage 1: At this stage, we find safety in our own authority, position and the rule book. We tend to use whatever power we have available to us, derived from the different roles we play in life, to protect our ego.

Stage 2: At stage two, we realise that using power tends to create adversarial relationships that threaten rather than protect us. We turn to an 'in-group' to protect our ego from people outside of the group. To ensure we are not ejected from the in-group, we tend to adopt the prevailing norms of behaviour, beliefs and values. Our identity becomes attached to these norms as we fuse with the in-group. An adult at stage two has an identity that is '**dependent**' on other people. This stage of consciousness development is aligned with the 'pre-modernist' era of collective consciousness.

Stage 3: As we grow and develop, we gradually acquire more knowledge, skills and expertise, which we are able to use to differentiate ourselves and add value. This increase in our competence gives us the confidence to separate ourselves from our 'in-group' and establish our own identity. However, this separation still makes us feel vulnerable and, as a result, we protect ourselves by investing our ego in our knowledge and expertise. Consequently, if our expertise is challenged, we will likely see this as a threat and respond with flight or fight.

Stage 4: By developing and using our skills to add value, we find our own way to perform at a high level and deliver results. This success gives us the confidence to be ourselves and be '**independent**'. At this stage, we feel the most authentic. However, this authenticity is aligned with our constructed identity, the 'me'. Our consciousness now has become significantly fused with our ego. If people critique, challenge or disagree with us, it can feel like our whole identity is being threatened. Consequently, by this stage, our ego has become quite large and vulnerable. Our ego now needs a lot of defending. It is the stage of the development of our consciousness where we are most likely to experience fragile high self-esteem and narcissism. This stage of consciousness development is also aligned with the 'modernist' era of collective consciousness.

Stage 5: As we face more complexity in our lives, we increasingly find our constructed 'me' identity is constraining our ability to respond in a suitable way. As we search for new ways of relating to the world, we realise we behave in different ways according to the various roles and relationships we have. These are what Assagioli called 'sub-personalities'. The realisation that we are made up of multi-personalities is really unsettling and can produce a high level of anxiety. We can feel out of equilibrium and keep asking the question 'Who am I?' When we discover that we can adopt multiple world views and see things from different perspectives, we realise we no longer have the right answer. To reduce anxiety, we search for our true authenticity and the right answer. This search attracts us to groups who are most aligned with what we would like to be our true identity. As more people develop to this level of consciousness, we see an upsurge in the 'identity politics' we discussed in Chapter 5. Society is increasingly fragmenting as we divide into groups according to race, gender, religion, politics, etc. We are becoming a society of competing activist groups. This stage of consciousness development is aligned with the 'postmodernist' era of collective consciousness.

Stage 6: By this stage, we are no longer fully invested in any one constructed identity, the 'Me', and we are consequently able to adapt our behaviour to meet the demands of a situation with great agility. Having let go of our constructed identity, we have less need to defend ourselves, and our ego tends to quieten. With a quieter ego, we now have more psychological space to include and connect with other people. As we are not attached to our ego, our sense of identity becomes '**interdependent**', which does not mean we become submissive. Instead, we tend not to see other people as threats and, therefore, we can just 'be' with people. This reduction in threat means we are better able to explore and understand different and often opposing views. We are able to use the differences between people as opportunities for listening and dialogue, enabling us to use the energy of difference to create change. Rather than focusing on the negative and what divides us, this stage of consciousness enables us to focus on the positive and what can unfold in the space between us as we come together. This stage of consciousness development is aligned with the beginning of the 'metamodernist' era of collective consciousness.

Stage 7: When we develop to this stage, we have come to terms with the idea that there is no right or wrong. We recognise that our judgements come from our worldview that our experiences have conditioned. Letting go of judgement gives us the ability to view ourselves, the situation and society simultaneously from an external perspective. We can hold a mirror up to situations and

> reflect back an unbiased view of reality. Having let go of our ego, we have gained the ability to hold contradictory views without conflict, enabling us to resolve a paradox by creating something new. Being no longer driven by our ego, we are better able to serve others. We then tend to focus primarily on the growth and well-being of people and communities. This stage in the development of our consciousness is aligned with the 'metamodernist' era of collective consciousness.

In the early stages, our ego is developing. Therefore, we are 'dependent' on others for support and protection. We observe successful people and try out their behaviour to see if it brings us success. In this way, we become socialised and conditioned into society. This conditioning is how we learn the norms of behaviour required to be an adult in our society.

By the time we develop to stage 4, our ego has fully matured, and we are 'independent'. Yet, due to the industrialisation of our consciousness, our ego has now become quite vulnerable. To maintain our independence, we need to find ways to support and defend our ego. This need allows businesses to sell us products and services that, we are told, will support and protect our ego. This message is implied by advertising messages and, obviously, not said explicitly.

Even with these products, the defence of our ego takes up so much psychological energy that we often have little energy to engage with other people. Consequently, we can become highly individualistic. The problems we face, caused by our industrialised, capitalist, consumerist and neoliberal economic system, are too complex for individuals to address working alone. Instead, we need to be able to draw on our collective intelligence and become more 'interdependent' to find solutions.

The characteristics of stage 4 development of consciousness are aligned with the modernist collective consciousness dominant in westernised societies today. In turn, this level of collective consciousness supports our capitalist, consumerist and neoliberal economic system. Most adults develop to stage 4 and not beyond. In fact, stage 4 has traditionally been viewed as the height of adult maturity. However, the world has now changed and has become much more complex. To quote Robert Kegan, 'we are now in over our heads'.[8]

If we are to establish a new, more sustainable economy, we need the consciousness of a critical mass of people in our society to develop beyond stage 4. This further development will require individuals to let go of their ego and, in doing so, free up a great deal of psychological energy. The energy released could then be invested in engaging with other people to develop solutions to the multiple crises caused by our current economic system. It is at this point in the development of our consciousness that we can become 'interdependent'.

Interdependence transcends the dualities of individualism and collectivism as well as dependence and independence. It allows us access to all of these qualities. Rather than 'either/or' it is 'both/and'. A consciousness that enables interdependence will enable us to hold both positions simultaneously without conflict. It is about recognising and valuing autonomous and emancipated individuals on the one hand, with the universal community of humankind on the other. People who have developed beyond stage 4 can easily co-create with others without losing their independence. It is co-creation rather than collaboration. When we collaborate, we are still trying to meet the needs of our own ego. Co-creation transcends the ego.

By letting go of our ego, we become less vulnerable and, thus, less susceptible to being conditioned into being consumers. Letting go of our ego is the first step in developing consciousness beyond consumerism. By employing developmental techniques, which I will introduce in the next chapter, it is possible to let go of our ego and develop our consciousness to stage 6. This stage is aligned with the emergence of the metamodernist collective consciousness we explored in Chapter 5. Stage 6 is the level of collective consciousness necessary for society to support a more sustainable economy.

MAPPING OUR JOURNEY

The Seven Stages of Adult Consciousness Development form just one part of the journey of consciousness development we can embark on during our lifetime. They can be overlaid on the mystical journey of consciousness development (see Figure 7.2).

Figure 7.2 *Staged Journey of Consciousness Development*

'Self'
'Soul'
Spiritual Connection
Fully
Formed
Ego
Transpersonal Development
Post-conventional Adult Development
Conventional Adult Development
Child Development
Inter-dependent
Independent
Dependent
7
6
5
4
3
2
1
Consciousness Development
Ego Dominance

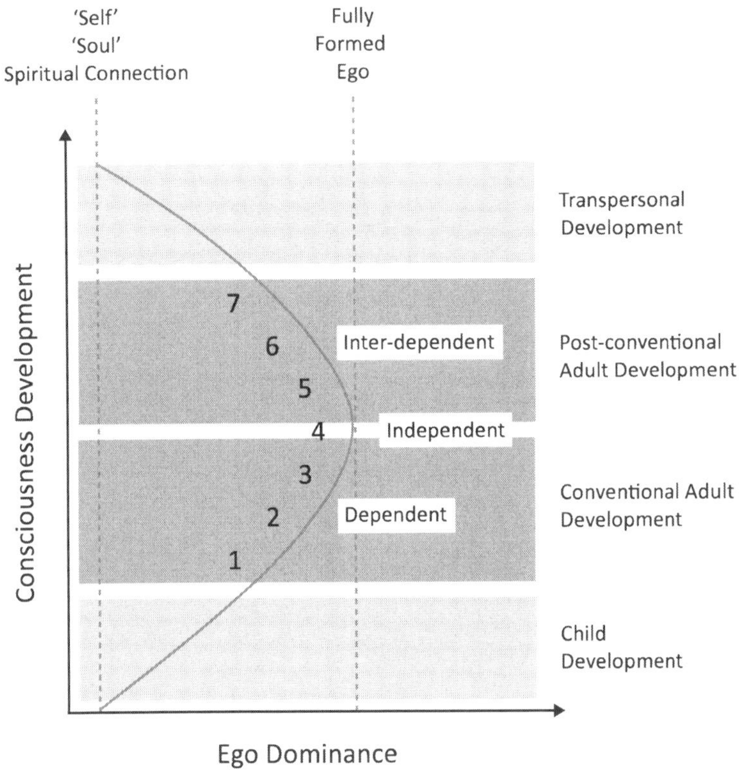

We can stop, slow down or accelerate our progress at any point. As adults, we tend to halt our journey of development when the complexity of our consciousness is aligned with the level of complexity in our lives. If the degree of alignment is working for us and we are not suffering significant psychological pain, we have no need to develop further. However, if life becomes more demanding than our stage of consciousness can deal with, it tends to provide a stimulus for psychological growth. At that point, we can accelerate the development of our consciousness. It is evident our society is now at the point where we need to develop our consciousness further. We now have to deal with the demands of economic and financial instability, climate change, mental illness, inequality and more frequent epidemics. These are examples of the pain and suffering species experience when their collective consciousness is no longer aligned with their environment. Our collective consciousness is clearly now out of alignment with our environment.

This section will walk you through the entire journey of consciousness development. It is a journey we all start, but few complete, at least in one lifetime. We will begin by looking at aspects of consciousness in relation to child development. Next, we will travel through both the conventional and post-conventional stages of adult development. I will then briefly introduce the transpersonal stages. There is no current need for people to develop beyond the post-conventional stages of consciousness, but the transpersonal stages are outlined to complete the full development journey.

At birth, we are totally fused with our environment. This comes from being in our mother's womb. Prior to this, we have no concept of having a 'self' separate from the womb and no sense of the duality of 'subject' and 'object'. When we are born, this 'non-dual' consciousness continues. When we are hungry, we cry, and we get fed, giving us the experience that nothing is separate. We are a part of one system, just like in the womb. It could be argued that we are born with the spiritual connection mystical traditions seek to attain. However, if this is the case, our consciousness is not sufficiently developed for us to realise or appreciate the connection. At this stage, we are simply sentient.

Gradually, as a result of our experience, our perception of subject and object starts to emerge. When we are hungry and do not get fed, we realise our food source is separate from us and beyond our control. This sense of separation continues through our early life experiences and culminates in the sense of self being separate from the world at around the age of 2 years old. This self is called the 'Existential Self' and what William James described as the 'I'. This development coincides with what is often called the 'terrible twos' when children start to assert their own will.

Once the 'I' has been established, the 'ego' starts to form. James described this as the 'Me', and it forms when a child starts to become attached to an identity. Children categorise themselves in terms of simple identity categories. At first, this is in terms of gender or age. As we grow older, this categorisation becomes more complex, such as in terms of our interests, abilities, race, class culture, our liking for a type of music, etc. This completes the child development phase of our life, and we enter a phase of conventional adult development.

As adults, we continue to develop our identity, essentially our self-concept. The development process consists of reflecting on memories of what has happened to us in the past and how we behaved. We make sense of and piece together these memories to form a consistent and integrated whole of who we are. In essence, our identity is formed by writing our own biography. This identity informs and guides how we go out into, perceive and experience the world. We start to determine what is important to us in terms of our values and beliefs. These essentially form our 'world view', which is the part of our identity the American psychologist Carl Rogers (1902–1987) termed the 'Personal Self'. Our memories also contain our perception of how we think other people view and experience us, which is the part of our identity Rogers termed the 'Social Self'. Over time, our memories, our perceptions of how people view us and our world view all come together to form our consistent and coherent identity. If we behave according to this identity, we feel we are authentic.

Gradually, our ego gets attached to our identity. We start to feel our sense of identity is important and needs protecting. The more our ego gets attached to our identity, the more we feel vulnerable and the more we need to find ways to keep ourselves safe. How we keep ourselves safe defines the first four stages of adult consciousness development. As mentioned in the previous section, stage 4 has been viewed as the height of adult maturity. Hence, stages 1–4 are called the 'conventional stages' of consciousness development.

To continue to develop and grow our consciousness, we need to quieten and let go of our ego. By transcending our ego in this way, we find we have more psychological space to access our intuition, connect with people and be open to new ways of behaving. The process of letting go of our ego defines the next three stages of adult development. These are called the 'post-conventional' stages of consciousness development.

The post-conventional stages need not be the end of our journey. We can progress through to the transpersonal stages. Nevertheless, given that most people reach stage 4, fewer people reach stages 5, 6 and 7, and developing to the transpersonal stages is extremely rare. A survey carried out by the management consultancy PwC in 2015, using a tool developed by Bill Torbert (derived from the Loevinger model), did not find any business leaders who had developed to stage 7.[9]

The transpersonal stages describe our psychology beyond the ego, the 'Me' identity and the 'I'. As we continue to let go of our ego, we increasingly experience 'pure consciousness'. This consciousness is awareness in the here and now, where we can observe our inner world of thoughts and feelings and our outer world without judgement. As we continue to develop, we start to transcend our 'I' identity. A variety of spiritual traditions suggest that when this happens, we start to enter a state of consciousness where subject–object duality disappears, described as non-dual or unity consciousness.

From researching a wide variety of contemporary psychologies, concepts from the Kabbalah (Judaism's esoteric tradition), Sri Aurobindo's writings (integral yoga), and several traditional Hindu and Buddhist systems of thought, Ken Wilber developed a spectrum of 17 levels of development.[10] These three, below, are stages in transpersonal development range:

Subtle: Characterised by states of imagination, reverie, daydreams, creative visions and visionary revelations.

Causal: Characterised by the capacity to 'witness' our internal and outer worlds with pure consciousness and so without influence of our unconscious drives and motivation.

Ultimate: Characterised by the transcendence of subject–object duality. In that what appears as hard or solid objects 'out there' are really transparent and translucent manifestations of our own being.

While western psychology has not been able to research these higher stages, due to the low numbers of people who would have developed to these stages, support for Wilber's view may be found in quantum mechanics. Wilber's description of the 'Ultimate' stage is similar to the Copenhagen Interpretation devised in the years 1925–1927 by Niels Bohr and Werner Heisenberg to reconcile the apparent dualism of 'wave' and 'particle'. As we have seen, this interpretation states 'a particle exists in all states at once until observed'. Therefore, it essentially asserts there are no solid states until they are manifested by our own being. Development of this nature is generally seen as a spiritual practice and beyond the scope of this book.

As we develop through the stages, we retain the qualities of the previous stages. We take on new attributes with each new stage, expanding our psychological capability and giving us greater flexibility. It can be likened to adding a new colour to a palette and creating more vibrant and complex pictures. We can go back and use the qualities of earlier stages when appropriate for the situation. We must do this mindfully to ensure it is a conscious choice rather than an unconscious reaction. When we are under sustained pressure and stress, we can have an unconscious reaction and fall down the stages. You may have noticed this reaction in work colleagues or friends.

CHARTING OUR JOURNEY

We all can chart the journey of our consciousness development. Although I have measured my own progress using diagnostic tools for assessment, I would not recommend this as it can hinder rather than facilitate development. In the past, when I have used tools to assess people who are at the post-conventional stages, I have found it sometimes re-energised their ego. Conversely, those assessed as being in conventional stages often became upset and rejected the assessment along with the whole seven stages model. None of us likes being assessed or judged by another person, especially if we perceive the result to be unfavourable. I have found the best solution is for people to self-assess by understanding the seven stages model and estimating what stage they are at by charting their development journey. People tend to be more honest with themselves and more comfortable with the result. This acceptance facilitates their ongoing development. Here is the story of my journey of consciousness development. I hope it may prove a useful example that helps you chart your own journey.

> I began my career in the construction industry, working for an extremely authoritarian site manager. He would get people to perform by shouting and using the power of his position. I learnt I could use the threat of his power to get people to work hard and, thus, I developed my own authoritarian style of managing. However, when the site manager took 2 weeks' holiday, leaving me to manage on my own, I found the limits of my authority. My authoritarian style of management did not work without the borrowed power. Threatened with being thrown through a window, I decided another way of managing was required. I realised the tradespeople did not need close management, or shouting at. All they required was sufficient work and materials. By adopting a facilitative style, I built a strong, trusting

relationship with them that enhanced my ability to influence.

As my career developed and I worked on larger projects with greater responsibilities, I found leading through relationships was constraining my ability to influence. There were too many people and I could not build trusting relationships with everyone. I had to make decisions that would not please everyone, and I felt my decision-making capability was being compromised. This tension led me to move from site management to more specialised roles. I developed expertise, knowledge and experience, which gave me a tremendous amount of influence. To gain more knowledge, I studied for a Master's in business administration (MBA). As a result, I was moved into Head Office, where I performed an internal consultancy role involving strategic planning, business development and, finally, culture change. To implement change properly, I needed to understand people better, so I studied psychology.

Leading change from the position of being an expert did not deliver results. Instead of providing advice, the role required me to inspire people. I needed to speak to people's hearts as well as their minds. By now, I realised my passion was psychology, and so I studied for a Master's degree in occupational psychology and, subsequently, moved to a business psychology consultancy.

By making this move, I instantly went from expert to novice and had to find another way to lead and quickly. Fortunately, my background in construction and my MBA differentiated me from my colleagues and enabled me to understand customers' needs quickly, propose solutions and win the business. I found I could lead a team to deliver business results and was quickly promoted to senior positions. Delivering results gave me sufficient confidence to bring my whole personality to work. While in construction, I had learnt to behave in a way that was aligned with the industry's culture and copy the behaviour of those who appeared successful. By bringing my whole personality to work, I was able to lead more authentically, which led to greater trust in the relationships I had with clients and my colleagues.

During this time, I enjoyed the benefits of my success – a big house, smart cars, pension, healthcare, and my wife could be at home with our two young daughters. I worked long hours, away from home all week and spending weekends recovering or preparing for the next week. One Saturday, after a particularly fraught week, I took our dog for a walk in the woods and found myself asking, 'Why are you doing this?' Unable to think of a suitable answer, it dawned on me that I had sacrificed my humanity. I was a cog in a machine that kept me away from my home and family. In that instant, I knew I would have to find the courage to make a change in my life. Back home, I told my wife, 'I am going to resign on Monday, and we will have to sell our house.' She said, 'Okay', and that was the end of the conversation. So, I resigned, and a few weeks later, we sold the house and moved into rented accommodation. As a family, this made us all incredibly vulnerable. To survive, I would have to use my imagination to create a new future. So, after a period of recovery, this is what I set about doing. Having the courage to be vulnerable, reawakening my humanity and my imagination enabled me to navigate this transition in our lives, during which I set up a consultancy business. The complexity of my working life increased significantly.

Running my own business meant I could invest in my own training and development. The course which had the greatest impact on my development was a 'Foundation in Core Process Psychotherapy'. This course combined Buddhism with psychology and applied it in a way that helped people develop and grow. As part of the course, I was required to work with a therapist every week. Both the course activities and the therapy enabled me to explore my own consciousness and grow as a result. After the 1-year foundation course, I continued to work on my self-development. I also explored other psychotherapies influenced by Buddhism, such as Psychosynthesis and Acceptance and Commitment Therapy.

As I mentioned in the Introduction to this book, one day, I read the poem 'Hieroglyphic Stairway' by Drew Dellinger, and it would not leave my mind. I realised that by developing leaders in large corporations, I contributed to our planet being plundered and the Earth unravelling. Realising I was part of the problem meant I could be part of the solution. To enable this, my colleagues and I established a not-for-profit co-operative to develop sustainable leadership, which helped people transition to the post-conventional stages of adult consciousness development. We researched, developed, practised and delivered various techniques, which I will outline in the next chapter.

My journey of consciousness development is told as an example of how we can review the path we have taken. I am still on this journey and always will be. Under sustained pressure, I tumble back down the stages like anyone else. My ego screams in pain when my pride is hurt, when I feel I have been treated unfairly or when I feel I am being ignored.

The post-conventional stages of development are not about getting rid of our ego. Instead, the focus is on letting go of our attachment to our ego. It is about 'having' an ego rather than 'being' our ego. By doing this, we can witness how our ego is reacting. We can see when it is in pain and wanting to be supported and defended. Witnessing our ego gives us a greater choice in how we want to behave, allowing us to transcend its constraints. It also, strangely, allows our ego to quieten down and be less demanding. Observing our ego pain helps that pain disappear as if our ego simply needs our recognition.

My journey of consciousness development has not been purposeful. I did not set out to develop my consciousness but have followed my interests. It is only in retrospect I see how the different challenges and courses have led to my development. While the path I have trodden has worked for me, it may not work for you. It may not continue to work for me in the future.

If, as a society, we are to develop consciousness beyond consumerism so we can create a more sustainable economy and society, we need to be more purposeful in our intention. We need to be able to chart the course of our own consciousness development from the past into the future. I hope my story has provided some guidance as you chart your own course.

SUMMARY AND CONCLUSION

In this chapter, I have taken you on a journey of human consciousness development. It is a journey we all start, but few of us fully complete in one lifetime. I began by demonstrating that while neuroscience has only recently recognised that our brain continually changes through our life, mystics have known this for centuries and psychologists for decades. By reviewing the work of both the mystical religious traditions and psychologists, I have demonstrated that the journeys of consciousness development roughly follow the same path.

I briefly explored aspects of consciousness concerning child development and then outlined the first four stages of adult development, the 'conventional' stages. This exploration took us to stage 4, where most people in western societies generally stop. I argued that if we are to create and implement a more sustainable economy, we need a critical mass of people to develop to the post-conventional stages of adult consciousness development. I outlined these stages before going on to discuss the transpersonal stages briefly.

Stage 4 is aligned with the 'modernist' era in our collective consciousness, which supports and maintains our neoliberalist, capitalist and consumerist economy. It represents our industrialised consciousness. The complexity of our consciousness at this stage is sufficient to deal with the complexity we have previously experienced in our environment during the Industrial Revolution. It has been a perfect fit. Consequently, there has been little need or stimulus for most people to develop beyond this stage.

Table 7.2 Alignment of Individual Consciousness, Collective Consciousness and Economic Systems

	Height of Maturing in Individual Consciousness Development (increases in psychological complexity)	Collective Consciousness Evolution (imaged order allowing a cultural code to be programmed into individual consciousness)	Economic Systems
Post-conventional	Stages 6 & 7 - Consciousness beyond consumerism	Metamodernism	New coherent economic system
	Stage 5 - Fragmented identity politics and activism	Postmodernism	Fragmented experimentation with new economic systems
Conventional	Stage 4 - Industrialised consciousness	Modernism	Neoliberal, capitalist and consumer-led economic system
	Stages 1–3	Pre-modernism	Feudal and market economies right through to the Industrial Revolution

At this stage, to protect our ego, we compete as individuals by striving to deliver the best results. It is about separating from other people, striving for success and achieving independently. This success is generally measured by the amount we produce and consume in society. It is the need to defend our ego and strive for success that has driven the growth in the economy. As we explored in Chapter 4, businesses have recognised this need to defend our ego and have used this vulnerability to condition us into becoming consumers. We are told if we buy their products, we will feel successful, look successful and other people will admire our success. This is the basis of conspicuous consumption.

Stage 6 consciousness is most aligned with the emergence of the 'metamodernist' collective consciousness required to support a new economic system and society (see Table 7.2). It represents our consciousness beyond consumerism. The complexity of our consciousness at this stage is what we need to be able to deal with the complexity we are now experiencing.

With increasing economic and financial instability, the impacts of climate change, increases in mental illness, tensions arising from inequality and the more frequent epidemics, our environment is becoming more complex than most people's consciousness can currently handle. To succeed in this environment and solve these problems, we need to be able to think in more complex ways, work with a wider range of people and behave with a higher level of agility. In order to create and implement a more sustainable economy, we need develop to stage 6 or beyond in our consciousness.

The evolution to consciousness beyond consumerism will, over time, happen naturally. We are already progressing along this evolutionary path. However, a critical mass of people operating at this level of consciousness has not yet formed. Can we wait for evolution to take its natural course? I believe not. Our industrialised consciousness is now doing far too much damage to our environment, communities and psychology. We now need to accelerate our evolution. We need to purposefully and intentionally develop our consciousness.

To accelerate the evolution of our consciousness, we must address three questions:

1. How can people's psychological growth be accelerated through the conventional stages?

2. How, in the conventional stages, can people develop their ego so it is secure and stable and, therefore, they are less susceptible to being conditioned into being a consumer?

3. How can people whose minds have already been industrialised continue to develop and grow into the post-conventional stages?

To answer these questions, in the next chapter I outline some of the techniques we, as individuals, can use to develop our consciousness into the post-conventional stages. So that we develop our consciousness beyond consumerism. Then, in the final chapter, I outline what we can do as a society to facilitate the evolution of our collective consciousness.

CHAPTER 8

METHODOLOGY FOR DEVELOPING YOUR CONSCIOUSNESS

As Sophia, still sitting beneath the tree, was contemplating how she could let go of her desire to possess all the gifts she had purchased, the early morning mist was getting thicker. From the mist, she could just make out Mimir walking towards her. He had returned to help. Her heart lifted. She felt waves of contentment surging through her body. He didn't say a word. Neither of them spoke. They just looked at each other. It was a look which said they both knew what the other was thinking. They didn't need to speak. They just knew. Then in an instant Mimir was gone. Now she knew he would always be with her, whispering in her ear when she needed him.

Sophia noticed the Green Man walking towards her. Seeing she was exhausted and hungry, he laid his hand on the bark of the tree trunk. With that, the roots of the tree broke from the ground and their tips gently touched her body. She immediately started to feel better, as if the tree were giving her sustenance. Gradually, the Green Man was absorbed into the bark. The Green Man and the tree had become one. Sophia remained for some time, resting against the tree, enjoying its restorative power.

Feeling fully restored, Sophia got to her feet, gathered up all the products she had bought and took them back to the market. She tried to return them to the stallholders, but they protested saying 'We don't give refunds.'

Sophia replied, 'I don't want a refund, these are a gift. I don't need them. You can sell them to people who do need them.'

'But what do you want in return?'

'They will help others,' replied Sophia as she left the goods and walked out of the market towards the dragon.

With the axe in one hand and a lasso in the other Sophia went eye to eyes with the dragon. They both stood looking at each other. Sophia didn't try to reason with it. She knew she was facing her own death. Her only plan was to lasso the dragon's three heads, one at a time, and chop them off. She knew she had a minuscule chance of success, but this was her purpose. Without a purpose, her life had little meaning. The dragon knew she meant business. Flames spurted from each of its three mouths and singed Sophia's hair. When it roared the ground shook, and Sophia had to steady herself to avoid falling. She was terrified, and finally the urge to run overwhelmed her; she turned to see a woman standing a few feet behind her. It was a woman from one of the groups who had helped her on the Way of People. A man appeared beside the woman, then a child. As Sophia turned to face the dragon once more, she could see more people approaching. Soon the dragon was surrounded. They'd come to help, but what were they going to do? Then she heard Mimir's voice in her ear, 'Turn away, turn away from the dragon,' said the voice.

Sophia dropped her axe and rope and turned her back on the dragon. Others followed and one by one they all turned away. As each turned its roars became quieter. Fewer flames erupted from its mouths. Gradually, the dragon faded away; its body vaporised and disappeared. When all was quiet, Sophia turned around and was astonished to see it had vanished.

The dragon had been tamed; it hadn't been killed. It could not be killed. It was a creature formed by the human mind. It had been tamed; not by violence, but by the mind. The dragon had been created by the collective consciousness of the people, an idea which everyone believed. If they no longer believed in the dragon, it could not exist. Its potential was unable to form into physical matter. Sophia had changed her state of consciousness, which led the way for others to do the same. When enough people turned away from the dragon, it could not continue to exist.

INTRODUCTION

> Do you know what you are? You are a manuscript of a divine letter. You are a mirror reflecting a noble face. This universe is not outside of you. Look inside yourself; everything that you want, you are already that.
>
> Rumi

I was recently introduced to a beautiful book written by Robert Macfarlane and illustrated by Jackie Morris called *The Lost Words*, and it deeply saddened me.[1] In 2007, the new edition of the *Oxford Junior Dictionary* introduced new words including broadband, wireless and Blackberry™, and removed others such as magpie, otter, dandelion, newt, adder, wren, bramble and bluebell. Even though I appreciate dictionaries need to be updated continuously, what upset me was that words describing nature were removed. As the philosopher A. J. Ayer (1910–1989) pointed out, 'Unless we have a word for something, we are unable to conceive it.' Without words for the natural world, our perception of the diversity of our flora and fauna will be lost. In the end, we will just see collectives of birds, plants and animals.

Although the natural world is being lost from the dictionary, is it being lost from us? We do not lose our soul simply because it is no longer recognised by science. Instead, we experience being separated from it. But is this separation just an illusion of consciousness perpetrated by our ego? Similarly, are we really becoming separated from nature and each other, or is this also an illusion?

I believe we cannot become truly separated from nature, each other and ourselves. The separation we experience is just an illusion of our ego. Deep down in our psyche the connection remains. We never lose this connection, but it is hidden behind our ego as our consciousness becomes industrialised. By transcending our ego, we can experience once again the connections we have with nature, each other and ourselves. This can happen naturally as we age. It can also be through purposeful psychological development.

As we transcend our ego, we can also uncover the higher stages of consciousness that are dormant within us. For these higher stages of consciousness to flourish, they need to be nurtured by our experience. As we saw in Chapter 3, many aspects of our experience in society have industrialised our consciousness. These have created a modernist collective consciousness that supports our economic system, which, in turn, conditions us to be consumers. If we are to release from within us higher stages of 'personal' consciousness, we need to allow ourselves to be conditioned by a higher level of 'collective' consciousness. As we explored in Chapter 5, there is a higher level of collective consciousness beginning to emerge called metamodernism.

Metamodernism has a new 'code system', which we can download and install in our personal consciousness so it can be programmed in line with a collective consciousness beyond consumerism. All we need to do is develop the psychological capability required to download and install this code system. You may feel uneasy about the thought of your consciousness being 'programmed'. You need not – it has been happening all your life. For a lot of your life, you have probably been downloading and installing the code system associated with modernism so that your consciousness can be industrialised. Our consciousness is being programmed all of the time. But, with awareness, you have a choice of what programming you want to download and install. Metamodernism is just an upgraded code system allowing you to develop your consciousness beyond consumerism.

Clearly, developing consciousness beyond consumerism is both nature and nurture. We need to prepare our 'nature', our psychology, so the new metamodernist code system can 'nurture' our inherent higher stages of consciousness. Preparing our nature means developing our psychology both in terms of quietening our ego and developing our ability to deal with a higher level of complexity.

This chapter outlines some techniques that can be used to develop our psychological capability in preparation for developing our consciousness beyond consumerism. These are techniques research has found to be effective in developing consciousness, many of which I have practised myself and employed numerous times in the development of leaders from all walks of life. The preparation consists of:

- Bringing forward your 'witness consciousness' so that you are better able to observe and manage your own psychology.

- Visiting and experiencing 'states of consciousness' that are aligned with the higher stages of consciousness, so their territory starts to become familiar.

- Developing 'lines of consciousness' such as your cognition, emotion and behaviour so that you can work with a higher level of complexity.

Once prepared, you will be ready to face experiences that allow you to start downloading the metamodernist code system. These are developmental challenges where your current way of perceiving and understanding will not provide a solution. After a period of anxiety, a new way of perceiving and understanding will emerge, a new level of psychological capability that will make you receptive to the metamodernist code system. To be receptive, you will need to ensure you are not becoming too anxious during the transition period. You will need to ensure you are getting adequate support. With the right type of preparation challenge and support, you will gradually develop your consciousness beyond consumerism.

As we explored in Chapter 7, we are all on a journey of consciousness development and we progress through different stages throughout our life. This chapter will guide you to ensure your preparation, challenge and support is right for your stage of consciousness development.

PREPARATION - WITNESS CONSCIOUSNESS

Developing our witness consciousness allows us to manage and develop our psychology purposely. It stands to reason that if we cannot observe the thing we want to change, we will not know what to change and whether the change has endured. Witnessing our psychology is about using one part of our psyche to observe another part. In Chapter 2, I outlined an exercise that allows us to experience one part of our psyche, witnessing another. That activity involved developing and using our witness consciousness.

There are several other ways in which we can develop our witness consciousness. This section outlines methods that develop three types of awareness: self-awareness, reflective awareness and reflexive awareness. Even though you can practise any one of these in isolation, they naturally build upon each other from self-awareness, through reflective awareness, to reflexive awareness.

Self-awareness

With this type of awareness, you will be able to predict the behaviour you are likely to demonstrate due to your personality. In many ways, your personality is your habitual behaviour. As your ego has developed, you would have experienced how different behaviours have brought success or kept you safe. These behaviours were likely driven by your genetics and reinforced by your social conditioning. Gradually, these successful and protective behaviours become habits integrated into your personality.

You can gain awareness of your personality through psychometric profiling or asking people for feedback. Remember, psychometrics only indicate how you are likely to behave, not how you will always behave. Also, most personality psychometrics only profile your ego, just one part of who you are. Nonetheless, psychometrics can be useful in allowing you to witness and then let go of your ego. Alternatively, you may find it useful to ask other people for feedback about how they perceive and experience your behaviour. You may have already received this type of feedback through performance appraisals or 360-degree feedbacks at work. If not, you can just simply ask people to describe how you typically behave. For instance, ask people for three words that best describe you.

Reflective Awareness

Once you have an awareness of your habitual behaviours, you can use 'reflective awareness' to determine how you actually behave. Reflective awareness involves periodically reflecting on your behaviour in different situations. An excellent method is to use a 'Reflective Learning Log'. Typically, you would ask yourself a set of questions after key events in the day, such as:

- What was the situation?
- How did I behave, and was it appropriate to the situation?
- What was the driver of my behaviour? How was I feeling and what was I thinking at the time?
- Were my thoughts, emotions and behaviours out of reactionary, habitual or conscious choice?

By regularly reflecting on your thoughts, emotions and behaviour, you can gradually build a picture of how you react and respond to different situations.

Reflexive Awareness

The continued practice of 'reflective awareness' often leads to the emergence of 'reflexive awareness', when you witness your thoughts, emotions and behaviour in the present moment. Reflexive awareness is often called 'mindfulness'. It is our 'witness consciousness' in action. By witnessing our thoughts, emotions and behaviours, we can observe our ego, in the present moment, as it does its work. This allows us to notice when it is feeling pain and the actions we take to defend it. We can observe how we try to support and boost our ego. By noticing all these, we have greater choice in how we respond to situations in our life. We can choose to continue to reinforce our ego, or we can choose to let it go. With awareness, we have a choice. Without awareness, we have no choice.

By continually practising reflexive awareness, you may develop what the British artist and writer Eugene Halliday (1911–1987) described as 'reflexive self-consciousness'.[2] Halliday believed that the goal and purpose of life are to grow towards an awareness of our true nature. This awareness is achieved by developing 'reflexive self-consciousness', which he described as a completely self-transparent consciousness continuously aware of its own presence and nature.

It can be useful to develop our witness consciousness before engaging in techniques to develop lines of consciousness such as cognition, emotion and behaviour, which are described later in this chapter. It is useful because the techniques used to develop lines of consciousness often require us to observe how we think, feel and act. Our development is accelerated and sustained through becoming consciously aware of our thoughts, emotions and behaviours, and ensuring they are appropriate for the situation we are facing.

PREPARATION - STATES OF CONSCIOUSNESS

As outlined in Chapter 6, we experience different states of consciousness every day, such as waking, sleeping and dreaming. You may have experienced an 'altered state of consciousness' brought on by alcohol, drugs (prescribed or not) or illness. We can also experience such a state without being intoxicated through using techniques such as meditation, prayer, dance, sensory deprivation, yoga, etc. It may also happen spontaneously when we are surrounded by nature, connecting with other people or just being with ourselves. Maslow called certain types of altered states of consciousness 'peak experiences'.[3] In 1964 he described these as being 'rare, exciting, oceanic, deeply moving, exhilarating, elevating experiences that generate an advanced form of perceiving reality and are even mystic and magical in their effect upon the experimenter'.

It is likely that we temporarily experience a higher stage of consciousness during some altered states of consciousness. These are short experiences of transcending our ego's constraints, which are associated with the post-conventional stages of development. However, once the experience is over, we tend to interpret and understand it from our current development stage. Nonetheless, if regularly repeated, these short experiences can help pave the way for developing to the post-conventional stages of consciousness, levels of consciousness beyond consumerism. It is like repeatedly holidaying in the same foreign destination. At first, you may feel out of place. But the more you visit, the more comfortable you feel and, gradually, the foreign destination begins to feel like home. It is the same with using altered states of consciousness to access and experience the higher stages of consciousness development. The more we visit these higher states, the more comfortable we feel and the easier it will be to develop to the higher stages and live there permanently.

Coincidently, the altered states of consciousness, which research consistently finds to be associated with the development of the post-conventional stages, are typically gained through connecting with nature, each other and ourselves. All of these enable us to let go of our ego. It is difficult to have a big ego when experiencing the awe and wonder of the wilderness; our ego dissolves when we truly connect with another person and when we connect with our soul, the ego needs to get out of the way. Therefore, practising techniques that reconnect us with nature, each other and ourselves can pave the way to developing to the post-conventional stages of consciousness.

Having a strong connection to nature, each other and ourselves can also help us develop a strong, stable and secure ego as we progress through the conventional stages of consciousness. This allows us to grow while not being so susceptible to businesses conditioning us into becoming consumers. Consequently, connecting with nature, each other and ourselves can help accelerate our progress through all the stages, no matter our current development stage.

Connecting with Nature

Substantial research demonstrates that connecting with nature is good for our mental health (some of which was outlined in Chapter 4). Whether it be in gardens, parks or the wilderness, nature can help us relax, restore our energy, gain clarity of thought and induce peak experiences that transcend our ego. Here are some examples of connecting with nature at different levels:

> **Forest bathing:** As an antidote to the tech-boom burnout in the 1980s, the Japanese developed a type of eco-therapy called 'forest bathing' (shinrin-yoku). It simply involves taking in the forest atmosphere. You can do this by walking in nature, purposely connecting with what is around you with all your senses. Focus your attention on what you see, hear, smell, touch and taste. It is not always necessary to be active. Just by being in the natural world, nature can work its magic. People often find this a restorative practice that maintains and restores their psychological resources.
>
> **Learning from nature:** Biomimicry is an approach to innovation that seeks sustainable solutions to human challenges

by learning from nature's forms, processes and systems. The goal is to create products, processes and policies (new ways of living) that are well adapted to life on Earth over the long haul. Numerous products have been developed using biomimicry, such as the bullet train, designed from observing a kingfisher entering the water. Biomimicry involves learning from, rather than about, an aspect of nature in terms of its form (what it looks like), its processes (how it survives and grows) and its ecosystems (how it lives with other aspects of nature). Learning from nature in this way can help us solve problems as well as guide our own psychological development. The act of engaging with nature in this way can bring us back to a closer connection with nature.

Listening to nature's wisdom: If you are really quiet, you can hear nature talking to you. You might think this utter nonsense! This is the reaction I often get when I ask people to listen to nature. However, once they have tried it, they realise it actually works. How and why is beyond our comprehension, but it does work. By being really quiet, I am referring to the constant chatter in our minds. It can take many hours of sitting in nature to quieten the mind. To hear nature's wisdom, all you need do is to go into nature and sit quietly. When the time is right, ask nature a question, one that you cannot easily answer. Then just sit, quietening your mind, and wait for the answer. It can take many hours. In my experience, when business leaders do this, they are often amazed nature can give them a solution to a problem they have been struggling with for a long time. So how does it work? Does nature really speak to us? Asking this question assumes we are separate to nature. If we assume that we are an intrinsic part of nature, then it does not matter if the answer comes from our intuition or nature. If we are all connected through our collective unconscious, then our intuition and nature's voice are the same. Believe whatever makes sense to you.

Peaking in the wilderness: According to Maslow, peak experiences are revelations or mystical illuminations that are generally short and involve both emotion and cognition. They are moments of highest happiness and fulfilment and generally carry some important meaning or insight. Research shows that peak experiences can be triggered by the awe and wonder experienced when in uninhabited natural areas or wilderness. If planning such a venture into the wilder side of nature, it is important to be properly prepared, guided and equipped.

Although each of these practices will take you to an ever-deeper connection with nature and increase the likelihood of having a peak experience, they will all give you some degree of an altered state of consciousness associated with letting go of your ego. They will all also be restorative in that they are the antidote to 'nature deficit disorder'. Consequently, they will all increase your mental health and reduce your susceptibility to your consciousness being industrialised and your ego being conditioned to be a consumer.

Connecting with Each Other

If when you are talking someone disagrees with you, what do you do? Most people will try to defend their point of view. If the other person does the same, a debate or argument will ensue. In this way, we compete because winning is an important way of defending our ego. Losing an argument reduces our self-esteem and is a threat to our ego. Debating and arguing can become all about the ego rather than finding the truth or creating something new.

The American quantum physicist David Bohm (1917–1992) recognised our tendency to argue and saw it as detrimental to science. He sought to understand the nature of reality as a coherent whole, which is never static or complete but continually unfolding. He felt conversations should be allowed to unfold continually. This way, something new can be created, rather than each person advocating what they already know. To enable this, he developed an approach called Bohm Dialogue.[4]

Bohm Dialogue is a free-flowing conversation within a group where each person gives voice to what is emerging from the group rather than speaking for themselves. It draws on the group's collective intelligence and allows new insights and meaning to unfold in the middle. Participants do not speak to each other but for the group and to the group. By practising this type of dialogue, people experience letting go of their ego and connecting with other people. However, it is not easy. We are so conditioned to speak for ourselves and argue or debate. So, when we enter into dialogue, we easily fall back into old habits.

To guide people, Bohm created parameters such as having no agenda or topic of conversation at the start, allowing this to unfold naturally. Some practitioners strictly adhere to Bohm's parameters, while others have allowed their own practice to unfold and evolve naturally.

When I engage a group in dialogue, I find it useful to give them some guiding principles. Without this, people often resort back to debating and arguing. The guiding principles I use are:

Non-judgemental listening: Being non-judgemental requires suspending certainty and recognising everything is continually unfolding. When we are certain about something, this fixes it in time and space without having the freedom to change and continually unfold. Listening involves us attending to both our inner and outer worlds. Judging our own thoughts and emotions fixes them just as much as when we judge others' ideas, views and insights.

Holographic participation: We experience what is happening to us in our consciousness. Therefore, while we are in the universe, the universe is in us. Consequently, dialogue enables the mutual unfolding of the universe. It can enable the whole to become manifest rather than fragments that attract our individual attention. As a result, dialogue can organise the processes that shape our collective future.

Unfolding thinking: We often confuse thinking with thoughts. Thoughts often come from our memory, while thinking creates something new. A new thought is the product of thinking. To think is to sense the emerging future and to let it unfold within us. Therefore, to think together is to co-create the future.

Voicing: This is not giving voice to our ego. Instead, it is sensing the potential future, which is starting to emerge in us. To perceive this potential and let it unfold within us, we need to let go of our ego. Our self-image and the need to maintain our self-esteem often distorts or constrains this potential.

Using these principles in dialogue will allow you to access a state of consciousness that connects you to other people and helps you let go of your ego.

Connecting with Self

The Self is the core of our being, not conditioned by our experiences, and it does not need defending. It is often referred to as the 'higher Self' or 'soul' and is the gateway to 'non-dualism' where the distinction between subject and object disappears. Everything becomes connected as one unifying whole. In this way, our Self can connect us to our spirituality.

Although it takes years of spiritual practice to identify more with our Self than our ego, we can experience our Self in operation. One way we can do this is to imagine we are getting a lifetime achievement award and, at the ceremony, the person giving the award is giving a speech about all we have achieved in our life. What would you like the speech to contain?

When writing this speech, it would be easy to write it from your ego. However, to connect with your Self, this speech needs to be written by your Self, which can be done in several ways, but it takes time. Here are some techniques you can try:

Sleep on it: Start writing your speech one day, but do not complete it. Instead, sleep on it and finish your speech the next day. Sleep will give space for your intuition to work. As your intuition is located in your higher unconscious it is more connected to your Self than your ego.

Interpret your dreams: As you 'sleep on your speech' keep a paper pad and your pencil next to your bed. Immediately when you wake in the morning, write down what you remember from your dreams. Writing down your memories has to be done immediately as we frequently forget our dreams within minutes of waking. Later in the day, review what you have written about your dreams and try to interpret it in terms of your speech. Remember, do not take your dreams literally; our dreams speak to us through symbols and metaphors. Carl Jung is quoted as saying: 'The dream is a little hidden door in the innermost and most secret recesses of the soul, opening into that cosmic night which was psyche long before there was any ego-consciousness, and which will remain psyche no matter how far our ego-consciousness extends.'[5]

Meditate: Meditation can quieten the chattering mind and give space for the soul to speak through our intuition. Just sit comfortably, but in an upright posture, so you do not fall asleep. Then spend some time just relaxing and quietening your mind by focusing your attention on your breathing. When you are ready, bring your attention to your thoughts. Just notice them and let them go. Imagine they are clouds floating across the sky. They come and they go without you getting attached to them. Gradually, your thoughts from your ego will quieten down, giving space for your Self to speak as thoughts through your intuition. Try not to analyse your thoughts; just write them down after your meditation session and put them to one side. Later in the day, review what you have written and try to interpret it in terms of your speech.

By writing your award speech from your Self rather than your ego, you will get a greater sense of what gives your life meaning and purpose. Practising these techniques regularly will help you access to a state of consciousness that has a greater connection with your Self than you would have ordinarily.

By experiencing states of consciousness brought on by connecting with nature, each other and ourselves, you will not only prepare yourself for developing to higher stages of consciousness, but you will also repair some of the damage done to your mind by the industrialisation process. Experiencing these states of consciousness will help to make you less susceptible to consumerism.

PREPARATION - LINES OF CONSCIOUSNESS

In Chapter 6, we saw how lines of consciousness are generally different aspects of our psychology, such as cognition, emotion, personality, values, motives etc. All of these can develop at different rates throughout our lives. As they develop, our psychological capability becomes more complex. This development enables us to expand our consciousness and download the programming from a higher level of collective consciousness. Also, by developing our lines of consciousness, we can prepare ourselves to face more complex challenges in our lives. In all these ways, developing our lines of consciousness will help prepare us to develop to our next stage of consciousness. In this section, we will focus on purposefully developing three critical lines of consciousness. These are how we think (cognition), feel (emotion) and act (behaviour).

Thinking (Cognition)

As we develop, the complexity of our thinking process needs to align with the increasing complexity of the challenges we are facing. Psychologists have identified several stages in the complexity of our thinking (see Table 8.1).

As we develop our cognition, the complexity of our thinking processes increases, allowing us to deal with more complex situations and problems. The Canadian psychoanalyst, social scientist and management consultant Elliott Jaques (1917–2003) found that people who do not deal well with uncertain and complex issues tend to think using declarative, cumulative or linear ways of processing information.[6] They prefer to draw more on rational analysis and their prior learning. In doing so, they are drawing on what the psychologist Raymond Cattell (1905–1998) called ‘crystallised intelligence’. In contrast, people who cope well with uncertain and complex issues are good at conceptual and abstract thinking, along with systems and parallel processing. They also tend to draw more on their intuitive insights and creativity. In doing so, they are drawing on what Cattell referred to as ‘fluid intelligence’.[7] This gives people the ability to solve novel problems where prior learning will not find a solution.

Fluid intelligence is also known as cognitive flexibility. It is essentially the ability to think about multiple concepts or solutions simultaneously by switching between them. This flexibility allows us to adjust our thinking or attention in response to changing goals and situations. To do this, we have to overcome our habitual beliefs, perceptions, ways of thinking and reactions. At the highest levels of cognitive flexibility, we can perceive new meanings and gain new insights that emerge from chaos and complexity.

Table 8.1 Stages in the Development of Cognition

Seven Stages of Consciousness Development	Stages in the Development of Cognition
Stages 1–3	▪ Declarative processing – concentrating on one task or unit of information ▪ Cumulative processing – gathering together units of information ▪ Linear processing – using cause-and-effect logic
Stage 4	▪ Systems processing – working with multiple relationships between multiple components
Stages 5–7	▪ Parallel processing – working with multiple systems all at the same time ▪ Emergent processing – tuning into the dynamic patterns that emerge from chaos

A good metaphor for cognitive flexibility is a television. Imagine each channel is a 'stream of thought' representing different beliefs, knowledge, understanding and habitual ways of thinking. Now imagine your mind is the television and you are stuck on one channel. In this situation, your cognition is inflexible, and your stream of thought cannot be updated or altered. Next imagine you possess a remote control and can rapidly change between channels. Changing channels opens you up to a wide range of 'streams of thought'. You can now see issues from a range of perspectives, gain new insights and understanding, consider paradoxical views without conflict and develop different ways of thinking. With the controller, you can access your cognitive flexibility.

If we are to create and implement a new economic system in an increasingly complex society, we need a critical mass of people who have the complexity in their thinking processes to match the complexity in our society.

Feeling (Emotion)

As we tend to be on the receiving end of our emotions, I appreciate it is a bit of a leap to believe we can develop them in the same way as we develop our cognition. I am talking about developing how we manage our emotions and manage the emotional content of relationships. As the complexity of the challenges we face increases, so too must our ability to manage emotions. Just as with cognition, the development of our ability to manage our emotions also goes in stages (see Table 8.2).

Table 8.2 *Stages in the Development of Emotion*

Seven Stages of Consciousness Development	Stages in the Development of Emotion
Stages 1–3	▪ Self-awareness – becoming aware of, and being able to label our own emotions ▪ Compassion – being aware of the emotional impact we have on ourselves and other people, and taking action to ease our own and others' suffering
Stage 4	▪ Emotional intelligence – working with the two-way interactions of the emotional content in relationships
Stages 5–7	▪ Moral reasoning – being aware of the emotional impact we have on other people across time and distance, and taking action to ease their suffering

As we develop our emotional line of consciousness, the range of our ability to manage emotional content gradually increases. In the early stages of development, we learn how to recognise our own emotions. This self-awareness often depends on emotional literacy. We need to be able to name the emotion so we can recognise and manage it. Managing our emotions is important for our cognitive functioning. We tend to believe we are rational beings able to make rational decisions and much economic theory has been built on this belief. Unfortunately, we are not as rational as we think we are.

In economic theory, the rational human is called 'homo economicus'. In *Principles of Macroeconomics*, Libby Rittenberg and Timothy Tregarthen define homo economicus (economic man) as being wholly concerned with maximising utility as a consumer and profit as a producer.[8] Homo economicus is then a rational person who pursues wealth for their own self-interest. The assumption that all humans make financial decisions in this way has been a fundamental premise for most economic theories. But does homo economicus really exist? Psychologist and economist Daniel Kahneman, and his long-term collaborator Amos Tversky, studied the effects of psychological, cognitive, emotional, cultural and social factors on the economic decisions of individuals and institutions.[9] Kahneman and Tversky found that even though we think our financial decisions are rational and designed to maximise the return, they are full of biases. It appears Homo economicus is a myth.

If you are to develop your cognitive consciousness, you must also develop your emotional consciousness. Otherwise, what you believe to be a rational decision may be emotionally driven without you knowing, especially when stressed or threatened. American author and science journalist Daniel Goleman calls this the 'amygdala hijack', or emotional hijacking.[10] The amygdala is an important structure within the limbic system, where our emotions are processed. When our flight or fight response is triggered, our brain's cognitive parts start shutting down, giving space for the amygdala to take over. With the amygdala in charge, it is extremely difficult to think clearly and make rational decisions. By developing your ability to recognise and manage your emotions, you will have a greater ability to use your developing cognitive processes.

With the ability to recognise and manage our own emotions, we can begin to recognise the emotions other people are experiencing, allowing us to be aware of the emotional impact we have on other people. With this awareness, we can take action to manage this impact. Emotional awareness and the flexibility of response are the foundations of emotional intelligence.

Emotional intelligence is essentially being aware of and understanding our own emotions when interacting with others, and being aware of and understanding other people's emotions. Emotional intelligence is extending our emotional self-awareness to include the awareness of other people's thoughts, decisions and behaviour based on their emotional responses. This awareness enables us to self-regulate our thinking, decisions and behaviour to build sustainable relationships based on understanding and trust rather than simple short-term transactions. Emotional intelligence works like a figure of eight on its side (see Figure 8.1).

Figure 8.1 Emotional Intelligence Figure of Eight

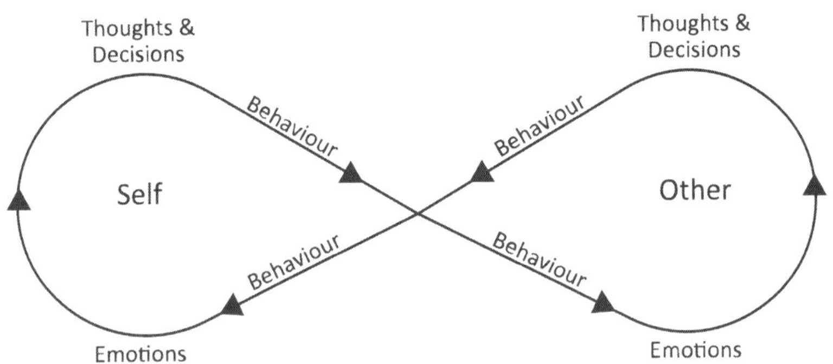

Once we develop to post-conventional stages, emotional intelligence extends to include people across time and space. This extension of emotional intelligence is often called moral reasoning. We use it when we make decisions that impact people we never meet, i.e. in different countries or future generations. The environmental, community and mental health crises we face today result from a lack of moral reasoning in society. People unknown to us are impacted by the decisions we make and how we live our lives. These include the products we buy, how we travel, the work we do, where we take our holidays and where we invest our money. Do you consider future generations when making these decisions? Most people simply consider the impact on themselves and those close to them.

To create and implement a sustainable future in terms of the environment, community and mental well-being, we need to develop moral reasoning in a critical mass of people.

Acting (Behaviour)

Our behaviour is a representation of our personality (habitual behaviours), values, motives, beliefs, defences, thoughts, emotions, etc. We can purposely develop our behaviour through three stages (see Table 8.3).

In the early days of our psychological development as adults, we experiment with a few different ways of behaving. Herminia Ibarra from INSEAD (Institut Européen d'Administration des Affaires) has described this process as experimenting with 'provisional selves' while a person forms a self-identity that feels authentic.[11] This can be likened to trying several pairs of shoes to find the most comfortable. We do this by observing people we admire and imitating their behaviour. This process enables us to fit within society and our community and is how we become socially and culturally conditioned. Each of the provisional selves is still us; we are not 'faking' our behaviour. It is simply who we are being at a particular stage in the process of becoming. By experimenting with provisional selves, we discover more about ourselves and who we want to be.

Table 8.3 Stages in the Development of Behaviour

Seven Stages of Consciousness Development	Stages in the Development of Behaviour
Stages 1–3	▪ Imitation – we observe role models, copy their behaviour, and learn how to assert ourselves in the world as part of our social and cultural conditioning
Stage 4	▪ Authenticity – we adapt what we have learned from other people and align with our own self-identity
Stages 5–7	▪ Agility – we become aware of and transcend the constraints of our self-image

Gradually, through experimentation, we find a self-identity that feels right. This alignment happens when one of the provisional selves best aligns with our personality's genetic aspects and how we have been conditioned during our childhood. At this point, we develop a high level of clarity in our self-identity, centred on a stable sense of self-knowledge and strongly held values and beliefs. At this stage, we feel our most authentic.

It is also the stage in our development when our ego is fully formed. It is when our self-identity and our ego become fused together. Consequently, when our ego feels threatened, our self-identity feels threatened. Therefore, to maintain our self-esteem, we need to defend our ego. With a high level of self-esteem, we feel confident enough to behave in accordance with what we believe to be our 'true self'.

Who is your true self? Philosophers have debated this for centuries, and the question now concerns psychologists. There is little consensus. A working definition is 'when behaviour is congruent with beliefs, values and personality'. Therefore, the first step in developing this sense of being true to ourselves is to gain greater awareness of our beliefs, values and personality.

> **Beliefs:** A belief is an opinion or conviction that something is true but which we have not proven. We understand the world through our beliefs, which are often unconscious assumptions. This understanding may not be perfect, but it is a pragmatic way of living.
>
> **Values:** Our personal values are how we operationalise our beliefs. Values provide us with an internal reference point for our decisions and actions. They are what we see as good, meaningful, beneficial, important, useful, beautiful, etc.
>
> **Personality:** Our personality is the characteristic patterns of thoughts, feelings and behaviours that make us unique. In many ways, our personality is the summation of our habits.

Clearly, all of these combine in a complex structure to form part of our own unique self-identity.

Even though we may be comfortable with our self-identity for years, providing us with a high level of self-esteem, there may come a time when we begin to feel constrained. Often, this feeling is brought on when facing increasing levels of VUCA (volatility, uncertainty, complexity and ambiguity). We find our habitual behaviours are too rigid and need greater agility. We become constrained by our own authenticity. In this situation, there are three choices: become increasingly defensive, behave inauthentically or behave with greater agility and contact a deeper place of authenticity.

We behave in different ways according to the various roles we play in life and our relationships. These are what Assagioli called 'sub-personalities'.[12] The realisation that we are made up of multi-personalities is unsettling and can produce high levels of anxiety. In her book *Developmental Coaching: Working with the Self*, Tatiana Bachkirova describes these personalities as mini-selves.[13] We develop a range of mini-selves as we successfully deal with different or complex situations throughout our life.

To access and deploy 'mini-selves' we need to let go of what we consider to be our authentic self-identity. Initially, we feel inauthentic but gradually find authenticity in a deeper place, in our values, which are strongly related to purpose and meaning in our lives. This deeper level of authenticity is associated less with ego and more with soul. As we let go of our self-identity, we have less need to defend ourselves, and our ego quietens. We have more psychological space to include and collaborate with other people.

At this stage, we can view ourselves, the situation and society simultaneously from an external perspective with an unbiased view, and can hold contradictory views without conflict. This capability enables us to resolve a paradox by creating something new. These qualities are vital for the creation and implementation of a sustainable future.

DEVELOPMENTAL CHALLENGES

Each stage in the 'Seven Stages of Consciousness Development' is a unified 'stage of consciousness' different in quality and nature to the other stages. Each is a new way of perceiving, experiencing and understanding the world. Within each stage, the qualities of the previous stages are embedded; nothing is lost. Instead, as we develop up the stages, we gain greater capability and psychological agility. We start to transition to our next stage when the world contradicts our understanding, and we are no longer able to 'make meaning' that is coherent. Following on from this experience, a new level of mental complexity emerges, which allows us to create our world in a meaningful way once again. We only fully inhabit this new stage of consciousness once we have changed how we perceive, experience and understand the world.

To develop to our next stage of consciousness, we must face a challenge where our existing way of perceiving, experiencing and understanding the world will not provide a solution. After a period of anxiety, we find a new way to perceive, experience and understand the world. However, our development depends on facing the right challenge, suitable for our stage of development, being well prepared and receiving the right type of support. Without the right preparation and support, it is like being thrown into the deep end of a swimming pool. We either sink or learn to swim.

Table 8.4 Appropriate Development Challenges

Transition to Stage	Appropriate Developmental Challenges
3	▪ Working in a team ▪ Taking a role that involves supervising other people ▪ Developing an area of expertise needed for the future
4	▪ Being responsible for the performance of a team ▪ Leading an organisational improvement project ▪ Launching something new
5–7	▪ Leading an area of the organisation where you have no previous experience ▪ Leading an organisation-wide change initiative ▪ Leading a project, initiative or organisation with global reach

The right challenge is essential for progress. One aligned with how we already view the world will not deliver any development. A challenge too far beyond our current stage of development will cause too much stress and force us to rely on existing skills and strengths. Here again, no development occurs. Table 8.4 provides some examples of the types of challenges suitable for transitioning to each stage of development. Inevitably, most challenges we face come from our working lives. Yet, this need not be in a business or paid work. We can find suitable challenging opportunities through volunteering or working in community organisations.

To determine which type of challenge is most appropriate for you, it is useful to consider the level of cognitive complexity inherent in the challenge. To develop to stage 3, the challenge should involve problems that can be resolved through linear, cause-and-effect thinking, i.e. A + B = C. To develop to stage 4, the challenge should involve problems that need to be resolved through systems thinking, where there are multiple components to the problem that all interact with each other. To develop to the post-conventional stages (5–7), the challenge should involve problems that need to be resolved through parallel processing. This is when multiple systems contribute to the problem and interact with each other, collide and create chaos. Solving these problems will require seeing patterns emerging from chaos. Even with the cognitive flexibility to work with chaos, you need to recognise there is not always a clear answer and adapt your behaviour to meet the demands of the situation with great agility.

When we step back and look at society's problems, we see that we are facing a chaotic challenge. Ecological, economic, political and psychological systems are colliding. Challenges such as climate change, mass extinction, inequality, mental illness and epidemics are interrelated. To face this challenge requires people able to handle this level of complexity.

SUPPORT

One-to-One

If we face the right developmental challenge, appropriate for our stage of development, we are likely to experience a significant level of anxiety before a new way of understanding of the world emerges. Although we may be well prepared to face the challenge, we still need to ensure we are being supported through the transition period. The level of support must match the level of challenge. Too much support and not enough challenge will create boredom. With too little support and too much challenge, we will get overly stressed. The balance of challenge and support is different for everyone, but the best advice is to work with a mentor, coach, counsellor or psychotherapist. Table 8.5 outlines the focus of support for each stage.

Table 8.5 Focus of Support

Transition to Stage	Focus of Support
2	Connecting e.g. teamwork and influencing
3	Problem solving e.g. interpersonal conflict, developing expertise
4	Performing e.g. leading a team, delivering objectives, identifying and leveraging strengths
5	Letting go e.g. dealing with ambiguity, gaining agility, facilitating agreement
6	Transcending e.g. anchoring authenticity in values, dropping the ego, holding paradoxical views
7	Transpersonal e.g. universal values, spiritual development

When making the transition to the post-conventional stages, we are best served by working with someone who can support us in letting go of our need for certainty and helping us transcend the constraints of our ego-attached identity. During this transition, we are likely to experience the loss of our sense of self, so we must work with someone who can hold us at our learning edge and reassure us that this is a natural part of adult development.

Group

Alongside one-to-one support, it can be beneficial to take part in an Action Inquiry Group. This process, developed by Bill Torbert, has been designed specifically to enable people to develop higher levels of consciousness.[14] An Action Inquiry Group consists of participants who share a common concern for developing their consciousness to a certain stage. A typical group will consist of between six and twelve participants engaging in cycles of action and reflection. In the action phases, participants experiment with new ways of thinking, feeling and behaving. In the reflection phases, they reflect on their experience critically, learn from their successes and failures, and develop new perspectives that inform their experiments in the next action phase. Action Inquiry Groups go through several cycles, meeting monthly during their lifetime.

SUMMARY AND CONCLUSION

You may have the impression that I think the ego is bad and the Self (soul) is good, and the conventional stages of development are bad and post-conventional stages good. They are simply different aspects of the same phenomena, like caterpillars and butterflies or valleys and mountains. Each aspect is critical for our growth and healthy functioning. Together the ego and the Self (soul) make us whole.

The problem with our ego is that it has become too industrialised and supports our unsustainable economic system. This industrialisation has resulted in our psychological growth becoming constrained or halted. Our consciousness supports the economy, and the economy conditions our consciousness. We are trapped in a vicious cycle.

In this chapter, I have argued there are two ways out. One is to ensure, as we grow, we develop a healthy, secure and stable ego, resistant to being conditioned by consumerism. To do this, we need to prevent our ego from being industrialised or repair the damage industrialisation does to the ego. I have suggested this can be achieved by reconnecting with nature, each other and ourselves. The second is to accelerate our consciousness development through the conventional stages, so more people reach the post-conventional stages at an earlier age. This acceleration would ensure we have sufficient people letting go of their ego and developing the consciousness required to cope with the increasing VUCA in our lives and to be able to create a new, more sustainable economic system.

Accelerating the development of our consciousness requires us to increase our psychological capability so that we can access the higher levels of consciousness already within us and download the programming from a higher level of collective consciousness. As explored in Chapter 6, there is a view that we are all connected by a sea of collective unconsciousness, and our individual unconscious is pulled out of this sea, like a wave, by our soul. By developing our psychological capability up the stages, we can access more of this unconsciousness and make it conscious. We literally expand our consciousness (see Figure 8.2). Developing our psychological capability also allows us to perceive and understand higher levels of complexity in our environment. As a result, our consciousness can be programmed by new emerging higher levels of collective consciousness.

Figure 8.2 Alignment of the Development of Individual and Collective Consciousness

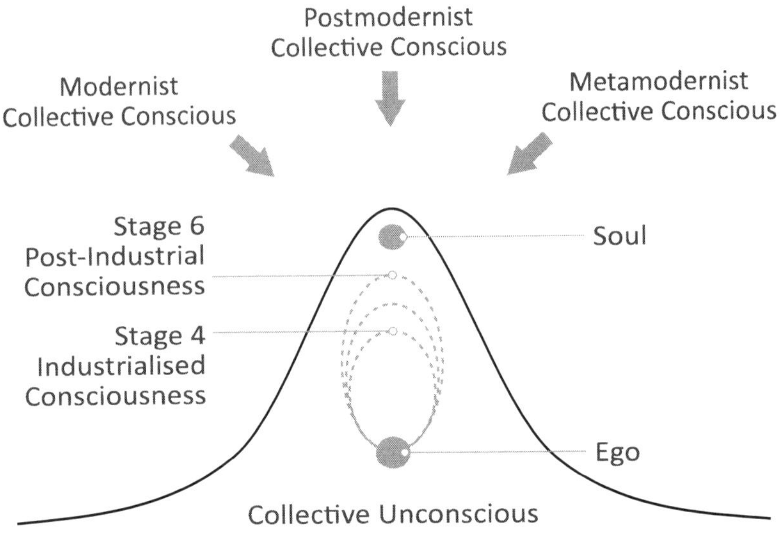

In the past, the height of adult psychological maturity was stage 4. This is the stage where we are most at risk of being conditioned to be consumers. In the future, through natural evolution, the height of adult maturity will be stage 6 or 7, which is the level of consciousness beyond consumerism. It is the stage a critical mass of people needs to reach if we are to create a new economic system that will solve the problems facing society. How long will this take? There is little progress currently. The PwC survey I referred to in Chapter 7 did not find any business leaders at stage 7 and only 8% had developed to stage 6 in 2015.[15] The majority still functioned at stage 4 (52%) in their consciousness development. It appears the evolution of our consciousness is stuck.

In this chapter, I have outlined the processes required to accelerate the development of our individual consciousness. This acceleration can be achieved by facing developmental challenges aligned with the next stage. We need to prepare our psychology for these challenges to develop our consciousness and be supported during the transition. I have provided some guidance on the necessary preparation, challenge and support for each stage. By actively engaging in these processes, we can accelerate our development. However, embarking on this task in isolation is unlikely to create sufficient mass. In the next chapter, I will explore how different aspects of our society could encourage more collective action.

CHAPTER 9

CREATING CHANGE

Could the people of Halkeld develop the type of collective consciousness which creates three-headed dragons? It's possible, thought Sophia. While it was a possibility, her town was in danger. She needed to return to her own town to pass on her knowledge and to help others develop the state of consciousness that tames three-headed dragons. But how could she return now having been on such a journey? How could she return to her old life in a town where nothing happens as regularly as clockwork? She no longer belonged there; she would be seen as mad or arrogant if she even began to explain how she had faced challenges and developed a state of consciousness which tames dragons. Sophia decided not to go back, but instead, she would roam far-off lands, developing her consciousness further and fighting more dragons. This way, she would serve the whole of humanity.

As she walked away from the great river towards whatever new adventure lay ahead, she heard a familiar voice in her ear.

'Go home, Sophia, go home.' She ignored the voice.

'Go home; your work is not complete, go home.' Still, she continued to walk.

'Go home, your town is in danger; you must return,' the voice repeated over and over.

Unable to bear it any longer she turned and headed for home cursing the voice in her head. At the market, the familiar vendors offered their wares, but Sophia took no notice. She had no desire to buy anything, even if she had any money.

'If you have no money, I can arrange some credit,' called one trader, but Sophia carried on walking.

Reaching the junction of the three paths, Sophia needed to decide which one to take, the Way of Nature, the Way of People, or the Way of Self. She wondered why the path in the mist was called the Way of Self and decided to take it.

This time the mist evaporated, and as she once more climbed the mountain, the land unfolded in front of her eyes. The higher she went, the more she could see. In the distance, the market was as busy as ever and the people appeared miserable. On the other paths, people were still racing, and others were tearing up nature and feeding the monstrous machine for products. From her vantage point, all their effort seemed futile. Nothing helped them progress along their chosen path. They were all fully occupied but not achieving much. She wondered if she should venture back down and try to help them. As that thought entered her mind, she spotted what looked to be another dragon on the horizon.

She heard Mimir, 'Your town is in danger, you must help them.'

She abandoned any thought of helping those on the paths. She wasn't sure how she could have helped the racers and the destroyers of nature. There was still the danger she'd get sucked back into their world and never escape. As she reached the mountain peak, Sophia glanced back a final time and could just make out the Green Man busy regenerating nature. Plants and seeds were pouring from his mouth.

As she descended, Sophia could see the great river in front of her and her town on the horizon. At the river, she found the ferryman.

'You're in luck,' he remarked.

'Why's that?' Sophia asked.

'This morning the river was all a torrent, then all of a sudden it went calm. Never seen anything like it. Still, I can get back to work ferrying good people like yourself back and forth.'

Halfway across the river, Sophia remembered she had no money. When she explained, the ferryman replied 'Don't worry, let this be my gift to you. I'm sure you've given gifts to people. When you give someone a gift, it always has a way of finding its way back. That's the way the universe balances itself. I think they call it karma.'

Passing through the gates of Halkeld, Sophia saw that everything was just as normal. People greeted her as if she'd never been away. But they didn't know, only her mother and father knew she'd gone. Nothing had changed; it really was as dull and as boring as when she left.

'So, you're back from chasing dragons then?' her father greeted her as she entered the little tailor's shop. 'I told you not to bother. I hear it vanished. Waste of time that was then. Best see your mother then get on with your work.'

'Best had,' Sophia replied, as she pricked her finger with a pin. I'm definitely back, she thought.

INTRODUCTION

> 'From now on I am thinking only of me.'
> Major Danby replied indulgently with a superior smile:
> 'But, Yossarian, suppose everyone felt that way.'
> 'Then,' said Yossarian, 'I would certainly be a damned fool to feel any other way, wouldn't I?'
>
> Joseph Heller, Catch-22

If everyone is anthropocentric, competitive, individualistic and defensive of their ego, would you be a damned fool to be any other way? Of course, I am making a sweeping generalisation. Nevertheless, the evidence I have presented in this book suggests that most people are anthropocentric, competitive, individualistic and defensive of their ego due to the industrialisation of our consciousness. So, what happens to people who are not? People who deviate away from the norm of consciousness tend to be ostracised by the mainstream. History has demonstrated that those who differ from the norm can step forward and lead people through a significant transition. Examples include Mahatma Gandhi, Nelson Mandela, Abraham Lincoln and Martin Luther King Jr. Today's examples include Greta Thunberg and Malala Yousafzai. It can be dangerous being the leader of societal change; many of these people have been imprisoned, shot or both!

If society is going to evolve the higher level of consciousness needed to create, implement and sustain a new, more sustainable economic system, we need leaders who can create catalysts in all aspects of society that will stimulate this evolution. These aspects of society include education, business and politics. This chapter will explore some of the changes that are already taking place. Leading these changes will require people who have not had their minds industrialised or have developed to the post-conventional stages of consciousness, a consciousness beyond consumerism. While they may initially be ignored or ostracised, with a critical mass of people leading these changes, a higher level of collective consciousness will evolve, and a new, more sustainable, economic system will be created. This new economic system, in turn, will reinforce the new level of individual consciousness.

If you are able to join groups in education, business and politics who are leading the changes that will engender consciousness beyond consumerism, you will be exposing yourself to a level of collective consciousness that will facilitate the development of your individual consciousness. However, there is a warning. As a result of the damage being done to our environment, communities and psychology, you may be opposed to business, industry, science or modernism. You may then join groups that share this opposition. As a critique of modernism, these groups tend to be postmodernist in nature. While the collective consciousness of the group is likely to facilitate the growth of your individual consciousness beyond consumerism, you may become stuck at a stage associated with postmodernism (stage 5). You will recall from Chapter 5 that postmodernism leads to fragmentation of society into tribes and a rise in identity politics. Although postmodernist groups have done fantastic work raising awareness of issues, they struggle to find ways to create societal change. Opposition often creates an equal and opposite reaction, which leads to a stalemate. While we are facing multiple existential threats, we are busy arguing amongst ourselves.

The collective consciousness associated with metamodernism (stage 6 of individual consciousness) offers an alternative approach. At this stage of consciousness development, you will be able to see the truth in both the modernist and postmodernist perspectives. While these truths may be contradictory, you will be able to hold both without contradiction. You may then be able to transcend both truths to create something new. If we are to create a new, more sustainable economic system before it is too late, we need a critical mass of people who have developed to stage 6. Their combined work will then increase the metamodernist collective consciousness that is now emerging in our society.

CHILD EDUCATION

I have two daughters. When they first started school, I was surprised they were given homework at such a young age. Helping them, I realised the homework consisted of worksheets similar to test papers. It dawned on me: my children were not being educated; they were being trained to pass tests. What was being done to inspire their love of learning? How were they being taught to learn? What about their creativity and emotional development? These questions began to concern my wife and me so much we decided to raise these issues at their parents' evening. You may be familiar with the format; you have 5–10 min with the teacher who quickly runs through the data in terms of how your child is progressing with their reading, writing and arithmetic. When the teacher had finished, I asked, 'How is our daughter developing emotionally?' A look of shock flashed across her face. I tried to help out by rephrasing; I asked, 'How is her social development progressing?' Clearly, I had asked something she had not anticipated. This response shocked me; obviously, no one else had asked this basic question.

Our children enjoyed being educated in the State system. They loved completing test papers and trying to be top of the class. Yet, we increasingly noticed their upset when they did not come first. At such a young age, they were becoming highly competitive, which the school encouraged. When I look back, I realise our children's minds were being industrialised, conditioned to serve the State's purpose, i.e. to serve industry and compete with each other.

The teachers were not at fault; they were under the direction of the government. This experience was over 20 years ago and things have changed since. However, for decades, our education system's focus has been on passing tests/exams in English, mathematics and science. It is believed this will make the country competitive in the global markets. To raise standards, the government introduced league tables where schools compete based on the pupils' results. Since 2000, when the Organisation for Economic Co-operation and Development (OECD) introduced league tables called the Programme for International Student Assessment (PISA) this competition has been global.[1] Students from different countries compete in standardised tests in mathematics, reading and science. In 2018, 94 countries/regions took part, and since it was launched, more than three million students have sat the tests. Governments see the results of their country's performance in the PISA tests as an indicator of their economy's future competitiveness. Forget about the arms race; it is now an education race!

To increase their performance in the PISA tests and hence the competitiveness of their economy, governments increasingly standardise and govern the education provided in schools by setting the curriculum. Literacy, maths and science are the top priority, followed by the humanities (such as history, geography and social studies), and, if there is time, the creative subjects (such as art, drama, music and crafts) can be taught. Sport has increasingly become the domain of after-school clubs. Although this prioritisation may help countries perform well in the PISA league tables, is it providing young people with the skills businesses need today? Sir Ken Robinson (1950–2020), British author, speaker and international advisor on education, argued that our current educational systems were set up to feed the Industrial Revolution and are no longer fit for purpose.[2] He found businesses increasingly complained their employees lacked the creativity and ability to adapt to change required in today's workplace. This lack of creativity and adaptability is perhaps why, in 2022, the PISA intends to include a new creative thinking test. Robinson also argued that our education system still employs the Industrial Revolution processes such as conformity, rejection of non-compliance and linear processing. During the Industrial Revolution, society valued machines and created education in the image of a machine. This metaphor still stands today. Mainstream education provided by the State processes children on a production line, rejecting those who do not come up to standard at various intervals and then spits out those who conform at the end.

Even though the introduction of creative thinking into the tests, and hopefully, the curriculum, is welcomed, where is the space for teachers to focus on each child's psychological development? It is our psychological development during childhood that will lay the foundation for our development as adults. Having our minds industrialised so young does not bode well for our ego's healthy formation in later life. This may be a contributing factor in the epidemic of mental illness we see in children worldwide.

Yet, I know teachers are taught child developmental psychology as part of their training. By drawing on Jean Piaget's (1896–1980) theory of cognitive development, they learn how children develop and grow; the work of Jerome Bruner (1915–2016) shows them how they can provide the scaffolding needed for a child to develop to their next stage; Lev Vygotsky's (1896–1934) Zone of Proximal Development can be used to determine the level of support needed to facilitate their psychological development. These, and many more, equip teachers to guide children through their psychological development to become healthy adults with secure egos. By governments taking control of the curriculum and focusing on testing and competition, there is no space for teachers to work with each child's unique needs, interests and talents, and facilitate their psychological development.

Some governments are loosening their grip on education. There are now free schools and academies that do not have to follow the UK's national curriculum. Nonetheless, these schools still have to abide by the government's testing regime, undergo inspections and have their results published in league tables. In Finland, all schools are required to follow a broad and balanced curriculum. However, there are no set texts or tests. Instead, the teachers are highly qualified, highly paid and highly trusted. They are given a high level of freedom in the classroom to decide what is right for their students. Rather than competition in league tables, there is a high level of collaboration between schools. This collaboration allows them to try the latest experimental techniques, draw on the latest research and share their experiences.

By losing the straight jacket imposed on teachers and students, it is possible to draw on alternative methods of education. Many of these alternatives tend to focus less on competition and more on collaboration; they take a holistic approach to teaching the child allowing the development of their mind, heart and spirit; and they are increasingly connecting children with nature. Here are some examples:

Forest Schools: Forest Schools have their roots in the 'free air life' (friluftliv) in Scandinavia. These are not necessarily physical places but can be regular outdoor learning sessions in any school. Yet, it is not just being outside that makes Forest Schools different. Practitioners take a supportive, child-centred and non-judgemental approach allowing children to try things out for themselves and take risks. In doing so, they seek to develop the children socially, emotionally, spiritually, physically and intellectually. The approach also seeks to inspire a meaningful connection with the natural world and help the children understand how they fit within it.

Steiner Waldorf: Grounded in Rudolf Steiner's philosophy, this education system gives equal attention to children's physical, emotional, intellectual, cultural and spiritual needs. It aims to provide an unhurried and creative learning environment where children develop a joy for learning. The learning activities are organised around Steiner's theories on the stages of child development to ensure each child takes on new challenges that are aligned to their stage in psychological growth. Steiner schools aim to balance practical and academic disciplines, emphasising creativity and co-operation rather than competition. The approach is known for developing well-rounded and balanced young people who are able to cope with the demands of a volatile, uncertain, complex and ambiguous world.

Montessori: This system of education was pioneered by Italy's first female doctor, Maria Montessori, in 1907 to educate poor children. It is fundamentally a model of human development, which has two basic principles. First, both children and adults engage in psychological self-construction by interacting with their environment, and second, we have an innate path of psychological development. Therefore, given the liberty to choose and act freely within a learning environment, we will act spontaneously for optimal psychological development. Consequently, at the heart of the Montessori system is self-directed activity, hands-on learning and collaborative play, where exploration and creativity are encouraged. A trained Montessori teacher, who is highly experienced in observing the individual child's characteristics, tendencies, innate talents and abilities, will follow the child and intervene to support their learning and development. It is an approach that seeks to develop the whole person.

These examples of alternative education systems demonstrate that children can be taught with highly trained and trusted teachers according to their current stage of psychological development. This can be done to develop their intellect and knowledge and meet their physical, emotional, social, cultural and spiritual needs. If this could be copied in mainstream education rather than preparing children to compete in literacy, maths and science, we would have an emerging society comprising young adults with secure and stable egos. It is highly likely that their psychological development would have been accelerated, facilitating society to evolve to its next level of collective consciousness, a metamodernist level of consciousness for the emergence and reinforcement of a more sustainable economic system.

ADULT LEARNING AND DEVELOPMENT

The majority of adult education, after college or university, takes place at work under the guidance of a 'Learning and Development' (L&D) department. What does this term mean? If you ask L&D departments what 'development' means, you will get a variety of vague answers ranging from gaining experience in different roles through to career development. The reality is that few companies do people development. Instead, most focus on teaching knowledge and training skills, with a little bit of career development for those they see as having the most potential. Real development is about developing people's psychological capability, which comes from developing our 'consciousness'.

Our consciousness is the source of our individual behaviour (what we do and how we do it). It is the source of our performance and results in business. Collectively, our behaviour creates our teams, organisations and, ultimately, our society. Businesses focus on what people 'know' and 'do' but neglect the 'source'. Development is about focusing on the source. To be successful in business, people need both learning and development – the two go hand-in-hand. A good analogy is that of a computer. We know what happens when we try to load increasingly sophisticated software without upgrading the hardware. The computer slows down and eventually crashes. With the increasing levels of mental illness in the workplace, we are probably seeing many people crashing because they have been overly trained and underdeveloped. Human Resources (HR) and L&D departments need to realise they cannot prepare people to be effective by teaching and training alone. They need to give people the means to develop their consciousness as well.

The teaching of knowledge and the training of skills is often called 'horizontal development', while consciousness development is called 'vertical development'. If horizontal development proceeds ahead of vertical development, the person cannot cope with the complexity and sophistication of the knowledge and skills. Consequently, they will oversimplify what they are being taught, or their brain will crash, and they will be unable to learn anymore. If vertical development proceeds ahead of horizontal development, the person will not have the tools needed to work with and communicate the complexity they are seeing. As a result, they are likely to become increasingly detached from other people and their organisation. To be effective, people in the workplace need both horizontal and vertical development, and they must proceed at equal rates.

Businesses need to develop the consciousness of their people for them to perform well in today's VUCA (volatility, uncertainty, complexity and ambiguity) world. People need to have higher levels of cognitive flexibility, emotional and moral intelligence, and behavioural agility to cope with increasing complexity. Through developing these lines of consciousness, they will be able to make better decisions. Consciousness development is like climbing a hill: the higher you go, the more you see and the better your decisions.

So why do HR and L&D departments not develop the consciousness of their employees? The desire for a quick return could be one reason why they focus on teaching knowledge and skills while neglecting psychological capability. The results of teaching can be seen almost immediately through tests. By observing people, it can be seen within days whether people are practising the new skills they have gained through training. Consciousness development can take years and is not easily seen.

Another reason it is neglected is that employees do not realise their psychological capability needs to be developed. How we perceive the world depends on our psychological capability. We construct our own reality. If our psychological capability has not developed sufficiently to enable us to perceive the increased complexity in our work environment, then we just do not see it. We filter out the complexity and perceive the world in much more simplistic terms. Therefore, if people cannot see the complexity in their work, they will not ask to be developed. Only when it is too late do they become aware that something is wrong, when their inability to perceive complexity causes a significant derailment of their performance. With flatter organisational structures and increasing VUCA, major derailments of this type are becoming increasingly common.

If our society is to create and implement a new, more sustainable economic system, we need more people in organisations who have developed their consciousness to the post-conventional stages. This higher level of consciousness will create businesses that are not only better able to serve a new emerging society but also perform better in VUCA markets. Developing the consciousness, along with traditional teaching and training, is a win–win for business.

BUSINESS

As a society, we fell in love with the great machines of the industrial age. Consequently, businesses were designed to behave like machines. The organisation of a machine-like business is broken down into its component parts – business units, departments, teams, etc. As work is divided through the division of labour, each person becomes a cog in the machine. As the cogs turn in unison, work is fed through and processed. By breaking the organisation and the workflow down into components, each can be easily managed and controlled. Practices such as management by objectives, performance appraisals, key performance indicators, budgeting cycles, strategic planning, etc. are used to increase predictability and control of the machine.

Businesses sold shares to investors to attract the capital necessary to invest in the Industrial Revolution. This way of securing investment led to businesses developing one over-riding purpose – to increase shareholder value. Each machine-like business clunked into action, scouring the land to hoover up the resources within its reach, whether they were natural, human or financial. It converted these resources into profit via the production and sales of goods and services.

With our society dominated by modernist collective consciousness (conventional stage 4), the control, certainty and progress that machine-like businesses can offer is very attractive. Consequently, their structures and processes are seen as best practice. Nevertheless, there has been a growing backlash against the damage they are causing. The postmodernist collective consciousness (post-conventional stage 5) does not accept the modernist notions of objective reality, morality, truth, reason and social progress. Instead, postmodernist consciousness creates and accepts a pluralistic society, giving us each space to perceive and understand the world differently according to our own diverse values. Our machine-like organisations have responded to this change, to some degree, with initiatives such as empowerment, inclusion, diversity and employee engagement.

But has this change been enough? Their pursuit of shareholder profit, above everything else, is blamed for rampant consumerism, environmental degradation, climate breakdown, inequality and psychological illness. As society's consciousness has continued to evolve, the metamodernist collective consciousness (stages 6 and 7) is beginning to make itself heard. Metamodernist consciousness does not see things as being fixed, separate and fragmented. Instead, it sees things as continually flowing, interconnected and whole. Rather than seeing a business as a machine, metamodernism sees a business as an ecosystem. To create and implement a new, more sustainable economic system, we need fewer machine-like businesses and more that are like ecosystems. Leaders and entrepreneurs who have developed to the post-conventional stages (6 and 7) of consciousness will be best able to create businesses that are aligned to the metamodernist consciousness. These businesses will accelerate the evolution of our collective consciousness and help to de-industrialise our minds.

As the metamodernist collective consciousness becomes the norm, society will increasingly value flow, emergence and unfolding.

Ecosystem businesses will need to evolve with these values in mind. To achieve this evolution, businesses will increasingly learn from nature's forms, processes and systems to allow them to work with wholeness and integrate relative truths. In an ecosystem business, change is a continuous natural process that cannot be managed. Instead, it needs to be nurtured and cultivated.

Ecosystem-like businesses have multiple and continually evolving purposes. These are related to planet, people and profit, often referred to as the 'triple bottom line'. To achieve these purposes, they seek to sustain and regenerate the resources they use to create goods and services by ensuring that the resources are returned to the environment in a replenishing form once used. Profit is realised through society valuing and rewarding the work of the organisation. The more effectively the ecosystem adds value to society, the more the triple bottom line is increased. To improve effectiveness, the ecosystem organisation uses a range of practices such as self-managed teams, personal inquiry, distributed and emergent leadership, organisational democracy, dialogue and listening to the organisation as it naturally unfolds its emerging purpose. All of these practices enable the natural flow of change.

One way for an ecosystem-like business to create organisational democracy is by becoming a co-operative. Traditionally the people who finance a business own it and hire workers. In a co-operative, it works the other way around. The workers own the company and hire in finance. Co-operatives are people-centred businesses owned, controlled and run by and for their members to realise their common economic, social, and cultural needs and aspirations.[3] The members can be the employees or the customers and are brought together democratically. Each member has an equal voting right, one member one vote, regardless of their position or the amount of capital they invest. All co-operatives are driven by and share the same values of fairness, equality and social justice, and their aim is to build a better world through co-operation. They are able to live these values as they are not owned by shareholders and are not driven to increase profit continually. Any profit is either reinvested in the business or shared amongst members. Therefore, co-operatives are generally more environmentally sustainable than other types of business.

Some co-operatives take the concept of organisational democracy further and operate through a process of sociocracy (also known as dynamic governance). This is a governance method grounded in collaboration, self-organisation and distributed authority. It seeks to achieve solutions that create harmonious social environments as well as productive organisations and businesses. Rather than decisions being made in accordance with the majority votes, they are made by consent through group discussion where individuals reason with each other until a conclusion is reached that is satisfactory to each of them.

Another form of organisational democracy is holacracy, which developed from sociocracy. Holacracy seeks to remove top-down management and to give individual workers and teams more control over processes. It does this by creating a holarchy of distinct self-governing teams that relate to each other in a symbiotic way. Workers have an equal voice while having shared authority for the direction of the business. As it differentiates the roles in the organisation from the people who work within it, workers can take one or more roles and have the flexibility to move between teams if they have skills beneficial to the business.

Following the work of Frederic Laloux, and his book *Reinventing Organizations*, ecosystem organisations are frequently called Teal organisations.[4] The Teal paradigm refers to the next stage in the evolution of human consciousness associated with the metamodernist collective consciousness and the post-conventional stages of development. Teal businesses see themselves as natural living systems and are characterised by:

- **Self-management:** Distributed authority and collective intelligence organised by structures that naturally emerge and dissipate depending on the situation.

- **Wholeness:** Workers are encouraged to 'drop the mask' of their work persona, reclaim their inner wholeness and bring all of themselves to work.
- **Evolutionary purpose:** Instead of trying to control the future of the business, workers are encouraged to listen and understand where it is naturally being drawn towards in terms of what it wants to become and the purpose it wants to serve.

By their very nature, ecosystem businesses seek to live in harmony with the environment, enable people to come together and collaborate, and enable individuals to find wholeness within their psyche. They reconnect us to nature, each other and ourselves. Research has found that to create and lead an ecosystem business, an entrepreneur needs to have developed into the post-conventional stages of consciousness. Otherwise, they are readily influenced to adopt business practices associated with modernism, and the business will begin to operate like a machine. Examples of ecosystem businesses include Patagonia, Spotify, Zappos, Buurtzorg, W. L. Gore and many more.

POLITICS

The way politics is conducted in most countries can best be described as adversarial. In western democracies, it is confrontational. Political parties in both government and opposition face each other in a debating chamber and verbally attack their opponents at every opportunity. Often televised, these attacks continue across all aspects of the media. To the average voter, this behaviour appears to have progressed little from the school playground, although children often engage in more collaborative behaviour than we see demonstrated by our politicians.

Undoubtedly, politics' adversarial nature serves an important purpose: it holds the current government to account. However, politicians are leaders of nations. They are role models. What is seen as acceptable behaviour in the debating chamber and in the media then becomes acceptable behaviour in the workplace, in bars and on the streets. The more an issue is debated in a confrontational way, the more everyone's views become polarised and entrenched. The more adversarial our argument, the more extreme and fixed we become in our views. The message we hear is that you are either with us or against us; there is no middle ground. As a society, we become polarised in our views and the nation divided.

Rather than leading from the post-conventional stages of consciousness development, all too often, we see politicians demonstrating the behaviour associated with the less functional aspects of the early conventional stages. These include commanding and controlling (stage 1), creating a 'them and us' mentality (stage 2), and rejecting feedback, not admitting mistakes and believing they know best (stage 3). These behaviours are deployed to protect their ego and perpetuate adversarial politics, which divides and does little to solve society's major problems.

Many politicians see the dangers. Often newly elected leaders promise to bring adversarial politics to an end. They endeavour to build cross-party consensus, where possible, and create ways to collaborate with different political parties. However, within no time, the political debates descend into attack, defence and counter-attack. Any trust between leaders is soon lost. Why does this happen? Why are political leaders unable to conduct their business in the way they desire?

The answers to these questions are many and varied. First, as we have already seen, if one person becomes competitive, then everyone else becomes competitive to defend and protect their own interests. Some politicians thrive on conflict. Landing a decisive blow on the opposition boosts their popularity. Creating polarised views gives their followers an identity and something to fight for. Second, consensus and collaboration do not sell newspapers or increase viewing figures. The media thrives on conflict and continually seeks to create division.

Third, under sustained pressure, we all descend to the lowest stages of our psychological development. Our survival mechanism kicks in and it becomes a matter of fight or flight. As most politicians cannot run away, they stand and fight. It takes a highly developed and resilient leader not to get sucked into adversarial politics in this environment.

Yet, if a new level of consciousness is to emerge in our society, we need our political leaders to demonstrate the behaviours aligned with this new level. This will require politicians to develop to the post-conventional stages of consciousness. In so doing, they will be able to draw on the collective intelligence of society and those around them, co-create the future with those who have different political ideologies and do what is right for the country rather than protecting their ego. Undoubtedly, this type of politician does exist, but they are often not well received by people who are less psychologically developed, who accuse them of 'flip-flopping' because they see both sides of an argument or call them weak when they miss an opportunity to attack a political rival. It looks inevitable that the evolution of consciousness will be held back by the way politics is conducted in western democracies. There has recently been one notable exception.

In Denmark in 2013, Uffe Elbæk and Josephine Fock launched 'The Alternative' party. It aims to harness citizens' collective intelligence to create ideas that will enable the transition to a more ecologically, socially and economically sustainable society. To achieve this, they invite citizens to engage in dialogue and gather ideas. The party was formed around a set of principles on how to conduct good political dialogue, which are:[5]

1. We will openly discuss both the advantages and disadvantages of a certain argument or line of action.

2. We will listen more than we speak, and we will meet our political opponents on their own ground.

3. We will emphasize the core set of values that guide our arguments.

4. We will acknowledge when we have no answer to a question or when we make mistakes.

5. We will be curious about each and every person with whom we are debating.

6. We will argue openly and factually as to how The Alternative's political vision can be realized.

The principles are enacted from the very start when new members of parliament commend the qualities and perspectives of the other political parties in their inaugural speeches.

The Alternative has developed into an international political movement in multiple countries. However, all has not been well in Denmark. In 2019, Elbæk announced he would stand down as The Alternative's political leader and left the party to become an independent member of parliament. After much controversy, Fock was elected as leader of the party. Clearly, creating a new way of doing politics has not been easy.

If our society is to create and implement a new, more sustainable economic system, we need more people in politics who have developed their consciousness to the post-conventional stages. This will enable them to role-model the behaviours associated with the next stage in our collective consciousness's evolution. To quote Gandhi, we need politicians who can 'be the change we want to see in the world'.

SUMMARY AND CONCLUSION

Today, the human race is facing an existential threat of climate breakdown. Yet, we appear to be powerless and unable to mitigate the threat. Despite our desires and intentions, we are collectively stuck. Our consciousness has created an economic system that is ravaging the environment upon which our lives depend. Our economy, in turn, is conditioning our consciousness. We are trapped!

Our capitalist, consumerist and neoliberal economic system, built during the Industrial Revolution, is supported by our modernist collective consciousness, aligned with stage 4 in the Seven Stages of Adult Consciousness Development. This is the highest of the conventional stages and has always been viewed as the height of adult psychological maturity. Modernist collective consciousness values rationality, objectivity, science and progress. For a new, more sustainable economic system to emerge, our society needs to evolve to the metamodernist collective consciousness aligned with stages 6 and 7. Metamodernist collective consciousness values difference, dialogue and interdependence; it brings people together to continually co-create the future.

To get out of our self-constructed trap, we need people who can separate from the norm and create the structures and mechanisms in our society that will facilitate the evolution of our collective consciousness. These include education, learning and development, business and politics. This chapter outlined where the levers of change are already being pulled in these areas.

In education, we have non-mainstream approaches that connect children with nature, each other and themselves. These connections help a child develop a stable and secure ego, making them less vulnerable to being conditioned into being a consumer, thereby halting our destructive consumerist economy. Consequently, these children are more likely to progress more quickly through the stages of adult development. They are likely to reach the post-conventional stages earlier in their lives than previous generations, and in greater numbers, heralding the evolution of a new level of collective consciousness.

In adult learning and development, some organisations engage their employees in both horizontal development (knowledge and skills) and vertical development (growth in consciousness). Vertical development supports horizontal development and enables the person to learn more complex and advanced skills and knowledge. It allows people to thrive during increasing VUCA in the workplace and in the organisation's markets. Focusing on vertical development alongside traditional training accelerates people's development to the necessary post-conventional stages of consciousness.

We see some businesses moving away from operating like machines towards operating as ecosystems. They seek to live in harmony with the environment, enable people to collaborate and find wholeness within their psyche. They reconnect us to nature, each other and ourselves. These new organisations will serve to accelerate our development to the post-conventional stages and the emergence of a metamodernist collective consciousness.

Although there is a desire to work more collaboratively in politics, we see politicians descending into adversarial relationships. In doing so, they demonstrate behaviour more aligned with the dysfunctional aspects of conventional consciousness. However, one political movement is trying to break from the norm. They are role-modelling the behaviours associated with stages 6 and 7 of adult consciousness development, which are aligned with the metamodernist collective consciousness.

These changes in child education, adult learning and development, business and politics are just the green shoots of a new emerging consciousness. On their own, they are insufficient to create the critical mass of people needed for the new collective consciousness to unfold across our society. For the main part, they are still seen as wild deviations away from the norm, but they are evidence of a change gradually gaining momentum.

Evidence can be seen in the companies now certified as 'B Corporations'. These are new kinds of businesses that balance purpose and profit. They are required to consider the impact of decisions on workers, customers, suppliers, community and the environment. B Corporations describe themselves as a community of leaders, driving a global movement of people using business as a force for good. Over 3,000 businesses are certified as B Corporations, including Ben and

Jerry's, Danone, Hootsuite, Amalgamated Bank and Patagonia.[6]

These green shoots will not be sufficient. To reach the critical mass necessary, society will need individuals to develop independently of these areas. We need people to create change in all aspects of our society.

EPILOGUE

As you have read this book, you have probably disagreed with some of what I have written. Some of my arguments could be perceived as controversial. If this is the case, I invite you to hold your views and mine in your mind simultaneously. Even though our views may be contradictory, could they both be right? You will recall being able to hold contradictory views without conflict is one of the characteristics of consciousness beyond consumerism. As you hold these views in mind, see if you can create something new that transcends their differences. It could be a new perspective, understanding or solution. This process can take time. It is good to let your unconscious, intuitive mind work on the problem. So, I recommend you sleep on it rather than trying to find an answer rationally.

With the problems our society is facing today, neither you nor I have all the insights, understanding and ideas needed for solutions. They are too complicated for one mind to navigate alone. Together, however, by drawing on our collective intelligence, we might find our way. When we work together, it is the differences in our views that point us in the right direction and give energy to our creativity. I hope one day we can meet, have a dialogue and co-create the future together.

If there is one thing we agree on, it will be that our society is unsustainable. While many eminent scientists, economists, activists and politicians are working hard to find solutions, I believe they will be found to be inadequate in the face of our current consciousness. Our current consciousness has created the problem, and it is this which we need to change to develop and implement the necessary solutions. Otherwise, with our industrialised consciousness, we will continue to industrialise any solutions and create even more unforeseen problems as a consequence. Our industrialised solutions of today will sow the seeds of tomorrow's industrialised problems.

Our economic system and our collective consciousness have

evolved, hand-in-hand, throughout the centuries. But we do not have time to wait for our collective consciousness to evolve naturally. It would be too late for humans and much of our biodiversity. But Earth will recover once we are gone. We are just a little bug Earth has picked up that made it feel unwell for a while. It will soon shake us off.

The evolution of our collective consciousness appears stuck in the Industrial Revolution. The materialism, reductionism, positivism and empiricism of the New Science movement paved the way for the Industrial Revolution bringing increases in the standard of living, but are now causing the catastrophic exploitation of our natural resources. Great machines were built, which could convert natural resources into products with high efficiency and productivity levels. To keep the machines turning, the products needed to be purchased and consumerism was born. To build machines, large sums of money were needed. Investors become the owners of business producing the products, and capitalism was born. To gain the highest return on their investment, businesses were encouraged to produce and sell products in ever-increasing quantities. Our natural resources started to be consumed at ever-increasing rates.

This love of the machine endures today, and since the Industrial Revolution, we have viewed everything as machine-like. Nature was seen as a machine; organisations were designed to operate like machines; even our minds came to be seen as machines. One of the dominant similes used today for how the mind works is like a computer, just one big machine. This deprives everything of a soul. Nature, organisations, communities and our minds have increasingly become psychologically dead. We lost our soul, spirit and, at times, even our consciousness. This is how our consciousness has become industrialised. It is a process that has left us psychologically vulnerable. Unfortunately, this vulnerability has been exploited by businesses to sell us products and services. Our economy now operates as one big machine, consuming our environment, our communities and our own psychology.

If we are to prise ourselves from the Industrial Revolution and stimulate the evolution of our consciousness, we need a new metaphor to replace the machine. This is starting to emerge with the term ecosystem being used for business. This may be an indicator that a new level of collective consciousness is emerging. In an ecosystem, there is no separation. Everything is connected to everything else. With the ecosystem metaphor in mind, we will be aware that everything we do ripples out across the universe, creating a myriad of consequences we will never be able to foresee. We will, therefore, act with greater caution and responsibility.

For our collective consciousness to evolve to a new level, to a post-industrial level, we need to put in place structures that will facilitate others' development. During our industrial era, society has viewed the height of adult psychological development to be stage 4, the highest of the conventional stages. However, we now need a critical mass of people at stage 6 and beyond if any sustainable change is to happen. This requires institutions and individuals to develop their consciousness to these post-conventional stages actively. This will take us as individuals, and collectively, into an era of post-industrial consciousness. An era of consciousness beyond consumerism. In this book, I have demonstrated how this could be done.

You may have already developed to the post-conventional stages. If so, I would encourage you to create structures and mechanisms to help others. If you believe you are currently in the conventional stages, like most people, then I hope this book has inspired you to focus on your psychological development actively.

In writing this Epilogue, I have realised I have subconsciously been using machine-like language to convey how we can create aspects of our society to operate more like ecosystems. I write about creating new 'structures and mechanisms'. This shows how far my mind has been industrialised, and I still have a lot more work to do.

I would just like to leave you with a quote by Aldous Huxley (1894–1963) from his book *The Doors of Perception*, referring to Henri

Bergson's (1859–1941) theory that brain, nervous system and sense organs are in the main eliminative and not productive:

> According to such a theory, each one of us is potentially Mind at Large. But in so far as we are animals, our business is at all costs to survive. To make biological survival possible, Mind at Large has to be funneled through the reducing valve of our brain and nervous system. What comes out the other end is a measly trickle of the kind of consciousness which will help us to stay alive on the surface of this particular planet.[1]

It is evident that our measly trickle of consciousness is no longer helping us to survive on this particular planet. In fact, it is now leading to our self-destruction. If we are to prosper as a species, now is the time to open up the value a quarter turn.

As a global society, if we do not focus on the development of our collective consciousness, I fear that a three-headed dragon will continue to ravage the Earth. Our economic system will continue to destroy our natural environment, our relationships and our psychology, causing increasing levels of environmental degradation, inequality and mental illness. Our consciousness created the three-headed dragon, and unless we change our consciousness, we will all suffer its wrath.

For further information and resources to facilitate the development of your consciousness visit:

www.consciousnessbeyondconsumerism.org.

APPENDICES

APPENDIX 1

PLANETARY BOUNDARIES (SOURCE: STOCKHOLM RESILIENCE CENTRE, STOCKHOLM UNIVERSITY)

Stratospheric Ozone Depletion

The stratospheric ozone layer in the atmosphere filters out ultraviolet (UV) radiation from the sun. If this layer decreases, increasing amounts of UV radiation will reach ground level. This can cause a higher incidence of skin cancer in humans as well as damage to terrestrial and marine biological systems. The appearance of the Antarctic ozone hole was proof that increased concentrations of anthropogenic ozone-depleting chemical substances, interacting with polar stratospheric clouds, had passed a threshold and moved the Antarctic stratosphere into a new regime. Fortunately, because of the actions taken as a result of the Montreal Protocol, we appear to be on the path that will allow us to stay within this boundary.

Loss of Biosphere Integrity (Biodiversity Loss and Extinctions)

The Millennium Ecosystem Assessment of 2005 concluded that changes to ecosystems due to human activities were more rapid in the past 50 years than at any time in human history, increasing the risks of abrupt and irreversible changes. The main drivers of change are the demand for food, water and natural resources, causing severe biodiversity loss and leading to changes in ecosystem services. These drivers are either steady, showing no evidence of declining over time, or are increasing in intensity. The current high rates of ecosystem damage and extinction can be slowed by efforts to protect the integrity of living systems (the biosphere), enhancing habitat and improving connectivity between ecosystems while maintaining the high agricultural productivity that humanity needs. Further research is underway to improve the availability of reliable data for use as the 'control variables' for this boundary.

Chemical Pollution and the Release of Novel Entities

Emissions of toxic and long-lived substances such as synthetic organic pollutants, heavy metal compounds and radioactive materials represent some of the key human-driven changes to the planetary environment. These compounds can have potentially irreversible effects on living organisms and on the physical environment (by affecting atmospheric processes and climate). Even when the uptake and bioaccumulation of chemical pollution is at sub-lethal levels for organisms, the effects of reduced fertility and the potential of permanent genetic damage can have severe effects on ecosystems far removed from the source of the pollution. For example, persistent organic compounds have caused dramatic reductions in bird populations and impaired reproduction and development in marine mammals. There are many examples of additive and synergic effects from these compounds, but these are still poorly understood scientifically. At present, we are unable to quantify a single chemical pollution boundary, although the risk of crossing Earth system thresholds is considered sufficiently well-defined for it to be included in the list as a priority for precautionary action and for further research.

Climate Change

Recent evidence suggests that the Earth, now passing 390 parts per million by volume CO_2 in the atmosphere, has already transgressed the planetary boundary and is approaching several Earth system thresholds. We have reached a point at which the loss of summer polar sea-ice is almost certainly irreversible. This is one example of a well-defined threshold above which rapid physical feedback mechanisms can drive the Earth system into a much warmer state with sea levels metres higher than present. The weakening or reversal of terrestrial carbon sinks, for example through the ongoing destruction of the world's rainforests, is another potential tipping point, where climate-carbon cycle feedbacks accelerate Earth's warming and intensify the climate impacts. A major question is how long we can remain over this boundary before large, irreversible changes become unavoidable.

Ocean Acidification

Around a quarter of the CO_2 that humanity emits into the atmosphere is ultimately dissolved in the oceans. Here it forms carbonic acid, altering ocean chemistry and decreasing the pH of the surface water. This increased acidity reduces the amount of available carbonate ions, an essential 'building block' used by many marine species for shell and skeleton formation. Beyond a threshold concentration, this rising acidity makes it hard for organisms such as corals and some shellfish and plankton species to grow and survive. Losses of these species would change the structure and dynamics of ocean ecosystems and could potentially lead to drastic reductions in fish stocks. Compared to pre-industrial times, surface ocean acidity has already increased by 30%. Unlike most other human impacts on the marine environment, which are often local in scale, the ocean acidification boundary has ramifications for the whole planet. It is also an example of how tightly interconnected the boundaries are, since atmospheric CO_2 concentration is the underlying controlling variable for both the climate and the ocean acidification boundaries, although they are defined in terms of different Earth system thresholds.

Freshwater Consumption and the Global Hydrological Cycle

The freshwater cycle is strongly affected by climate change and its boundary is closely linked to the climate boundary, yet human pressure is now the dominant driving force determining the functioning and distribution of global freshwater systems. The consequences of human modification of water bodies include both global-scale river flow changes and shifts in vapour flows arising from land-use change. These shifts in the hydrological system can be abrupt and irreversible. Water is becoming increasingly scarce – by 2050 about half a billion people are likely to be subject to water stress, increasing the pressure to intervene in water systems. A water boundary related to consumptive freshwater use and environmental flow requirements has been proposed to maintain the overall resilience of the Earth system and to avoid the risk of 'cascading' local and regional thresholds.

Land System Change

Land is converted to human use all over the planet. Forests, grasslands, wetlands and other vegetation types have primarily been converted to agricultural land. This land-use change is one driving force behind the serious reductions in biodiversity, and it has impacts on water flows and on the biogeochemical cycling of carbon, nitrogen and phosphorus, and other important elements. While each incident of land cover change occurs on a local scale, the aggregated impacts can have consequences for Earth system processes on a global scale. A boundary for human changes to land systems needs to reflect not just the absolute quantity of land, but also its function, quality and spatial distribution. Forests play a particularly important role in controlling the linked dynamics of land use and climate, and are the focus of the boundary for land system change.

Nitrogen and Phosphorus Flows to the Biosphere and Oceans

The biogeochemical cycles of nitrogen and phosphorus have been radically changed by humans as a result of many industrial and agricultural processes. Nitrogen and phosphorus are both essential elements for plant growth, so fertiliser production and application is the main concern. Human activities now convert more atmospheric nitrogen into reactive forms than all of the Earth's terrestrial processes combined. Much of this new reactive nitrogen is emitted to the atmosphere in various forms rather than taken up by crops. When it is rained out, it pollutes waterways and coastal zones or accumulates in the terrestrial biosphere. Similarly, a relatively small proportion of phosphorus fertilisers applied to food production systems is taken up by plants; much of the phosphorus mobilised by humans also ends up in aquatic systems. These can become oxygen-starved as bacteria consume the blooms of algae that grow in response to the high nutrient supply. A significant fraction of the applied nitrogen and phosphorus makes its way to the sea, and can push marine and aquatic systems across ecological thresholds of their own. One regional-scale example of this effect is the decline in the shrimp catch in the Gulf of Mexico's 'dead zone' caused by fertiliser transported in rivers from the US Midwest.

Atmospheric Aerosol Loading

An atmospheric aerosol planetary boundary was proposed primarily because of the influence of aerosols on Earth's climate system. Through their interaction with water vapour, aerosols play a critically important role in the hydrological cycle affecting cloud formation and global-scale and regional patterns of atmospheric circulation, such as the monsoon systems in tropical regions. They also have a direct effect on climate, by changing how much solar radiation is reflected or absorbed in the atmosphere. Humans change the aerosol loading by emitting atmospheric pollution (many pollutant gases condense into droplets and particles), and also through land-use change that increases the release of dust and smoke into the air. Shifts in climate regimes and monsoon systems have already been seen in highly polluted environments, giving a quantifiable regional measure for an aerosol boundary. A further reason for an aerosol boundary is that aerosols have adverse effects on many living organisms. Inhaling highly polluted air causes roughly 800,000 people to die prematurely each year. The toxicological and ecological effects of aerosols may thus relate to other Earth system thresholds. However, the behaviour of aerosols in the atmosphere is extremely complex, depending on their chemical composition and their geographical location and height in the atmosphere. While many relationships between aerosols, climate and ecosystems are well established, many causal links are yet to be determined.

APPENDIX 2

ABRAHAM MASLOW'S 'HIERARCHY OF NEEDS'

Stage 1: Physiological: Breathing, food, water, sex and sleep.

Stage 2: Safety: Security of body, employment, resources, family, health and property.

Stage 3: Love/Belonging: Friendship, family and belonging to a group.

Stage 4: Esteem: Self-esteem and respect from others.

Stage 5: Self-actualisation: Achieving full potential.

LAWRENCE KOHLBERG'S 'STAGES OF MORAL DEVELOPMENT'

Stage 1: Obedience and Punishment Orientation. People demonstrate moral behaviour by abiding by the rules to avoid being punished.

Stage 2: Individualism, Instrumental Purpose and Exchange. People demonstrate moral behaviour by negotiating the course of action with others so they can pursue their individual interests – 'If you scratch my back, I will scratch yours.'

Stage 3: Good Interpersonal Relationships. People demonstrate moral behaviour by adhering to what their social consensus has deemed to be right. In doing so, people are receptive to approval or disapproval from other individuals as it reflects the views of their immediate social circle.

Stage 4: Maintaining the Social Order. People demonstrate moral behaviour by abiding by the wider society's rules and upholding the law. At this stage people believe there is an obligation and a duty to uphold laws and rules so that society can continue to function.

Stage 5: Social Contract and Individual Rights. People demonstrate moral behaviour by considering 'What makes for a good society?' At this stage they believe that while society's rules and laws might exist for the good of the greatest number, there are times when they will work against the interest of particular individuals. Instead, they conceive a good society as being a social contract into which people freely enter to work towards the benefit of all.

Stage 6: Universal Principles. People demonstrate moral behaviour by adhering to their own set of moral guidelines which may or may not fit the law. At this stage they believe laws are only valid when they are grounded in justice and a commitment to justice carries with it an obligation to disobey unjust laws. Instead of adhering to society's laws, they adhere to the principles of justice that require us to treat the claims of all parties in an impartial manner, respecting the basic dignity of all people as individuals. They believe these principles of justice to be universal and apply to us all.

ROBERT KEGAN'S 'SUBJECT-OBJECT THEORY OF DEVELOPMENT'

1st Order: Impulsive Mind (approximately 2–6 years old) – Perceives and responds by emotion.

2nd Order: Imperial–Instrumental Mind (approximately 6 years old through adolescence) – Motivated solely by one's desires.

3rd Order: Interpersonal–Socialised Mind (post adolescence) – Defined by the group.

4th Order: Institutional–Self-Authoring Mind (variable, if achieved) – Self-directed.

5th Order: inter-individual–Self-Transforming Mind (typically >40, if achieved) – Interpenetration of self-systems.

CLARE GRAVES' 'EMERGENT CYCLIC LEVELS OF EXISTENCE THEORY'

Level	Learning System	Thinking	Motivational System	Specific Motivation	Means Values	End Values	Nature of Existence	Problems of Existence
A–N	Habituation	Automatic	Physiological	Periodic physiological needs	No conscious value system	No conscious value system	Automatic	Maintaining physiological stability
B–O	Classical conditioning	Autistic	Assurance	Aperiodic physiological needs	Traditionalism	Safety	Tribalistic	Achievement of relative safety
C–P	Operant conditioning	Egocentric	Survival	Psychological survival	Exploitation	Power	Egocentric	Living with self-awareness
D–Q	Avoidant learning	Absolutistic	Security	Order, meaning	Sacrifice	Salvation	Saintly	Achieving ever-lasting peace of mind
E–R	Expectancy	Multiplistic	Independence	Adequacy, competency	Scientism	Materialism	Materialistic	Conquering the physical universe
F–S	Observational	Relativistic	Affiliation	Love, affiliation	Sociocentricity	Community	Personalistic	Living with the human element
G–T	All learning systems open	Systemic	Existential	Self-worth	Accepting	Existence	Cognitive	Restoring viability to a disordered world
H–U	All learning systems open	Differential	Experience	?????	Experiencing	Communion	Experientialistic	Accepting existential dichotomies

JANE LOEVINGER'S 'THEORY OF EGO DEVELOPMENT'

Impulsive: The young child is driven by its emotions, including sexual and aggressive drives.

Self-protective: The child at this stage begins to develop some rudimentary self-control so as not to get caught and be punished.

Conformist: The child becomes more aware of society and the need to belong to a group through compliant behaviour.

Self-aware: The adult becomes self-critical and is able to see the difference between the 'real me' and the 'expected me'.

Conscientious: The adult has internalised the rules of society and sees life in terms of the choices and responsibilities.

Individualistic: The adult has respect for individuality in oneself and a tolerance towards the individual differences in others.

Autonomous: The adult is driven to achieving a sense of self-fulfilment rather than achievement and self-acceptance is increasing.

Integrated: The adult has inner wisdom, deep empathy for others and a high degree of self-acceptance. Loevinger says that few people make it to this stage.

GLOSSARY OF TERMS

Animism: Attributing a soul to animals, plants, inanimate objects and natural phenomena.

Anthropocentrism: The assumption that all phenomena should only be interpreted through human values and experiences.

Behaviourism: A psychological approach concerned only with observable behaviour, its stimulus and its reinforcement.

Capitalism: An economic and political system in which most means of production are privately owned, and prices, production and the distribution of goods are determined mainly by competition in a free market.

Collective unconscious: Structures of the mind that are shared amongst beings of the same species.

Collectivism: A social theory which argues that the cohesiveness of the group takes precedence over the individual.

Consciousness: There is no agreed definition of consciousness. Some scientists and philosophers believe it does not exist, while others believe it is one of the fundamental building blocks of the universe. This book takes consciousness to be the ground from which we think, feel and behave. It includes both conscious and unconscious influences along with the personal and collective.

Consumerism: A social and economic order that sees the ever-increasing consumption of goods as being economically desirable and, therefore, encourages people to consume so that they can be better off.

Conspicuous consumption: The practice of acquiring goods of a higher quality or quantity than practically needed to display wealth and status.

Dualism: A theory of consciousness where it is believed that at least some aspects of consciousness fall outside the brain's physical structures.

Earth stewardship: An approach that sees entities in nature as being psychologically alive, but humans as being their superior. Its goal is not to protect nature from people but to protect nature for human welfare.

Ecocentrism: The belief that there is no tangible division between human and non-human entities and, therefore, all life is equal and has the same value.

Ego: The constructed identity that we like to present to the world. It is our self-image or mask. In everyday language, when we use the word 'me', we are often referring to our ego. It is our self-identity.

Eliminism: A theory of consciousness that believes our understanding of the mind is false and the mental states we believe we experience do not exist. Instead, it is believed they can be traced back to neural activity and are simply down to chemistry and physics in our brains.

Empiricism: A philosophical theory which states that all knowledge can only be based on experience derived from the senses.

Gaia theory: A theory which asserts that living organisms and their inorganic surroundings interact to form a complex system.

Higher unconscious: A part of the psyche that contains the positive aspects of our psychology, such as inspiration, intuition, altruism, spiritual energy, etc. It is where our flashes of brilliance and genius come from.

Humanistic psychology: An approach that treats people as unique individuals and focuses on their psychological growth. It is concerned with areas of growth such as increasing self-awareness, self-efficacy, self-worth, creativity, free will and wholeness.

Idealism: A philosophy which holds that the physical reality of matter is in some way indistinguishable or inseparable from consciousness.

For idealists, everything is psychologically alive, and everything is interconnected.

Individualism: A social theory which argues that the individual's interests should take precedence over the state or a social group.

Lines of consciousness: Different aspects of our psychology, such as cognition, emotion, values, moral reasoning, motives, etc.

Lower unconscious: A part of the psyche which contains the psychological activities that control our bodily functions, our fundamental and primitive drives and urges (survival and sexual). It includes things we do not like about ourselves, disturbing memories that we have suppressed or repressed, our phobias and delusions, etc.

Materialism: A philosophy which holds that matter is the fundamental substance in nature, and that all things, including consciousness, are results of material interactions.

Metamodernism: A cultural movement, or era of collective consciousness, that values acceptance and thrives in our society's paradoxical and self-contradictory nature. It takes a 'both–and' rather than an 'either–or' perspective on life. Therefore, it accepts both modernist and postmodernist perspectives and unites them.

Middle unconscious: A part of our psyche where we put memories, skills and, to some degree, perceptions, etc., which are not currently within our field of conscious awareness. Yet by directing our attention, we can make these conscious.

Modernism: A cultural movement, or era of collective consciousness, that assumes everyone can be the author of their own mind and be independent of any external influences.

Monism: A theory of consciousness where there is no separation between mind and matter.

Narcissism: An exceptional interest in, or admiration of, oneself. It lies on a continuum from healthy to pathological. Healthy narcissism is self-love and confidence gained through increasing self-esteem. It becomes a problem when a person becomes preoccupied with themselves and needs excessive admiration from other people.

Neoliberalism: A political and economic system that favours free-market capitalism and reduction in government spending. It seeks to achieve this through privatisation, deregulation, globalisation, free trade, austerity and increasing the private sector's role in the economy and society.

New Science: A philosophical and scientific movement of the 17th and 18th centuries that emphasised materialism, empiricism, reductionism and positivism.

Objectivity: Reasoning in a way that is **not** influenced by a person's feelings, opinions, prejudices, moods, etc.

Panpsychism: A theory that views consciousness as permeating every aspect of reality rather than being a unique feature of the human experience. It believes that consciousness is the foundation of the universe and is present in every quantum particle, i.e. all physical matter.

Perfectionism: Endeavouring to do a good job and get things exactly right so that you can feel good about yourself.

Personal unconscious: Our own individual part of the collective unconscious.

Positive psychology: An approach that focuses on how individuals can build a life of meaning and purpose so they can flourish rather than just survive. It is believed this is achieved through focusing on, and utilising, their individual strengths.

Positivism: A philosophical system which states that only that which can be scientifically verified or proven by logic or mathematics can be seen as genuine knowledge.

Postmodernism: A cultural movement, or era of collective consciousness, that is a critique of modernism, questioning whether people are truly independent and, therefore, whether the truth can be verified. It is characterised by scepticism, which critiques the generally accepted notions of objective reality, morality, truth, reason and social progress.

Pre-modernism: A cultural movement, or era of collective consciousness, characterised by religions and philosophies establishing a 'universal truth' or the 'word of God', which provides a guide for morality, behaviour and thought.

Productivity: A measure of efficiency in terms of producing more with fewer resources, including labour.

Psyche: The entirety of our psychological life. It is the totality of the human mind. Our psyche contains our ego, soul and witness consciousness as well as our thoughts, emotions and desires. It includes what is conscious and unconscious.

Psychodynamic psychology: An approach that emphasises the dynamic psychological energy and forces that underlie and motivate our behaviour, emotions and cognitions.

Reductionism: The practice of breaking down a complex phenomenon into its fundamental component parts so they can be studied, analysed and described.

Scientific management: A theory and practice designed to increase labour productivity by analysing workflows.

Self (capital 'S'): The core of our being, not conditioned by everyday life experiences, and it does not need defending. It is often referred to as being the 'higher Self' or the 'soul'. It is also the gateway to 'non-dualism'. This is where the distinction between subject and object disappears. Everything becomes connected as one unifying whole. Our Self can, therefore, connect us to our spirituality.

Self-actualisation: The process by which a person achieves their full potential and becomes self-fulfilled.

Self-denial: The act of letting go of the ego, forgoing personal pleasures and being critical of your own needs, desires and pleasure-seeking.

Self-esteem: The feeling resulting from a person's self-evaluation of their own worth.

Servant leadership: Puts the needs of followers first and helps them develop and perform as well as possible. The servant leader tries to develop other people to become wiser, freer and more autonomous servant leaders, allowing them to share power.

Social comparison: How a person determines their social worth and self-worth based on how they believe they compare to other people.

Social dominance: A theory that proposes people with power will always seek to get more of what they desire in life at their subordinates' expense.

Social liberalism: A political and economic philosophy that seeks to balance individual liberty and social justice. It views the common good as harmonious with the freedom of the individual. It endorses a regulated market economy and the expansion of civil and political rights.

Soul: The immaterial part of a being, a distinct entity, separate from the body.

Spirit: The 'life force' or the spark of life, present in every living thing and, therefore, connecting us.

Spiritual ecology: A movement that recognises the unity and interrelationship of all creation.

Stages of consciousness: Adult psychological growth in terms of periods of transition, followed by plateaux of stability.

States of consciousness: Different qualities of awareness such as waking, sleeping, dreaming, hypnosis, sensory deprivation, transcendence, etc.

Subjectivity: Reasoning in a way that is influenced by a person's feelings, opinions, prejudices, moods, etc.

Transcendence: The process of expanding your personal boundaries, connecting with something beyond your ego, considering yourself to be an integral part of a unifying whole and acting accordingly.

Transformational leadership: When leaders and followers make each other advance to a higher level of morale and motivation.

Transpersonal psychology: An approach that includes the transcendent and spiritual aspects of the human experience. It assumes the psychology of the individual extends beyond ego to include the soul and beyond to connect with a form of a collective soul (the spirit).

Tribalism: When society is divided into smaller groups and these groups are actively hostile towards one another.

Witness consciousness: The awareness of both our external and internal worlds; often called 'pure awareness' or 'conscious self'.

Utilitarianism: An ethical theory that promotes the greatest amount of good for the greatest number of people. It aims to foster the maximum happiness and well-being for all affected people.

NOTES

INTRODUCTION

1. Dellinger, D. (2003). *Hieroglyphic Stairway*. Available at: https://drewdellinger.org/ (accessed 15 April 2021).
2. Jung, C. (1991). *The Archetypes and the Collective Unconscious*. London: Taylor & Francis.

CHAPTER 1

1. *Treaty on Principles Governing the Activities of States in the Exploration and Use of Outer Space, including the Moon and Other Celestial Bodies*. Available at: https://www.unoosa.org/oosa/en/ourwork/spacelaw/treaties/introouterspacetreaty.html (accessed 24 January 2021).
2. Stockholm Resilience Centre. *Planetary Boundaries*. Available at: https://www.stockholmresilience.org/research/planetary-boundaries.html (accessed 2 January 2020).
3. UN Intergovernmental Panel on Climate Change (IPCC). (2018). *Special Report: Global Warming of 1.5°C*. Available at: https://www.ipcc.ch/sr15/ (accessed 2 January 2020).
4. Global Footprint Network. (2017). *Earth Overshoot Day*. Available at: https://www.overshootday.org/ (accessed: 1 November 2017).
5. United Nations. (2018). *Responsible Consumption and Reduction: Why It Matters*. Available at: https://www.un.org/sustainabledevelopment/wp-content/uploads/2018/09/Goal-12.pdf (accessed 2 January 2020).
6. United Nations Environment Programme (UNEP). (2020). *Preventing the Next Pandemic – Zoonotic diseases and How to Break the Chain of Transmission*. Available at: https://www.unenvironment.org/resources/report/preventing-future-zoonotic-disease-outbreaks-protecting-environment-animals-and (accessed 2 January 2020).
7. OECD. (n.d.). *Inequality*. Available at: https://www.oecd.org/social/inequality.htm (accessed 2 January 2020).
8. Oxfam International. (n.d.). *It's Time to End Extreme Inequality*. https://www.oxfam.org/en/take-action/campaigns/fight-inequality-beat-poverty/its-time-end-extreme-inequality (accessed 24 January 2021).
9. Wilkinson, R. and Pickett, K. (2009). *The Spirit Level*. London: Penguin Books.
10. *Diagnostic and Statistical Manual of Mental Disorders* (DSM; latest edition: DSM-5, publ. 2013). Philadelphia, PA: American Psychiatric Association.
11. Research and Markets. (2019). *The Market For Self-improvement Products & Services*. Available at: https://www.researchandmarkets.com/reports/4992351/the-market-for-self-improvement-products-and?w=4 (accessed 2 January 2020).
12. Global Wellness Institute. (2015). *Wellness Now a $3.72 Trillion Global Industry – With 10.6% Growth from 2013–2015*. Available at: https;//globalwellnessinstitute.org/press-room/press-releases/wellness-now-a-372-trillion-global-industry/ (accessed 2 January 2020).

13. Marketdata Enterprises Inc. (2017). *$1.2 Billion U.S. Meditation Market to Grow Strongly, Following Path of Yoga Studios*. Available at: https://www.marketdataenterprises.com/wp-content/uploads/2018/03/Meditation-Mkt-2017-Press-Release.pdf (accessed 2 January 2020).
14. World Health Organization (WHO). (2016). *Investing in Treatment for Depression and Anxiety Leads to Fourfold Return.* Available at https://www.who.int/mediacentre/news/releases/2016/depression-anxiety-treatment/en/ (accessed 2 January 2020).
15. Mental Health Foundation. (n.d.). *Mental Health in the Workplace*. Available at: https://www.mentalhealth.org.uk/our-work/mental-health-workplace (accessed 2 January 2020).
16. Gov.uk. (2017). *Thriving at Work: A Review of Mental Health and Employers. An Independent Review of Mental Health.* Available at: https://www.gov.uk/government/publications/thriving-at-work-a-review-of-mental-health-and-employers (accessed 2 January 2020).
17. World Health Organization (WHO). (2017). *Adolescents and Mental Health.* Available at: https://www.who.int/maternal_child_adolescent/topics/adolescence/mental_health/en/ (accessed 2 January 2020).
18. NHS Digital. (2020). *Mental Health of Children and Young People in England, 2020: Wave 1 Follow Up to the 2017 Survey*. Available at: https://digital.nhs.uk/data-and-information/publications/statistical/mental-health-of-children-and-young-people-in-england/2020-wave-1-follow-up (accessed 2 January 2021).

CHAPTER 2

1. Wohlleben, P. (2017). *The Hidden Life of Trees.* London: HarperCollins.
2. Perry, B. (2016). Why land rights for indigenous peoples could be the answer to climate change. *The Guardian.* https://www.theguardian.com/commentisfree/2016/nov/29/land-rights-indigenous-peoples-climate-change-deforestation-amazon (accessed 2 May 2021).
3. Lovelock, J. E. (2000). *Gaia: A New Look at Life on Earth.* New York: Oxford University Press.
4. Bentham, J. (1823). *An Introduction to the Principles of Morals and Legislation.* London: Pickering. p. 2
5. Harding, S. (2009). *Animate Earth: Science, Intuition and Gaia.* Totnes: Green Books Ltd.
6. Hofstede, G. (1983). Culture's consequences: International differences in work-related values. *Administrative Science Quarterly* 28(4): 625–629.
7. Camerer, C. F. and Fehr, E. (2006). When does 'economic man' dominate social behavior? *Science* 311(5757): 47–52.
8. Spencer, H. (2012). *Principles of Biology, Volume 1.* Charleston, SC: Nabu Press (first published 1864).
9. Kropotkin, P. (2017). *Mutual Aid: A Factor of Evolution (The Kropotkin Collection)*. New York: McClure, Phillips & Co (first published 1902).
10. Maslow, A. H. (1954). *Motivation and Personality*. New York: Harper & Row.
11. Tauer, J. M. & Harackiewicz, J. M. (2004). The effects of co-operation and competition

on intrinsic motivation and performance. *Journal of Personality and Social Psychology* 87(2): 245–245.

12. Rhea, M. R., Landers, D. M., Alvar, B. A. and Arent, S. M. (2003). The effects of competition and the presence of an audience on weight lifting performance. *Journal of Strength Conditioning Research* 17: 303–306.
13. Tajfel, H. (1970). Experiments in intergroup discrimination. *Scientific American* 223(5): 96–103.
14. Santos, H. C., Varnum, M. E. W. and Grossmann, I. (2017). Global increases in individualism. *Psychological Science* 28(9): 1228–1239.
15. Ostry, J. D., Loungani, P. and Furceri, D. (2016). Neoliberalism: Oversold? *Finance & Development* 53 (2). p.38
16. Neff, K. (2011). *Self-compassion: Stop Beating Yourself Up and Leave Insecurity Behind.* New York: HarperCollins.
17. Curran, T. and Hill, A. (2019). Perfectionism is increasing over time: A meta-analysis of birth cohort differences from 1989 to 2016. *Psychological Bulletin* 145(4): 410–429.

CHAPTER 3

1. Harari, Y. N. (2015). *Sapiens: A Brief History of Humankind.* London. Vintage.
2. Smith, A. (1759). *The Theory of Moral Sentiment.* Strand & Edinburgh: A. Millar; A. Kincaid and J. Bell. Smith, A. (1776). *An Inquiry into the Nature and Causes of the Wealth of Nations.* London: W. Strahan.
3. Bailey, C. and Madden, A. (2016). What makes work meaningful — Or meaningless. *MIT Sloan Management Review*. Available at: https://sloanreview.mit.edu/article/what-makes-work-meaningful-or-meaningless/(accessed 16 April 2021).

CHAPTER 4

1. Brickman, P. and Campbell, D. (1971). Hedonic relativism and planning the good society. In M. H. Apley, ed., *Adaptation Level Theory: A Symposium*. New York: Academic Press, pp. 287–302.
2. Louv, R. (2010). *Last Child in the Woods: Saving Our Children from Nature-deficit Disorder.* London: Atlantic Books.
3. University of Derby and The Wildlife Trusts. (2020). *30 Days Wild*. Available at: https://www.derby.ac.uk/news/2020/new-review-says-get-long-lasting-feel-good-factor-from-30-days-wild/ (accessed 3 January 2021).
4. White, M. P., Alcock, I., Grellier, J. et al. (2019). Spending at least 120 minutes a week in nature is associated with good health and well-being. *Scientific Reports* 9: 7730.
5. Cigna. (2020). *Cigna Takes Action to Combat the Rise of Loneliness and Improve Mental Wellness in America.* Available at: https://www.cigna.com/about-us/newsroom/news-and-views/press-releases/2020/cigna-takes-action-to-combat-the-rise-of-loneliness-and-improve-mental-wellness-in-america (accessed 3 January 2021).
6. Ford. (2020). *Looking Further with Ford Trends Report*. Available at: https://media.ford.com/content/fordmedia/fna/us/en/news/2019/12/11/ford-releases-2020-global-trend-

report (accessed 3 January 2021).

7. Frankl, V. E. (2004). *Man's Search for Meaning*. London: Rider (first published 1946).
8. Kobau, R., Sniezek, J., Zack, M. M., Lucas, R. E. and Burns, A. (2010). Well-being assessment: An evaluation of well-being scales for public health and population estimates of well-being among US adults. *Applied Psychology: Health and Well-being* 2(3): 272–297.
9. Luchner, A. F., Houston, J. M., Walker, C. and Houston, M. A. (2011). Exploring the relationship between two forms of narcissism and competitiveness. *Personality and Individual Differences* 51(6): 779–782.
10. Twenge, J. M., Konrath, S., Foster, J. D., Campbell, W. K. and Bushman, B. J. (2008). Egos inflating over time: A cross-temporal meta-analysis of the Narcissistic Personality Inventory. *Journal of Personality* 76(4): 875–902.
11. MacDonald, P. (2014). Narcissism in the modern world. *Psychodynamic Practice: Individuals, Groups and Organisations* 20(2): 144–153.
12. Transcript available at https://www.jfklibrary.org/learn/about-jfk/the-kennedy-family/robert-f-kennedy/robert-f-kennedy-speeches/remarks-at-the-university-of-kansas-march-18-1968 (accessed on 17 April 2021).
13. Fleming, D. (2016). *Surviving the Future*. White River Junction, VT: Chelsea Green Publishing.
14. Wilkinson, R. and Pickett, K. (2009). *The Spirit Level*. London: Penguin Books.
15. Bernays, E. (2004). *Propaganda*. New York: IG Publishing (first published 1928), p. 10.
16. Shah, A. (2014). *Consumption and Consumerism*. Available at: https://www.globalissues.org/issue/235/consumption-and-consumerism (accessed 3 January 2021).
17. Sidanius, J. and Pratto, F. (1999). *Social Dominance: An Intergroup Theory of Social Hierarchy and Oppression*. Cambridge: Cambridge University Press.
18. Milfont, T. L., Bain, P. G., Kashima, Y. et al. (2017). On the relation between social dominance orientation and environmentalism: A 25-nation study. *Social Psychological and Personality Science* 9(7): 802–814.

CHAPTER 5

1. Legatum Institute. (2015). *Prosperity for All: Restoring Faith in Capitalism*. Available at: https://li.com/wp-content/uploads/2019/03/prosperity-for-all-restoring-faith-in-capitalism-pdf.pdf (accessed 4 January 2021).
2. Schumacher, E. F. (1993). *Small Is Beautiful: A Study of Economics as if People Mattered*. London: Vintage (first published 1973).
3. Brown, C. (2017). *Buddhist Economics: An Enlightened Approach to the Dismal Science*. London: Bloomsbury Press.
4. Jackson, T. (2011). *Prosperity without Growth: Economics for a Finite Planet*. Abingdon: Routledge.
5. Raworth, K. (2018). *Doughnut Economics: Seven Ways to Think Like a 21st-century Economist*. London: Random House.
6. Freinacht, H. (2017). *The Listening Society: A Metamodern Guide to Politics, Book One:*

Volume 1 (Metamodern Guides). Metamoderna.

CHAPTER 6

1. Chalmers, D.J. (1995). Facing up to the problem of consciousness. *Journal of Consciousness Studies* 2(3): 200–219.
2. Schaie, K. W. (1998). The Seattle Longitudinal Studies of adult intelligence. In M. Powell Lawton and T. A. Salthouse, eds. *Essential Papers on the Psychology of Aging*. New York: New York University Press, pp. 263–271.
3. Van Lommel, P. (2011). *Consciousness Beyond Life: The Science of the Near-death Experience*. New York: HarperCollins.
4. Assagioli, R. (2012). *Psychosynthesis: A Collection of Basic Writings*. Amherst, MA: The Synthesis Center Inc.
5. Sheldrake, R. (2009). *Morphic Resonance: The Nature of Formative Causation*. Rochester, VT: Park Street Press.
6. Creswell, J. D., Bursley, J. K. and Satpute, A. B. (2013). Neural reactivation links unconscious thought to decision-making performance. *Social Cognitive and Affective Neuroscience* 8(8): 863–869.
7. Wilber, K. (2000). *Integral Psychology: Consciousness, Spirit, Psychology, Therapy*. Boulder, CO: Shambhala Publications Inc.
8. Maslow, A. H. (2010). *Toward a Psychology of Being*. Mansfield Centre, CT: Martino Publishing. (first published 1962).
9. Maslow, A. H. (1954). *Motivation and Personality*. New York: Harper & Row.

CHAPTER 7

1. James, W. (1985). *The Varieties of Religious Experience: A study in Human Nature*. London: Penguin Books.
2. Van Eyk McCain, M. (2010). *Green Spirit: Path to a New Consciousness*. Winchester: Earth Books.
3. Maslow, A. H. (1954). *Motivation and Personality*. New York: Harper & Row.
4. Graves, C. (2004). *Levels of Human Existence*. Publisher unknown.
5. Kohlberg, L. (1981). *The Philosophy of Moral Development: Moral Stages and the Idea of Justice* (Essays on Moral Development). New York: HarperCollins.
6. Kegan, R. (1982). *The Evolving Self: Problem and Process in Human Development*. Cambridge, MA: Harvard University Press.
7. Loevinger, J. (1987). *Paradigms of Personality*. New York: W. H. Freeman & Co.
8. Kegan, R. (1994). *In Over Our Heads: The Mental Demands of Modern Life*. Cambridge, MA: Harvard University Press.
9. PwC. (2015). *Under Your Nose: Ten Ways to Identify and Retain Transformational Leaders*. Available at: https://www.pwc.co.uk/services/human-resource-services/human-resource-consulting/under-your-nose-ten-ways-to-identify-and-retain-transformation-leaders.html (accessed 3 November 2017).
10. Wilber, K. (2000). *Integral Psychology: Consciousness, Spirit, Psychology, Therapy*.

Boulder, CO: Shambhala Publications Inc.

CHAPTER 8

1. Morris, J. and Macfarlane, R. (2017). *The Lost Words: A Spell Book.* London: Hamish Hamilton.
2. Halliday, E. (2019). *Reflexive Self-Consciousness.* Melchisedec Press.
3. Maslow. A. H. (2012). *Religions, Values, and Peak-Experiences.* BN Publishing (first published in 1964).
4. Bohm, D. (2004). *On Dialogue.* Abingdon: Routledge.
5. Jung, C. (1933). The meaning of psychology for modern man. In *The Collected Works of C. G. Jung* Vol. 10: Civilization in Transition. Princeton, NJ: Princeton University Press, p. 304.
6. Jaques, E. (1996). *Requisite Organization: A Total System for Effective Managerial Organization and Managerial Leadership for the 21st Century.* Fleming Island, FL: Cason Hall.
7. Cattell, R. B. (1963). Theory of fluid and crystallized intelligence: A critical experiment. *Journal of Educational Psychology* 54(1): 1–22.
8. Rittenberg, L. and Tregarthen, T. (2009). *Principles of Macroeconomics.* Boston, MA: Flat World Knowledge Inc.
9. Kahneman, D. and Tversky, A. (eds). (2000). *Choices, Values, and Frames.* Cambridge: Cambridge University Press.
10. Goleman, D. (1996). *Emotional Intelligence: Why it Can Matter More Than IQ.* London: Bloomsbury Publishing.
11. Ibarra, H. (1999). Provisional selves: Experimenting with image and identity in professional adaptation. *Administrative Science Quarterly* 44(4): 764–791.
12. Assagioli, R. (2012). *Psychosynthesis: A Collection of Basic Writings.* Amherst, MA: The Synthesis Center Inc.
13. Bachkirova, T. (2011). *Developmental Coaching: Working with the Self.* Buckingham: Open University Press.
14. Torbert, W. R. and Cook-Greuter. S. R. (2004). *Action Inquiry: The Secret of Timely and Transforming Leadership.* Oakland, CA: Berrett-Koehler.
15. PwC. (2015). *Under Your Nose: Ten Ways to Identify and Retain Transformational Leaders.* Available at: https://www.pwc.co.uk/services/human-resource-services/human-resource-consulting/under-your-nose-ten-ways-to-identify-and-retain-transformation-leaders.html (accessed 3 November 2017).

CHAPTER 9

1. OECD. (n.d.). *What Is PISA?* Available at: https://www.oecd.org/PISA/ (accessed 8 January 2021).
2. Robinson, K. (2016). *Creative Schools: Revolutionizing Education from the Ground Up.* London: Penguin Books.
3. ICA. (n.d.). *What Is a Co-operative?* Available at:https://www.ica.coop/en/cooperatives/

what-is-a-cooperative (accessed 24 January 2021).

4. Laloux, F. (2014). *Reinventing Organizations: A Guide to Creating Organizations Inspired by the Next Stage in Human Consciousness: A Guide to Creating Organizations Inspired by the Next Stage of Human Consciousness.* Fownhope: Nelson Parker.
5. The Alternative. (n.d.). *Debate Principles.* Available at: https://alternativet.dk/en/politics/debate-principles (accessed 8 January 2021).
6. B Corporation. (n.d.). *B Corporation Directory.* Available at: https://bcorporation.net/directory/find-a-b-corp (accessed 8 January 2021).

EPILOGUE

1. Huxley, A. (1954). *The Doors of Perception.* New York: Harper & Row, p. 23.

INDEX

ABOUT THE AUTHOR

Before becoming a business psychologist, Terence worked for 12 years in the construction industry. Starting as a site manager, he performed many roles before becoming the leader of a major culture change programme for a large international contractor. Since then, Terence has gained 20 years' experience working as a business psychologist in a wide range of industries. He mainly works with leaders, engaging them in executive profiling, executive coaching and leadership development. in recent years, his focus has been on sustainable leadership and he has co-founded a not-for-profit co-operative to develop leaders for a better future.

When working with leaders, Terence facilitates the development of their consciousness alongside increasing their skills and knowledge. In doing so, he converts psychological theory and research into practical application. While his prime interest is psychology, Terence has also extensively studied in a wide range of areas such as philosophy, economics, religion, quantum physics, sustainability, management and business. Through studying all these areas, Terence has become convinced that we need to collectively develop our consciousness if we are to create a sustainable society.

Terence is a member of the British Psychological Society and a fellow of the Royal Society of the Arts (FRSA). He has been a guest lecturer at the University of Kent and the Centre for Alternative Technology. Terence holds a BSc Hons in psychology, an MSc in occupational psychology and an MBA. He has trained in Gestalt coaching, Buddhist psychotherapy and psychosynthesis. Terence has also gained a Certificate in Leadership and Facilitation from Schumacher College.

Terence is passionate about helping people to develop their consciousness and frequently gives talks, facilitates workshops and delivers consultancy. To find out more about Terence's work, visit www. aqumens.com.

Printed in Great Britain
by Amazon